Albert Réville

Prolegomena of the history of religions

Albert Réville

Prolegomena of the history of religions

ISBN/EAN: 9783337131937

Printed in Europe, USA, Canada, Australia, Japan

Cover: Foto ©Lupo / pixelio.de

More available books at **www.hansebooks.com**

PROLEGOMENA

OF

THE HISTORY OF RELIGIONS.

BY

ALBERT RÉVILLE, D.D.

PROFESSOR IN THE COLLÉGE DE FRANCE, PARIS; AND HIBBERT LECTURER
FOR 1884.

TRANSLATED FROM THE FRENCH

BY

A. S. SQUIRE.

WITH AN INTRODUCTION BY PROFESSOR F. MAX MÜLLER.

WILLIAMS AND NORGATE,
14, HENRIETTA STREET, COVENT GARDEN, LONDON;
AND 20, SOUTH FREDERICK STREET, EDINBURGH.

1884.

LONDON:
PRINTED BY C. GREEN AND SON,
178, STRAND.

PREFACE.

THIS book is the reproduction, in a condensed form, of Lectures which I gave at the Collége de France during some months of the last spring and summer. I have not reproduced them literally, *in extenso*, because it seems to me that the same forms which are suitable to an oral lesson are not so suitable to a book. That which the Professor says in a lecture in order to be well and clearly understood by his audience, is apt to degenerate into redundancy and prolixity in a book. Reading allows of more reflection than hearing; it requires also more rapidity in development.

I do not claim to have exhausted in these chapters all that might come into a general Introduction to the History of Religions. There are subjects which those who are familiar with this kind of studies could easily point out which are not even approached, because it is only later that they could be usefully dealt with. At the beginning of a course in which his powers would fail the Professor long before the matter he has to treat of is exhausted, I have sought simply to bring together data and judgments which are most necessary for those who wish to follow it profitably. It is a digest to which I may from time to time be allowed to refer, in order not to lengthen the way by fatiguing repetitions or digressions. Misunderstandings will thus be avoided by this statement of the principles and of the tendency which direct my researches in a domain where confusion of ideas and of words is as easy as it is frequent. I would venture to hope that, in default of any other merit, the mark of that strictly scientific spirit which should preside over studies of this kind will be found here. I do not consider the very real sympathy which I openly profess for their object as in any way opposed to that spirit. I believe, on the contrary, that the love of religion within one's-self—like the love of nature to the naturalist, like the love of art to the theorist of the beautiful—is indispensable to the historian of religions. These various affections are not at war; on the contrary, they nourish and inspire the love of truth.

ALBERT RÉVILLE.

INTRODUCTION.

I WAS delighted when I heard that M. Réville's excellent *Prolégomènes de l'Histoire des Religions* were to be translated into English, and if I hesitated before acceding to the request that I should add a few lines by way of introducing his book to the English public, it was simply because I remembered the old English saying that good wine needs no bush.

I do not doubt that all real students of the History of Religion have by this time read M. Réville's book in the original. But the interest in the Science of Religion is spreading rapidly and widely, and there are large classes of English readers who seldom see a book which is published abroad, and who are more easily reached by an English translation.

I hope, therefore, that M. Réville's book in its English translation will be read even more widely in England than it has been; and I trust that it may help to remedy the injury which has of late been done to the Science of Religion in this country, both by its indiscriminate enemies and by its indiscriminate admirers.

Its indiscriminate enemies have often represented that new science as entirely hostile to religion. The author of our book, however, has not only been an active clergyman, but he is not afraid, as the first Professor of the History of Religions at the *Collége de France*, to confess his real love of religion.

But the indiscriminate admirers of the Science of Religion have proved almost more mischievous than our enemies by raising a prejudice against us among men who, though few in number, always tell in the end, and who, from the unscientific way in which the history of religion, or, I should rather say, the evolution of religion, has often been treated in recent publications, have naturally been led to believe that this new so-called science is rather an amusement for amateurs than a study for scholars. Long ago, I ventured to apply to the study of religion what Goethe had said of the study of language, that he who knows one knows none. A man may know his own religion very well, but he is not thereby a theologian, as little as a man is an astronomer because he knows the sun and the moon and the stars that rise above his own horizon. Now in M. Réville we have a writer who has carefully studied, not his own religion only, but most of the really important religions of mankind, and who never forgets the duty of the true historian to treat all religions, the lowest as well as the highest, with perfect impartiality and fairness.

But greater mischief even than has been done by those who know or who recognize one religion only, has been done to our young science by those who profess to know all religions, whether ancient or modern, whether savage or civilized. This comprehensive treatment of religions may have its advantages, and may no doubt claim its proper place in anthropological and psychological works. It is full of interest, and even of amusement, but it is simply intolerable in the Science of Religion. In Comparative Theology, no less than in Comparative Philology and Mythology, it is necessary before all things that whosoever wishes to do any real good, should make himself a scholar, and should acquire not only the knowledge, but also the conscience of a scholar. What should we say of a writer who undertook to teach us anything about Zeus, and was not able to spell his name rightly? Yet men venture to write about the religions of literate and illiterate nations without attempting to learn even the alphabet or the grammar of their languages. *C'est magnifique, mais ce n'est pas la guerre.*

Lastly, our young science has suffered much from the embraces of that philosophy which tries to know how everything ought to have been, without first trying to know something of what really has been, and which, if facts happen to run counter to its postulates, disposes of all difficulties with a self-complacent *Tant pis pour les faits*. Having been myself one of the earliest and most outspoken admirers of Darwin's work, and having stood up, even before Darwin, for the theory of evolution, which nowhere, I believe, has achieved greater triumphs than in the Science of Language, I cannot protest too strongly against degrading the name of Darwin by applying it to that pseudo-philosophical sciolism which tries to put evolution in the place of history, and which, instead of descending from the known to the unknown, imagines that we can ascend far more easily from the unknown to the known. Before we have recourse to the theories of evolution in religion, language, or mythology, we ought surely first to learn what history has to teach us. When that is done, but not till then, there will be time for reasoning out what is required as necessarily antecedent by the very facts which are still within our reach. Let us by all means study history in order to show that there is a unity of purpose, that there is the evolution of an idea in it. But let us not imagine that evolution can defy the authority of history. It was one of the glories of our century that in the study of the earliest history of mankind we had shaken ourselves free from the *à priori* theories of the last century, the Euhemerism of Banier, the Fetichism of De Brosses, the Infantism of Voltaire, the Animism of Rousseau, and the Savageism (*sit venia verbo*) of Lord Monboddo. If the Science of Man is to descend once more to that low level, it will become again a subject for dabblers, but not for students who have patiently tried to learn the great lessons which the true antiquities of the world, the tools of man, the languages of man, the religions of man, the earliest laws and literatures of man, are able to teach.

That is the spirit in which M. Réville's Prolegomena are written—Prolegomena of the history, not of the romance, of religion. We find ourselves throughout its pages, as well as in his other works, *Les Religions des Peuples Non-civilisés*, and his excellent *Hibbert Lectures*, under the guidance of a scholar and an historian; though he also shows us, when we have come to the Land's End, those dim and distant regions in the growth of the human mind which no history and no scholarship can reach, and where the philosopher finds ample scope both for his reasoning and for his imaginative powers. It is quite true that the human mind must not shrink from embarking on that dark ocean which beats everywhere against the shores of our historical knowledge. All I say is, that those who venture on that perilous voyage which is to lead them to the discovery of the oldest world, should possess not only the boldness of the psychologist, but likewise the caution of the scholar and the tact of the historian, as the only safe compass to guide them across mists and darkness from the safe shore which they leave to the unknown harbour which they hope to reach.

F. MAX MÜLLER.

OXFORD, OCT. 17, 1884.

CONTENTS.

	PAGE
M. Réville's Preface	v
Professor Max Müller's Introduction	vii

FIRST PART.

I.—Religion	1
II.—Definition of Religion	25
III.—The Primitive Revelation	35
IV.—Primitive Tradition	49
V.—Other *a priori* Theories of Religious History	58
VI.—Religious Development	65
VII.—Classification of Religions	89

SECOND PART.

I.—The Myth	103
II.—The Symbol and the Rite	117
III.—The Sacrifice	128
IV.—The Priesthood	139
V.—Prophetism	150
VI.—Religious Authority	165
VII.—Theology	175
VIII.—Philosophy	187
IX.—Morality	198
X.—Art	209
XI.—Civilization	219
XII.—Science	225

ERRATA.

Page 4, line 20, insert "the word" before "religion," and for "religion" read "*religio*."
,, 4, ,, 34, for "religion" read "*religio*."
,, 11, ,, 18, for "I" read "we."
,, 12, ,, 4, dele "yet."
,, 14, ,, 23, for "feelings" read "feeling."
,, 27, ,, 19, for "vexation" read "perplexity."
,, 27, ,, 33, for "I" read "we."
,, 27, ,, 35, for "I" read "we."
,, 28, ,, 13, for "I" read "we."
,, 29, ,, 24, insert "may be" before "conceived," and "of" after it.
,, 29, ,, 28, for "relation" read "position."
,, 31, ,, 7, insert "who is the" before "object."
,, 31, ,, 16, insert "but" before "that it is."
,, 33, ,, 22, dele "the" before "eminent."
,, 44, ,, 16, for "the" read "its."
,, 57, ,, 16, for "sprung" read "sprang."
,, 69, ,, 3, for "mankind" read "man."
,, 87, ,, 13, dele "already."
,, 96, ,, 25, insert "in the" before "Mosaism."
,, 169, ,, 11, insert "do" between "to" and "that."
,, 184, ,, 3, for "defiance" read "distrust."
,, 189, ,, 5, for "themselves" read "himself."
,, 195, ,, 10, for "saw" read "sees."
,, 211, ,, 9, for "their" read "its" in each case.
,, 212, ,, 12, for "at" read "of."
,, 227, ,, 35, for "moreover" read "however."
,, 228, ,, 26, for "occupied" read "occupies."

PROLEGOMENA
OF
THE HISTORY OF RELIGIONS.

First Part.

I.

RELIGION.

A.—Antiquity and the Middle Ages.

Of all subjects of study, Religion is perhaps the one which has suffered most from misapprehension. There is none more constantly under discussion by those who do not possess even the simple elementary knowledge which is indispensable for the formation of a competent judgment. There are hundreds of thousands of minds to whom "Religion," "Christianity," "Catholicism," "Theology," are synonyms which they use indifferently one for the others. Religion is one of those domains in which the accident is continually confounded with the substance, the accessory with the essential. That is attributed to all humanity which is true of only a fraction, and that which endures but for a moment is held to be eternal.

Hence the necessity, before entering on the historical task which we have set ourselves, of a sort of general survey which may help us in our long journey by defining notions and terms which are far from being sufficiently understood. We shall travel from the surface to the centre, in order to return from the centre to the surface, and so determine with more accuracy the meaning and bearing of certain general phenomena which met us at the outset, but which it was impossible to understand fully apart from their common source.

The first thing that strikes us on glancing over a map of the religions of the globe, is their multiplicity and diversity. Creeds, rites, moral precepts or simple religious observances; fetichism, animism, polytheism, dualism, monotheism, pantheism; ritual obligations passing from crime to heroism, from prostitution to spotless purity, from cruel immolation of others to complete sacrifice of self—all, principles and forms, produce at first sight the effect of a confused mingling of incongruous phenomena, to which it seems very rash to ascribe beforehand any element in common.

More than this: we may lay down as a general rule that nothing is so tenacious as a religion, nothing more obstinately defies proscription and all attempts at extirpation, nothing resists with more constancy the contradictory demonstrations of palpable reality. History supplies examples of this which are almost appalling. Nevertheless, the number of religions which have become extinct or have disappeared is great. Buddhism, after having been for ages the popular and official religion of Hindostan, from a certain date almost suddenly vanishes, and that, as it would seem, without any persecution having been directed against its votaries. The grand religion of Zoroaster, one of the most interesting and beautiful of antiquity, at present numbers only a few hundreds of professors, and is on the verge of extinction. In France, our religious history presents at least four successive stages—the old religion of the soil, on which was grafted a mystic Druidism; then the religion of the conquerors, who absorbed one and proscribed the other; and at last Christianity, in its turn the point of departure of new evolutions. The Greco-Roman, Germanic and Scandinavian mythologies— the Semitic polytheisms of Nineveh, Babylon, Biblos, Tyre and Carthage—the rich pantheon of ancient Egypt—the solar worship of the Incas—all these are dead, gone for ever. And we could add to this funereal list other names less known. So that religions exhibit this double phenomena of a vitality which we might suppose indestructible, and of a tendency to decay which frequently ends in complete annihilation. Later, we shall have to examine the hidden causes of this contradictory manifestation; at the moment we content ourselves with noticing a fact which is brought more prominently forward through this very contradiction.

It is this, that if religions are mortal, religion never dies, or we may say, it dies under one form only to come to life again under another.

There is, then, underneath and within this multicoloured development a permanent and substantial element, something stable and imperishable, which takes a firm hold on human nature itself. It is like the tendency of man to live in society, or like the faculty of speech, two things which subsist through all changes, all governments, all revolutions of states and races. If we were called upon to write a comparative history of legislation, or a general history of art, we should begin by defining the idea of law or of art. In like manner, our first effort now ought to be devoted to ascertaining what *Religion*, the common cause of all these fluctuating, varied and successive phenomena, is in itself.

If the question is elementary, it is far from being easy of solution. It is with religion, in the abstract sense of the word, as with man himself, as with the state, art, philosophy, and so many other subjects of reflective thought. Their rigorous definition demands sustained effort, which is not always rewarded by success. We must bear this in mind in our summing up of what may be called the history of the definition of Religion.

The etymological meaning of the word itself does not throw much light on the question, though it contains an indication which we must not overlook. In spite of the objections of some philologers, we persist in thinking that the word *religion*, derived from the Latin *religio*, conveys the idea of a bond, of something which attaches and binds, and, as a matter of fact, we shall find this idea in the definition which will result from our inquiry.[1]

[1] The Greek does not possess any term exactly corresponding to the Latin *religio:* θρησκεία, θεοσέβεια, εὐσέβεια, relate rather either to a ritual form of worship, or to the disposition which we call piety. The Greek expression, τὰ περὶ τοὺς θεούς, or περὶ τὸν θεόν, that which concerns the gods or god, is too vague to serve as an equivalent. The German *Gottesdienst*, which we find in all the languages of the Germanic family except in English, literally signifies *service of God*, that is, religious practice rather than religion itself. This is why the philosophers and theologians of Outre-Rhin borrow from us the term *religion* in their technical works. This, we may say in passing, singularly weakens the force of the reasoning in virtue of which it is often desired to insist upon the absence of a notion, or of a faculty, or of a moral disposition among certain peoples, founding this argument on the fact that their language did not contain the precise word for designating it.

Etymologists, whose opinion we do not share, refer the term religion to *re-legere*, to collect anew, re-collect, to take again something in order to devote one's attention to it. It is thus, it is added, that *intelligere* means to collect several things, to dispose them, arrange them, comprehend them; that *nec-ligere* (*negligere*) means not to collect, to leave aside, neglect; that *di-ligere* supposes that one has collected, but has put something apart from the others, whence the meaning of liking, preferring, cherishing. *Relegere* would be equivalent to the French word *repasser, revolve* (in mind or memory), and in fact this is the meaning which the Latins themselves have assigned to religion. Cicero, for example (De Nat. D. ii. 28, 72), says, in reference to this: *Qui omnia quæ ad cultum deorum pertinerent diligenter retractarent et tanquam relegerent, sunt dicti* RELIGIOSI *ex* RELEGENDO, *ut eleganter ex eligendo, tanquam a diligendo diligenter, ex intelligendo intelligenter; his enim in verbis omnibus in est vis legendi eadem quæ in religioso.*

With all deference, however, to Cicero, whose etymologies often leave much to be desired, his comparison is open to very grave objections. The greater number of substantives formed with *intelligere, diligere, eligere, negligere*, take the termination *entia, intelligentia, diligentia, elegantia, negligentia;* consequently *religere* ought to give *religentia*, not *religio*. *Religiosus* has so little the meaning of *repassant, revolving*, reviewing carefully, that another Latin, quoted by Aulus Gellius (iv. 9), clearly distinguishes between the meaning of *religens* and that of *religiosus*, this last being understood as the equivalent of our word "superstitious:" *Religentem esse oportet, religiosum nefas*. Finally, the word religion is employed in Latin in the sense of a sacred or solemn bond which it is not lawful to break, a meaning which is preserved in such phrases as "*Religion du serment,*" "*Religion du drapeau.*" *Religione jusjurandi ac metu Deorum in testimoniis dicendis commoveri*, said Fonteius, ix. 20.

Agreeing with Servius, Lactantius and Augustine, we think that the word religion must be connected with *religare*, to bind, to connect with. Pott (Etymol. Forsch. i. 20) objects that *religare* ought to give *religatio*, as *obligare* makes *obligatio*. But we may reply that the termination *are* of Latin verbs of the first conjugation is not primitive; it represents *a-ere*. This is why the penultimate of substantives formed out of these verbs may vary. We have, for example, *opinio* by the side of *opinari, optio* by the side of *optare, rebellio* by the side of *rebellare*. Nothing, then, is philologically opposed to the derivation of *religio* from *religa-ere*, or rather from the root *lig*, which is common to them. M. Max Müller, from whom we borrow several of the preceding observations, also appears to prefer this etymology.

But while admitting that religion may be a bond, that tells us nothing of what that bond consists in, nor especially of what it unites or attaches.

The ancients concerned themselves with religion itself, independently of its historic forms. For them, in fact, religion had no history. It would be impossible to give this name to myths relating how younger gods were substituted for more ancient deities, like those which told of the dethronement of Uranus, to be replaced by Kronos, and of Kronos again dispossessed by Zeus or Jupiter. These revolutions among their deities formed a part of the traditional mythology which the thinkers of antiquity rarely openly combatted. They saw in it something established, secular, venerable and inevitable, to which they had to accommodate themselves, even while they discerned its puerile and fabulous character. The Greek philosophers knew little of the world, and those who began to know it somewhat better were neither Greeks nor philosophers. What the former knew of Asia, of Egypt, of the regions of the North, showed them nothing which differed essentially from that Hellenic polytheism in the bosom of which they had been born and would die. Religion, as distinguished from religions, and as constituting the internal spring of their development, could not be to them an object of study.

Whenever they did not yield to scepticism or to a grosser materialism, they sought to form a rational idea of the normal relation necessarily existing between man and that higher Power whose will or whose nature determines human destiny. The popular religion appeared to their minds as a form adapted to the intellectual weakness of the masses, in which to present to them the highest truth under a disguise which would render it accessible to uncultivated intelligences. The almost total absence of dogma from the mythological traditions greatly facilitated this position, half scornful, half benevolent. It is especially in the Platonic school, as well as in the Pythagorean societies, that we find this philosophical notion of religion, one which it has been sought to revive in our own day, but with no great success, inasmuch as it is with religions infinitely more systematized, more dogmatic and more dominant than the old Paganism that we have to do.

According to Plato, the Absolute is the ideal and real good, the *intelligible sun*, the action of which results in the formation of matter by means of *ideas* which impart to it whatever it possesses of reason, order and beauty. The human soul, a combination of the divine and of the material, participates in divine things through the divine element in its nature; while in like manner, through the material element, it is dragged down to the troubled region of blinding and hurtful passions. The mythological tendency of his mind causes Plato to mix with this fundamental notion various elements which find a place rather in the regions of poetry than in the severer atmosphere of a system purely rational (reminiscences of an anterior life, prophetic ecstacy, &c., are among these); but it is evident that in his view the religious destiny of the soul, the essence and the end of religion, is ὁμοίωσις τῷ Θεῷ, likeness to God, founded on the co-essentiality of the human soul and of the Deity.

This mode of comprehending religion, already indicated by Socrates and implied in the Pythagorean reform, is typical in the history of the ancient philosophy. We meet it again, with variations which in no way affect the principle, in Stoicism, Alexandrian Judaism, Christianity of the same name, and in Neo-Platonism. It is easy to understand how relations on the whole sufficiently amicable might be established between the philosophical point of view and the popular faith. We must take care not to apply the intolerance of our modern logic to these ancient relations between philosophy and religious tradition. Where we should at once have seen two religions distinct and hostile, the ancients saw but one. It is true that Socrates, Anaxagoras, Plato and others, aroused in a certain number of minds fears which found their relief in actual persecution. This, however, was partly due to political animosity, partly because

the popular polytheism at the time believed itself to be attacked
in principle. But the proof that these passing emotions never
penetrated very deeply, is found in the fact that the very doctrines
which had excited them continued to be taught and propagated
without any serious opposition being made to them by either the
state or the priesthood. The question of the true or false in
religion was not then submitted to the conscience of the people,
as it has been since. Thence a certain serenity, a benevolent
optimism, prevailed in the mutual relations between philosophy
and the popular faith. The ancient religions were utterly destitute of all spirit of propagandism. The philosophers did not
distinguish themselves from the people in their observance of
traditional rites. The people, on their side, did not look too
closely into matters. They were quite contented that poetry,
the drama and comedy should be associated with the old myths
and the hereditary deities. The philosophers readily sought
support to their systems by pointing out the analogies in form
or in origin which the popular tradition offered. Their language
is almost always half-mythological. They delighted in personifying abstract ideas, a tendency which dates from the time of
Hesiod. A personified idea would be indeed unlucky if in the
traditional pantheon it could not find some deity whom it resembled. Plato could raise his voice against the efficacy which
superstition attributes to sacrifices, and against the employment
of scandalous myths in the education of youths; Cicero could
exhibit his scepticism in regard to divination, oracles, auguries.
This did not prevent either of them from offering sacrifices or
taking part in the ceremonial of divination. Herodotus among
the Greeks, and Cæsar and Tacitus among the Romans, furnish us
with familiar examples of the facility with which they identified
the gods of strange or barbarous nations with those of the Græco-
Roman polytheism. As to the grotesque or the decidedly im-
moral elements of the mythic tradition, it is to be presumed that
the sages applied to them a treatment analogous to that which
many Christians in our day use to remove from their consciences

the painful impression which many passages in the Old Testament are likely to cause them. They either do not consider them at all, or they complacently interpret them allegorically or in a modified sense; in no case do they accord to the real sense any influence on their thoughts or life.

The school of Epicurus is always held to be irreligious, because, in spite of the πρόληψις, the *antecæpta quædam informatio Deorum* which he recognized to exist in the human soul, Epicurus, by banishing the divine power into space without admitting any actual bond between it and humanity, suppressed at the same time all religious relation between the two terms. There was no longer any actual relation between man and the Deity. But the Epicurean in his daily life showed himself scrupulously conservative in regard to the established religion. With Lucretius, it is true, philosophical thought took a higher flight. Lucretius is not an atheist, as he has been called: he is rather a pantheist; and one often feels, in reading his great poem, as it were a breath of profound and mystic piety. It is untrue, a wide-spread notion to the contrary notwithstanding, that he was the author of the famous verses which attribute to fear the origin of the earliest beliefs. But while recognizing, in his contemplation of the universe, the *mens agitans molem*, which separates him entirely from Epicurus, he exhibits, in a far higher degree than the other independent thinkers of the period, a violent repulsion against the popular religion, and he delights in reproaching it with all the evil it has done to men. This negative point of view could not then, any more than it could now, prepare him for the serious study of what we may call "the natural history" of religion.

To sum up, the ancients did not and could not acquire an experimental and historical notion of religion in itself, still less of the common cause of its various manifestations. The materials for study were wanting; and that sort of intellectual simplicity which is induced by the absence of contradiction, disabled them from recognizing even the existence of the problem.

The situation was greatly changed when a new religion placed itself in antagonism to the old. One thing especially affected the minds of those who, brought up in polytheism, were accustomed to attach only a minor importance to the question of truth in religion. The new faith offered itself to their acceptance in these terms: "Your religion is error, and I am truth; you are plunged in darkness, while I soar in the brightest light; your gods are false; your myths are lies; your faith is no longer needed on the earth." Such language had never before been heard in the Western world.

By the time that the Christian Church was in a position to speak authoritatively, she was already in possession of an orthodoxy, that is, of a canonical list of doctrines, which it was necessary to profess under pain of exclusion. Although this orthodoxy was then very modest in comparison with what it afterwards became, it none the less contributed to widen the gulf of separation between the two powers. More, the Church had inherited from Judaism a peremptory mode of accounting for the existence and prevalence of the mythological religion. It was purely and simply the work of the devil; and if any one remarked that, nevertheless, even from her own point of view, the Church ought to recognize the presence of certain divine rays in the thick darkness of popular traditions, she replied by the mouth of her most approved apologists, that the devil, this imitator, this "ape" of God, had purposely introduced these into the mass of corruption and lies in order the more easily to seduce mankind. In truth, it was not a religion which she had to oppose; quite the contrary; there was but one religion, her own.

It is evident that such an antagonism, softened only in the great Christian school of Alexandria, was no more favourable to a true historical science of religion than the previous state of things. In fact, there was no escape from this narrow dualism until modern times. The Platonizing theory of Alexandria, which numbered amongst its most illustrious representatives Clement of Alexandria and Origen, might have been able to extend the horizon of religious thought. By developing the Phi-

Ionian idea of the divine word, of the divine thought, embodied, it is true, in the Old and New Testaments, but having disseminated always and everywhere the germs of truth and of morality, it would have been possible to arrive at a comprehensive notion of the religious development of humanity, which might at least have suggested the idea of preparing a history, in the serious meaning of the word. But the Church, with whom orthodoxy became more and more the chief passion, borrowed from the Alexandrian theories only so much as served to support her absolutist pretensions. That is to say, that she identified the Logos, or the divine Word, with her Founder and permanent Chief in such a manner as to claim a monopoly of all religious and moral truth, and she haughtily declined any concession which could have formed a link between her and any religions which had preceded her, or which continued to subsist by her side. Islamism itself was treated as any other Paganism, and the Christianity of the middle ages held that Mahomet was a false god, an idol, a sort of Asiatic Jupiter, raised up by the devil in order to destroy the only religion which had any right to exist. Men did not know any more of the real world in the middle ages, perhaps rather less, than in ancient times. Humanity, that is to say the fraction about whom they knew anything, was Christian and Catholic; the old Paganism was supposed to be slain, absolutely dead. Within the Church were certain miserable sectarian movements, of no importance; without, on the frontier of the unknown, was Islamism, always menacing, but always beyond the reach of law: these were the only opposing forces which had to be taken into account, and they did not seem to be of a nature to shake the implicit confidence inspired by the grandeur, the incomparable majesty, of the Catholic Church. The possibility of a distinction between Religion in itself and Catholic Christianity was never for a moment entertained.

B.—Modern Times.

One of the laws of religious history, which it is the most easy to verify, is that which always, sooner or later, establishes a close relation between the religious ideas of men and the knowledge which they have of the world. The various mythologies would never have existed, if men in the earliest times had possessed a scientific knowledge of nature. Christian orthodoxy would never have been formulated as it was, if at the time of its elaboration it had been possible to take into account the real place which our poor little planet occupies in the immensity of space. The Church would never have boasted of her universal character, if it had been known in the middle ages that as a matter of fact she embraced only a fraction, relatively very small, of humanity. It is true that a belief, once formed, propagated and invested with traditional prestige, may long resist those facts of a non-religious character which either scarcely agree or are in open conflict with the suppositions on which it is based. But the slow and direct action of these facts is not the less felt in the long run. Already the Crusades had resulted in a diminution of that which I will call the security of faith.

From the beginning of the fifteenth century, all was changed. The resurrection of a world, the discovery of the globe, the opening up of the heavens, took place almost simultaneously. Greek and Roman antiquity comes forth from its grave; the princes of the Church themselves approve, and can no longer attribute purely and simply to the devil this splendid culture, which is eagerly sought after, and the literary monuments and works of art of which are studied with passionate devotion.

The earth, in its turn, unrolls itself beyond the range of sight; the immensity of ancient Asia is discovered with a surprise not unmingled with awe; the outlines of Africa are traced, but no one as yet dares to sound its mysterious depths; and there is America, with its two peninsulas. If at least in these countries, until yesterday unknown, there had been met only savages, brutish beings, or those scarcely emerging from animalism, in whose presence our Christian and civilized Europe could still have cherished the thought that she was humanity *de jure*, if not yet *de facto!* But no! Navigators found old societies, ancient civilizations, in Mexico, in India, in China; old religions also, with their institutions, their rites, their priests, their claims to the possession of divine truth. Added to all these observations were those which result from the progress of physics and astronomy; that silence of space which appalled Pascal; the insignificance of our planet amid the grand spheres scattered in profusion throughout immensity; the blue vault of the firmament which is merely the limit of our atmosphere, and which has nothing in common with the celestial seat on which the simple poetry of the middle ages imagined the sun in blissful repose. It is thus easy to understand the anxious gaze with which a thoughtful man at this epoch would look upon the world and upon himself. Can we contemplate the *Melancolia* of Albert Dürer, that handsome and robust woman seated among all the instruments of the new knowledge, and watching gloomily and thoughtfully a sun which disappears behind the horizon, without seeing there the reflection of that involuntary sadness which seizes the spirit when it must say adieu for ever to the dreams of infancy and to the illusions of youth? May it not be the shattering of the security in which he had hitherto lived which explains the amiable and contagious scepticism of Montaigne? In him, and in many others, arose a feeling, which continually gained strength, of a disproportion between the absolutist pretensions of the Church and that reality which demonstrates that in the world it is the relative which governs.

It is in effect since then that the elements of the history of religions begin to accumulate. But much time must still elapse before such a history can be morally possible. The mind for a long time yet will be held back by theological prejudices, or will be rendered cautious, at least as much by the fear of attacking so difficult a subject, as by the severities of the dominant orthodoxies. Samuel Bochart, Bishop Huet, Jurieu, endeavoured to systematize the knowledge acquired in their time. These attempts are absolute failures. Moreover, no one as yet would venture to break loose from the idea that the religions opposed to that which is taught in the Bible were anything more than that religion distorted and disfigured. The violent quarrels between Catholics and Protestants absorbed the attention of religious thinkers. Cartesianism occupied itself very little, or, to speak more accurately, not at all, with history. Classical studies were limited to the literary form, to the æsthetics of the old civilization. The Greco-Roman mythology was of value only to supply graceful symbols, subjects of noble or gallant art, elegant types of architecture or of statuary. No one imagined that they contained any elements worthy of the notice of thoughtful men. Much travel, many discoveries, added to what was already known, were needed to compel attention to the wide panorama of religions which began to be unfolded. At first these were studied only from the outside, superficially; they were treated as a repertory of curiosities, as in the great work in seven folio volumes which appeared in 1741 under the title of *Cérémonies et coutumes religieuses de tous les peuples*, the chief authors of which were Picart and Antoine Banier.

The eighteenth century at length emancipated historical science from all those trammels which, especially in the domain of religion, had hindered its development. But it must be borne in mind that this emancipation, inasmuch as it was recent, very imperfectly prepared the mind for undertaking the history of religions with that impartiality which is absolutely necessary to the task. Whatever knowledge was possessed was most often employed in making a breach in Christian tradition. In its desire to make a clean sweep of the errors and abuses which it everywhere discovered, the eighteenth century deemed it necessary in everything, and especially in religion, to return as much as possible to nature. But it little imagined that natural religion, the religion which humanity was bound to profess in this age of idyllic virtue, in which *le contrat social* had been elaborated before it became corrupted by the artifices of priests and kings, was nothing else but philosophic deism. It did not perceive that this pretended natural religion was merely an extract subtly derived from Christian tradition, the fruit of a civilization already old and artificial, already saturated with criticism and rationalism, quite the opposite of a religion springing up spontaneously in the human mind, still influenced by its primitive inspirations.

Meanwhile, many of the elements of positive research were already germinating in public opinion. Look at the chapter entitled *Religion*, in the *Dictionnaire Philosophique* of Voltaire. We find there glimpses of great promise. For example, Voltaire likens the state of mind of the first men in matters of religion to that which we may observe in children. True, he falls immediately afterwards into very grave historical errors. He confuses the Semitic polytheism with others. He believes in a primitive monotheism. He imagines that the sages of Greece and Rome were deists like himself. There is here, nevertheless, from the point of view which we indicate, an intuition of profound justness. Jean Jacques Rousseau, inferior to Voltaire in historical insight, surpasses him in analysis of religious fact, in which he attaches to feelings a quite special importance. It is thence that he became the father of a new kind of mysticism, which was not slow in spreading through Germany, and which had this advantage, that, detached from traditional dogma, it was in a position to include the non-Christian mysticisms. Nevertheless, in order to form an idea of the chaos which prevailed in the matter of religious history, it will suffice to look through the crude truth of the *Monde Primitif* of Court de Gébelin, one of the best men, the most worthy of esteem, and the most devoted to science, of his own age. When, with new light and more logical precision, Dupuis writes his *Origine de tous les cultes* (1801), we see again in this last product of the mind of the eighteenth century the perpetuation of its great error, which consists in making calculation and subtle reflection intervene where the simple spontaneity of the human mind displays itself without counterpoise.

Another error of the eighteenth century, not unlike the preceding, is, that it sought in all religion only for its moral teaching; then, governed by polemical interest, it attributed a higher morality to many religions of which their chief title to its esteem was their remoteness in place. It believed, or appeared to believe, with a marvellous docility, in the virtues of bonzes, of mandarins, of lamas, and of talapoins. It desired a religion consisting only of moral precepts, identical with morality. It was too much what Kant calls *statutory*, that is to say, the age was too ready to think that beliefs and religious institutions could be settled by decrees. Wise men, legislators, enlightened priests, decide that it is for the general good to profess such a belief, to practise such a rite; they enact, they decree, and all things move of themselves in the desired direction. This was, we know, one of the illusions of our great Revolution.

It was in Germany that the intellectual and scientific progress to which we at length owe a just notion of religious history and of what religion essentially is, took place.

Lessing led the way by familiarizing his readers with an idea as yet very little understood, that of the religious development of humanity. Religious history with him is only the education of the human race, which rises gradually to purer notions of God and of duty. Each historical religion will thus mark a phase or a halting-point in this development. Here is a new idea, which goes far beyond the antithesis of the middle ages, between revealed religion, alone worthy of the name of religion, and the *soi-disant* religions, daughters of lying. There is no longer the *salto mortale*, the impassable gulf, between the religions. Every religion has its relative legitimacy. But, like a true son of his age, Lessing seeks too exclusively the essence of religions in morality. He everywhere distinguishes between the *positive*, that is to say the moral teaching, and the *conventional*, that is to say the dogmas, the rites, the sacerdotal or disciplinary institutions, which he deems the accessories. In this he is in error. There is no more of the conventional in the dogmas or the ritual precepts of a settled religion than in its moral precepts. Both alike are derived from the religious principle which constitutes its essence.

Kant shared the same error. We know how this powerful thinker, after having crushed under the teeth of his dialectic harrow all the arguments of anterior theodicies, found the idea of duty alone unyielding and invincible, and how on the immovable basis of the categoric imperative he built up the famous trilogy—God, Virtue and Immortality. It is thus easy to comprehend how he found no other substantial element of religion but moral doctrine. But how was it that he did not perceive the contradiction? His definition of religion in itself consists in saying that "religion is the recognition of our duties as *divine* commands"! *Divine* commands—that is to say, commands which owe their august, irresistible character to their divine origin—in other terms, to their religious character! Is it not clear that that which was to be defined has been included in the professed definition?

Still more than Lessing, whose artistic nature often rebels against the rigour of his theories, and who had also his own mysticism, Kant despised the element, so essential in religion, of feeling. The sort of voluptuousness with which the religious soul can relish the absurd, if the absurd is necessary for the satisfaction of its wants, remains without any possible explanation in his system; and it is especially the too exclusive intellectualism of his religious views which provoked the reaction of the mystic sentiment of which first Hamann, "the Magian of the North," an original but eccentric and obscure thinker, and afterwards Jacobi, were the representatives. The latter claimed that the immediate intuition, the sudden possession of the soul by a higher truth, should be the criterion and pre-eminently the revelation of divine realities, and he found a way of grasping "intuitively" the greater part of orthodox doctrines.

Neither his philosophical nor his religious opponents spared him the well-merited reproach of being arbitrary. His influence as a thinker was small beside that of Herder, the eloquent and poetic founder of the Philosophy of History. At least he shares this glory with Vico. Dying in 1803, we may say that he inaugurated in Germany and in Europe the knowledge of antiquity. He it was who first saw clearly that our processes of reasoning, our mode of feeling and of understanding things, should not be applied to antiquity, if we wished to form a true idea. It is thus that he has caused poetry to flow abundantly from a thousand unknown springs, and has prepared us to breathe the perfume of the old traditions. If the too frequent wandering of his thoughts renders the study of his writings somewhat tedious to French readers, always delighting in clearness and precision, we must not the less admire this disciple of Rousseau, who prepares the way for Hegel. He had in the highest degree the sentiment of that continuous divine action, without interruption or weakness, of which the world is the theatre. History is to him only the prolongation of nature, and the attentive contemplation of the one, as of the other, enables him to grasp their constant laws.

His notion of religion is in close relationship with this dominant principle of his philosophy. Religion, he says, is the internal appropriation (*das Innewerden*) of the divine activity, which ordains all things in such a manner that we knowingly submit ourselves to this divine order; or rather, religion is in us the inner consciousness of what we are, as men forming part of the universe. We specially remark in this double definition, the obscurity and vagueness of which are to be regretted, the very legitimate intention of doing justice to that indispensable factor, the world, the *not I*, of which the theories of Lessing and of Kant took so little account. Nevertheless, we can scarcely content ourselves with so little. Supposing that we could discover the exact sense of the German abstraction, the *Innewerden*, what becomes of this abstruse definition in face of the simple religions of nations destitute of all culture? And what becomes of "the internal appropriation of the divine activity" in the presence of that religion which occupies so great a place in religious history, Buddhism, in which the divine perfection consists entirely in not possessing the least activity, just as human perfection is found in renouncing every kind of activity? Remember, we are seeking for a notion of religion in itself which may find its application, and consequently its justification, in all the historical forms which it may assume.

Fichte, at first very Kantian in his idea of religion, understood later the synthetic character of all religion so far as the practical reconciliation of the *I* and the *not I*. But the abstract and cloudy character of his thought, always dominated by a subjectivism which never allowed him to affirm unreservedly the real existence of the *not I*, prevents us from forming a clear and positive notion of what he understood by this reconciliation. According to Schelling, religion was nothing else but God seeking himself through all the series of intermediaries from brute matter to mind; it was God in the course of formation, or rather of re-constitution, for the system so original and so eccentric of the great theosoph had as its foundation the idea of a divine fall. In the midst of these speculative orgies, Schleiermacher spoke words of great significance. Applying to religious fact his marvellous power of analysis, Schleiermacher joined Jacobi and Herder in showing that feeling was rightly the seat of religion; but he limited the vagueness of this thesis by pointing out that it led up to the consciousness of our absolute dependence on a power which influences us, and which we cannot influence. This definition is in its turn too narrow. If the celebrated theologian had said that in all religious sentiment we find the sentiment of dependence, he would have maintained an undeniable fact. But the sentiment of dependence by itself does not constitute the religious sentiment. Other elements also form an integral part of it, such as admiration, veneration, confidence, love. Purely negative, the sentiment of dependence remains in opposition, in antithesis, and religion distinctly aims at conciliating opposition.

And besides, without saying coarsely, as Hegel does, that if religion consisted essentially in the spirit of dependence, the dog would be the most religious of all beings, we are justified in objecting to a definition of a fact so specifically human as religion is, when that definition sums up everything in a sentiment which holds so large a place in purely animal life.

Comte in France, and Feuerbach in Germany, gave importance to another element of religious fact which also they understood in a too limited sense. They relied on the anthropomorphism inherent in all religions to introduce into them all the worship of man by man. Comte, it is true, did not make the individual man the object of the normal worship; he proposed for our adoration man as a species, as humanity, and succeeded in founding a true mysticism on this narrow base. Feuerbach was less of a poet. He boldly propounded the thesis that man could do nothing else in religion than egotistically worship himself. God, he said, is never anything but egoism rejoicing in itself, the *Selbstgenuss des Egoïsmus*. Man idealizes himself; he creates his God by making him in his own embellished image.

We know that as far as regards the first Positivism, the chapter relating to religion was the part which had the least success. There is a very profound feeling of religious reality in this *unknowable*, enveloped in impenetrable mystery, which, in spite of their divergencies, such thinkers as M. Littré and Mr. Herbert Spencer discover on the confines of the field accessible to our knowledge. There, at least, we meet again that which is indispensable to every religious notion, the sentiment of the object obtruding on the subject, even though it must obtrude only as the most tormenting and the most insoluble of problems. It is for religious philosophy to investigate whether the necessity of a certain anthropomorphism leads the human mind as by a fate in the sense of error or in that of truth. For our own part, on the historical ground to which we confine ourselves, we must say that neither the theory of Comte nor that of Feuerbach is in harmony with the facts of history. In religion, man has always sought,

and with reason, to worship another than himself. Grant for a
moment that this worship has always been the result of an illusion,
yet this illusion remains as the historical fact, and we seek to
know exactly what constitutes it. It is vain in a definition of
religion to limit ourselves to man, and to exclude the world as
an abstraction. All religion supposes man on the one part, the
universe on the other, and aspires to furnish to the former the
principle or the method of harmony between him and destiny.

It is to Hegel, rather than to his system, discredited like so
many others, and to the views which he has disseminated in the
conscience of our age, that we must revert in order to find the
philosophical notion of religion which best accords with the facts
of history.

In conformity with his system, Hegel defines religion as "the
knowledge which the finite mind possesses of its essence as an
absolute mind." To put it more clearly, the mind of man carries
with it the consciousness of being *de jure* superior to all the
limitations which are obstacles to its full development. It tends
to become absolute. If it is objected that thus the absolute mind
is only the product of the finite mind, that is true, replies Hegel,
only from a dialectic point of view, which necessarily starts from
the finite mind; in reality, it is the absolute Mind, which is at
once the first cause and the final cause, which influences things
in order that they may rise to its own height. On this point,
we may say in passing, the true view of Hegel has been often
misrepresented.[1] Historical religions will thus be so many
degrees of development of the mind tending to realize the absolute which it possesses potentially. It is for the historian to
determine for each of these the central idea which assigns to it
its logical place in the ascending movement of humanity. He

[1] Compare in this connection the enlightened investigation to which Professor
Pfleiderer, of Berlin, has subjected the various systems of religious philosophy in his
remarkable work entitled *Religions-philosophie*, Berlin, 1868; second edition, revised
and corrected, 1878. We are indebted to him for many of the preceding observations;
on other occasions we have recorded the coincidences of opinion on which the learned
Professor will allow us to congratulate ourselves.

will distinguish the religions of infancy, those of peoples without culture; those of youth, in which the mind already claims a certain liberty, such as Judaism, which is the religion of the sublime; Hellenism, which is the religion of the beautiful; the Roman religion, which is that of law and of finality. Christianity, which is with Hegel the absolute religion, corresponds with the mature age of humanity. To philosophy belongs the task of disengaging from the symbols, the myths, the dogmas of each epoch, the idea which they seek to express, but of which they can give only the imperfect formula. For religion and philosophy have the same contents; they teach fundamentally the same thing; only religion, the daughter of sentiment, of feeling, of imagination, expresses under a symbolic, and consequently inadequate, form the same truth which philosophy will present under a severer form, strictly rational and scientific. We know how, on the strength of this theory of the relations between philosophy and religion, Hegel found means to re-constitute the greater number of the dogmas of Christian orthodoxy. The latter, for a moment enchanted with this unhoped-for aid, enthusiastically adopted the new costume. But the first infatuation over, she bethought herself to look in the glass of independent criticism, and discovered that she had become unrecognizable. Strauss showed her with a master's hand that she was no longer herself, and the charm was broken.

We can see in all that has gone before the constant effort of the human mind to attain to a clear and positive notion of this great fact of religion, which it may study henceforth free from prejudices, and of which it more than ever recognizes the importance, the universality, and the profoundly human character. We might say that each of the thinkers whose personal point of view we have recalled, has been specially struck with that one of the constituent elements of fact which he has concerned himself in analyzing, and that his error has been rather to exalt this element than to give it a too exclusive place. The definition proposed by Hegel, the most comprehensive of all, has, however, the defect of being too closely bound up with his metaphysical system, and of yielding with difficulty to the exigencies of history. How, for example, can we, without forcing its terms, apply it to Buddhism? Is it in accordance with reality to apply to the religious development of humanity as a whole these categories of infancy, of youth, of maturity, which would infer a continuous and simultaneous development? Is there a difference of form only between religion and philosophy, and does the Hegelian philosophy take sufficient account of that practical realism, so different from theoretic abstraction, whence it results that a religion may become philosophical, but that no philosophy has ever founded a religion possessing true historical power? And does not the illusion under which the illustrious master fell, when he believed that he had victoriously re-constituted Christian orthodoxy, already prove that there was much that was arbitrary, not only in his method, but also in the principle of identity from which he set out?

It is no doubt as a reaction against the too intellectualist character of previous definitions that, without recurring to the sentimental quaintness of the romantic school, M. Max Müller, whose name is justly entitled to great authority when he treats of religious history, has chosen to put forward as the essence of religion the human faculty of "apprehending the Infinite" under different forms. "Religion," says the eminent Orientalist,[1] "is a mental faculty which independently, nay, in spite of sense and reason, enables man to apprehend the Infinite under different names and under varying disguises. Without that faculty, no religion, not even the lowest worship of idols and of fetiches, would be possible; and if we will but listen attentively, we can hear in all religions a groaning of the spirit, a struggle to conceive the inconceivable, to utter the unutterable, a longing after the Infinite, 'a love of God.'"

M. Max Müller himself warns us that he offers his religious

---

[1] "Lectures on the Origin and Growth of Religion as illustrated by the Religions of India:" London, 1878.

formula rather as a characteristic than as a definition of religion, and he maintains that he is right in putting in relief an element too much neglected by his predecessors, that of mystery, in which the object of religions is enveloped, and which attracts the curious and anxious mind of man by the very reason of its impenetrability. According to the Oxford Professor, the infinite is only the highest generalization of all that is indefinite, supra-sensible, supernatural, absolute or divine. The infinite, he says, is not a simple abstraction,[1] since we cannot deduce it from the finite; it is a reality which we necessarily affirm in affirming the finite, since we cannot place the limited without placing the unlimited, the visible and palpable without supposing the invisible and impalpable, &c. No doubt the philosophical conception of the infinite has not been present to the human mind from the beginning. But we meet in it the *not yet*, the presentiment in the oldest traces of man on the earth. It is only a question of development.[2]

We incline, however, to think that here again we find ourselves in the presence of an element of religions put forward in a too exclusive manner. Yes, there is in all religion, if not the idea, at least the feeling, the perception, more or less vague, of the infinite, just as there is in all something which appears in the sentiment of dependence, of obligation or of supreme synthesis. But is the feeling of the infinite purely and simply religious? Observe that the infinite appeals to the religious sentiment only as the attribute of something or of some one. Abstract infinities, infinite time, infinite space, are empty notions, silent to the religious soul. There is need, then, of a reality having for its pre-

---

[1] "Lectures," &c., p. 28.

[2] M. Max Müller believes he has found a historical confirmation of his opinion in the name of the ancient Vedic divinity *Aditi*, the personification of dawn. This name signifies the *ab-soluta* from *a*, negative, and *diti*, feminine participle of *dâ, dyati, nectere*, to bind. In the twilight, when the dawn brings back light and the sun from mysterious regions, primitive thought darted into the *beyond*, into unknown, illimitable space, where all was preparing. This was a revelation of the infinite. The explanation is poetical and charming. But the name *unbound*, might it not simply signify that the dawn or morning light was represented as detained in the prison of night, and freed from its bonds at the moment in which it should re-appear?

dicate the infinite, in order that its infinity may add to the religious impression which it was already prepared to make on the human mind. That which we retain of the characteristic of religion formulated by M. Max Müller, is the necessity of doing justice, in the definition which we in our turn are about to propose, to this element of mystery and to its powerful attraction, which hold an incontestable and eminent place among the various factors, the convergent action of which has for its result religion.

II.

DEFINITION OF RELIGION.

In these Prolegomena of Religious History, it must be borne in mind that the question above all others is, not to define religion such as it might or could be, but to disengage its essence and central idea in such a manner that we shall be able to recognize it under all the forms which it may assume in history.

On this strictly historical ground, and taking into account all that has seemed to us true or defective in previous definitions, we say that *Religion is the determination of human life by the sentiment of a bond uniting the human mind to that mysterious Mind whose domination of the world and of itself it recognizes, and to whom it delights in feeling itself united.*

I take in turn each of the terms of this definition in order to show its legitimacy.

What is a determination of human life?

Life is made up of a series of multiple determinations of simple existence. All the determinations which modify it, in one sense or another, have for their common cause the *need of living*, the most imperious of all—that is to say, of preserving existence, of avoiding that which may injure or destroy it, of exercising those active faculties the germs of which are born with us. If we examine the matter carefully, we shall see that the highest morality is involved in the definition. To a certain point in his development, man repels moral evil with the same horror with which, as a matter of course, he does his best to avoid physical suffering and the action of agencies likely to prove fatal.

It is thus that we can connect with this primordial tendency the determinations arising from physical necessities; then those which, less immediate, nevertheless are much of the same kind, such as lodging, clothing, the perpetuation of the species. As a consequence, man finds himself impelled to procure for himself that with which nature has not immediately furnished him—arms defensive and offensive, means of protection against vicissitudes of climate and against dangerous animals, tools, instruments, furniture. He invents the art of making a fire, he stores provisions, he observes nature, he sees that fruits ripen at the end of a certain period after the plant which bears them has flourished, and that this plant itself flowers only at the end of a certain period after it has borne seed. Thence he imitates nature; he sows seed, and he waits. Sociable, he develops the chief social faculty, language; the family, the clan, the tribe, later the city, the nation, spring from that. And then, when his elementary needs are satisfied, man becomes an extremely curious animal. He manifests a strange desire to know everything, even those things the knowledge of which cannot benefit him in any way. This is the point of departure of science. Again, he experiences a special pleasure, in regard to which he constantly grows more fastidious, in seeing things combined according to certain laws of harmony and of contrast. This is the beginning of art. Finally, he feels certain sensations of pleasure or of displeasure according as it is a question of one mode of action or of another, independently of any profit which he may derive from either, and he is never more fully conscious of these impressions of a quite special kind than when he feels displeasure after having satisfied a selfish desire at the expense of another, or than when he deprives himself of some wished-for pleasure in order not to injure another. This is the commencement of morals.

These are the determinations which are among the most general and which have the greatest influence on existence or on human life. The varieties of application belonging to each of them are innumerable.

But have we done?

Suppose that an inhabitant of Saturn or of Sirius, endowed

with intelligence, capable of judging of all that passes among us, but absolutely limited as to his faculty of knowledge to notions of physical wants, of provident labour, of social life, of art, science, morals, had found means to come down to our earth, and to be present invisibly at all that is going on there. He would see that our species has laboured hard since it has been upon our planet; he would observe our societies, our armies, our governments, our arts, our sciences, our manners, and he would understand all that. He would, however, have a group of terrestrial facts which would be to him absolutely incomprehensible. He would see numerous buildings of various forms opening on certain days at certain hours. Wherefore? He would see multitudes given to odd movements, genuflections, with hands joined, with heads bowed, their food regulated or even abstained from, speaking, or singing, or silent, some men clothed differently from others, images, some hideous, others ravishing, sacrifices, processions, discussions, books, perhaps punishments, perhaps bloody wars,—and the motive, the reason of all this, would escape him absolutely. In vain would he exercise his ingenuity in conjecture. His vexation would be increased if some one should tell him that there is in all this only the quite external surface of a world apart which goes down into the very depths of terrestrial life, whether collective or individual. He would be compelled to return to his star having understood everything in terrestrial life except these manifestations, which are religion.

What is then the specific nature of this direction of human life?

We say that it is connected with the feeling of a *bond*, not merely of a relation which exists only in theory, logically, philosophically, but of a bond positive, concrete—as real, for instance, as the force of gravitation which detains us on the surface of the earth, or as the affinity which exists between our blood and those elements of like composition with which we furnish it by nutrition and respiration. I do not at the moment give any opinion on the question as to whether this sentiment is well founded or illusory. I simply attest that it has for the religious man as convincing evidence and as deep intensity as the consciousness of living in the midst of other men, or of being lighted by the rays of the sun.

This bond unites the human mind, we say, to another mind. Here let us detach our inquiry from adjacent questions, however grave they may be. We are not going to plunge into the discussion of the great problem of spiritualism or materialism. Let us endeavour to make our meaning clear. In the world of realities two great divisions stand out—that of realities which our senses perceive, or which they may perceive provided they are sufficiently qualified, and that of realities which absolutely escape our means of sensible perception even when we multiply their power indefinitely by instruments. I class in this second category the facts of conscience, impressions, feelings, thoughts, volitions, reasonings, dispositions, intellectual, moral, æsthetic, &c. There is a whole series of facts or of realities, imperceptible to our senses, which we range in the category of mind. Attribute it to what you will, say that it is only a form of matter, at the same time taking care that it is not more easily demonstrated to you that matter is only a form of mind, or rather admit that which is our conviction, that for him who would know all and understand all, there is in the depths of our being no irreconcilable dualism, and that this division can be only provisional, conditional on the limitations of our faculty of knowledge. You have the choice. But you cannot prove in the *chiaro oscuro* in which we are compelled to live and to reason, that there is any hard and fast line drawn between invisible and impalpable realities and others. Well! We say that the first are the domain of mind. But we add that this domain is not confined to the interior of man, but that it extends also to the world around him.

Here, again, let us systematically exclude all metaphysics. Let us maintain simply that which no instructed person can dispute, that the things of the external world are not a confused mass, a medley, a chaos. They have among them fixed relations of all kinds—relations of proportion, of affinity or of repulsion,

DEFINITION OF RELIGION.   29

of antecedent and of consequent, of reciprocal concomitance or exclusion. Science from the beginning has sought only to know what lies *beneath* and *within* the visible and tangible surface of being in order to formulate these relations. Man, on his side, from the beginning also has been led to believe that there is in the world in which he lives, even though he himself can observe only a small part of it, something more than a motley and confused mass of sounds, of colours and of forms, that there is through all a certain order, a certain succession, something which his intelligence recognizes as being like itself. And however gross may be the errors into which he may fall in representing to himself this intelligence or cause which reveals itself in things which he has called law, divinity, cosmic order, secret cause, or even *fatum*, genius, *numen*, *mens agitans molem*, it still remains that for man, listening as yet only to his instinct, there is face to face with his spirit another spirit manifested in matter, a spirit in affinity with his own—for otherwise he would not even suspect its existence ; and religion is essentially the bond which unites his spirit to that spirit.

In fact, the supposition with which science sets out, and which she verifies at each step in advance, is identical with that which religion instinctively makes.

Let us add that spirit, the object of religion, may be taken in a collective or in an individual sense, conceived as impersonal or personal. This distinction, so important in history, in no way modifies our definition.

This granted, religion springs from the feeling that man is in such a relation in regard to this spirit that for his well-being, and in order to gratify a spontaneous impulse of his nature, he ought to maintain with it such relations as will afford him guarantees against the unknown of destiny. Man, in presence of the world, feels himself little, confined, miserable. It is an opposition which imperiously demands its synthesis. For the spirit whose existence man recognizes through and above that which surrounds him, is a superior spirit (we do not at present say infinite or absolute or perfect, in order not to go beyond the data of strict experience), and of a superiority such as, if he feels himself in harmony with it, he becomes, even he, if not the master, at least the superior, of this destiny, of this unknown, which limits and disquiets him. Assuredly we cannot exaggerate the amplitude of the angle which would contain the innumerable modes in which this relation is represented and realized. Observe only, that from the worship paid by the savage to the fetich to which he attributes the power of securing good hunting or fishing—from the penitent Buddhist, who seeks in the renunciation of all earthly desire the infallible method of attaining to the supreme felicity of being no longer conscious of living, to the Roman making the safety of his country, outside of which he could not imagine life possible, depend upon the punctuality with which the rites celebrated by the Flamens were performed— to the pious trust in a God of mercy of the Christian spiritualist,— all these varieties of religion are to be found between the lines which we have just traced.

There is, however, a side of the question which is too much neglected in contemporary theories of the origin of religions. It would be very inexact to see in even the earliest form of religion only a calculation based on the need of arriving at a good understanding with the superior being whose favour we wish to gain in order to govern destiny. This is certainly one of the factors of religion, but not the only one. Always bear in mind that, if man is religious, he is so, not only because he thinks he will find his advantage in being so, but also because he likes to be religious, independently of anything he may gain by it. Those who do not understand this double element of the religious conscience, are thereby excluded from understanding anything of either the genesis or the permanence of religion in humanity. This assertion may seem paradoxical; it is, nevertheless, an incontrovertible truth. Man *likes* to worship even gods which frighten him, even those whom he represents to himself under all sorts of appalling forms. We shall return to this point; at present we will only say to those whom this enunciation may surprise, Explain why men love the tragic, that which shocks, that which moves them, that which at a certain point fills them with dread? Why do they, while unwilling to shed a tear, yet resort in crowds to spectacles where they can expect nothing else? We touch here upon that other element of religion which we call mystery. The spirit, object of religion, is mysterious.

Man ardently aspires to become more intimately acquainted with, to understand, the governing spirit or spirits which he discerns through things, and which he likes to know as his allies against fate, but he soon perceives that he cannot succeed in this. If he rises to the notion of an individual mind, sovereign director and *ultima ratio* of everything, it seems to him for a moment that all is explained. But soon he is forced to confess that this individual spirit is himself incomprehensible, impenetrable; that his superiority is not merely very great, that it is immense, infinite, overwhelming, and all the more so when contemplated apart. The angel himself, in the poetic symbolism of the Christian mythology, covers his face with his wings while passing before the throne, the splendour of which he cannot look upon; and we can see no better in the light which blinds than in the darkness. Man must and can apply to this superior spirit the most exalted idea of which he is conscious. This divine spirit no doubt possesses, in full and complete reality, all the perfections of which the human spirit contains the germ or conceives the idea. But these perfections themselves only augment the mystery. Reason may despair, but religion loses nothing. It is thence that she causes mysterious chords to vibrate in the soul, chords which seem to tremble in unison with the distant harmony reserved for the eternal spheres. We speak here of a religion already purified, already cleared from the original dross. But we find already very early, as a confused feeling of this truth, that the attraction which the notion of God has for us is due to the very mystery in which his ineffable majesty is enveloped. Do we not see it inspire one of the myths, at once one of the rudest and the richest in meaning of Hebrew antiquity, that nocturnal struggle of the patriarch with the mysterious being who refuses to tell his name, to allow himself to be seen, and who leaves him wounded and blessed? (Genesis xxxii. 24—29.)

This is why it is an error to believe that religion is the daughter of fear, engendered by ignorance. If it was so, when once the object of fear had vanished, religion should disappear also. Assuredly fear had a place, especially in the beginning, in the motives which provoke in man the rise of religion. But it is not alone, any more than is calculation. Let us say, further, that we must take largely into account a sort of secret voluptuousness, capable of acquiring an extraordinary degree of intensity, and which, even when reduced to slender proportions, is none the less one of the chief creative causes of religion. He who allows himself to be entirely subjugated by mysticism will be very ill prepared for the rational study which we undertake. But he who has not known by experience at least something of this charm sovereignly sweet to the soul, will be no better fitted. We must have the religious ear in order competently to study phenomena of the religious order. How could the man who has no sense of the beautiful ever write the history of art?

Religion, such as we define it, is inherent in the human mind and *natural*. We are justified in applying these terms to that which throughout history and over the whole surface of the habitable globe shows itself inseparable from human nature. The ancients, when they began to look beyond their own country, were greatly struck by this *consensus gentium*, the result of which was, that in spite of all diversities, they found everywhere a religion. The more acquaintance with the world has been extended, the more this observation has been confirmed. Ancient Asia, America, Africa, Malaisia, Polynesia, Australia, the Polar regions, have successively furnished their testimony. Religion is a human fact in the strictest sense of the word, and here we are in accord with Benjamin Constant, who, in a work as remarkable for the shrewd and penetrating views which are occasionally found in it, as it is insufficient and out of date owing to the progress of religious history, has enunciated this principle, constantly verified ever since, that religion is an indefectible and perfectible attribute of our species.

It is true that in the present day this universality has been disputed. Of late years, we have often heard of savage tribes which are described as being quite destitute of any kind of religious ideas. The detailed discussion of such assertions will come in its place when we approach the religious history of peoples devoid of all culture. At the moment, we will weigh only these two considerations.

1st. The reports of travellers on the subject of peoples whom they have found without any kind of religion, ought to be received with the greatest circumspection. Too often they base their judgment either on inaccurate information or on very superficial observation. Many of them, strangers to all religious criticism, from the absence of those forms to which they have been accustomed to attach the idea of a religion, infer the absence of the religion itself. The number is already relatively great of peoples of whom such things have been said, and in regard to whom later more attentive and better directed inquiry has afforded evidence of the contrary. Sometimes even the eminent narrators fall into the strange contradiction of describing the belief in magic, sorcery, divination, of natives to whom a few pages previously they have denied any kind of religious faith.[1]

2nd. *A priori*, nevertheless the fact itself cannot be denied. The human mind can rise very high, but it sets out very low down. There is nothing to show that man has not passed through an initial period in which, while already possessing some features of its distinctive physiognomy, he did not yet possess what we call religion. But that would not prove anything against the

---

[1] This contradiction is especially manifest in the work of Sir John Lubbock, "The Origin of Civilization." Professor Roskoff, of Vienna, has peremptorily refuted this kind of ethnographic error in his book, *Das Religionswesen der rohesten Naturvœlker:* Leipzig, 1880.

naturally *human* character of religion. Might there not have been among the very numerous families of which humanity is composed, some specimens yet existing who might have remained stationary below the level at which the human mind becomes religious? Or else, that which cannot be denied beforehand, that some of the disinherited tribes may have degenerated into a state akin to that of the brutes? Or, once more, must we maintain in regard to the human family, that which is so easy to maintain among ourselves, that men are endowed very unequally from a religious point of view? There are men whose soul trembles at the breath of religion like the Æolian harp in the breeze, men with whom religious feeling, religious convictions and religious enthusiasm, attain an absorbing intensity. Others, on the contrary, are cold as ice, and remain deaf to that which speaks so powerfully to the first. It is as if a sense were wanting. Exceptional and accidental facts can never be converted into permanent and fundamental characteristics of the human race. The mathematical capacity of the human mind is not destroyed by the fact that children are still incapable of employing it, and that certain savages, it is said, cannot learn to make calculations that are to us elementary. The same may be said of art, of science, of politics, all essentially human. Never allow to the abnormal, the doubtful exception, the weak point, such a value as will cast a slight on the characteristic features of the whole. If we wished to describe the European type, it would not be among the goitrous of the Valais that we should seek our models.

In beginning, then, the history of Religion, we start from the fact that religion is a thing essentially human. Unfortunately, before going further, we find ourselves face to face with a theological doctrine which throws itself across our path, and which we must discuss. For according to the solution given to this, the history which we are about to write will completely change its aspect. It is the hypothesis of a *primitive revelation*.

III.

THE PRIMITIVE REVELATION.

If we were writing the history of art, or of civilization, or of philosophy, the question which now meets us would not arise. We should begin with the early and imperfect rudiments of each of these higher products of the human mind, and we should need only to follow their continuous development.

Our history, on the contrary, is met at the outset by the claim of those who will have it that, in the very beginning of the human race, the creative power revealed to the first men by supernatural means the essential principles of religious truth. If this claim be well founded, our history, for a very long time at least, can be nothing more than an exposition of the degradations and corruptions of this revealed truth. It is only in the event of the case being otherwise that we recur to the conditions of all history.

It is altogether in spite of ourselves that we engage exceptionally in one of those theological discussions which we should prefer to avoid. There might be, it is true, neutral ground on which agreement would perhaps be possible. If God has so constituted human nature that at some moment in its development it must awake to the recognition of a reality superior to purely sensible phenomena, and if this first awaking of the religious feeling must, in virtue of this same constitution of the human mind, lead it by a series of experiences, of reflections, of genial aspirations, to the notion of a Power supreme and superlatively adorable, it is evident that this moment, august above all others, in which a human soul feels itself pervaded, as it were, by a spirit the existence of which it had not previously suspected, is the initial point of a development which must fill history. It matters little, from this point of view, that this dawn of the religious sentiment in the human soul may have been associated with simple and rude notions of the world and of the object of faith. The point of departure is fixed, and the journey begins. In substance, it comes to precisely the same thing to say, God revealed himself in the beginning to man, as soon as man had reached a certain stage in his psychic development; as to say, Man was so constituted that, arrived at a certain stage in his psychic development, he must become sensible of the reality of the Divine influence. In this sense, which leaves perfect freedom to history, we also could accept the idea of a primitive revelation.

But in view of the very narrow interpretation which is habitually given to this doctrine, we should seem to be playing with words, and to be clothing our ideas in an orthodox dress which does not become them. In fact, the religious schools which maintain the truth of a primitive revelation, are guided by a very evident theological interest. The Catholics hope thus to lay the foundation-stone on which later they will raise the dogma of the infallibility of the Church; while Protestant orthodoxy believes this doctrine to be taught in the Bible, and that its maintenance is necessary to the authority of the holy book.

This distinction is connected with the two modes in which the question itself may be looked at. It may be taken at once on its purely theoretic, abstract side, independently of all direct relation with the Church or the Bible; it may also be sustained directly on what is believed to be read in the first book of the Bible, in Genesis.

The first method has found an ingenious and subtle defender in M. de Bonald. The originality of his system consists in his making a primitive supernatural revelation the absolute condition of human life, such as it is unfolded in history. It is not only religion which is supposed to have been miraculously given to man, but also language and even the art of writing. And as, according to the essential conditions of this system, man thinks only if he is able to speak, it would follow that without this supernatural endowment we should have known nothing, we should have remained sunk in animalism, incapable even of thought.

We might reply to this theory by the plea in bar with which science is always justified in opposing views which rest on an appeal to the supernatural. Here we have, in the first instance, man as yet in all points like an animal, incapable of speech or of thought. Some time after, this man is found speaking and thinking. It is supposed that we are absolutely unable to mark the point of transition from the primitive state to this last and higher state. Have we, therefore, in sound logic, the right to conclude that a supernatural intervention has taken place, and that it has worked this inexplicable change? By no means. When we were ignorant of the physical causes of rain, that was not a rational explanation which accounted for the phenomena by attributing them to the special action of the Divine will, and saw the finger of God where we now speak of refrigeration, of currents of air, and of condensation of vapours.

But, moreover, how, according to this hypothesis, could the Divine power have communicated ideas to man, as yet incapable of speech and thought? To reveal anything to any one, is to speak to him. It matters little here whether the language be external, striking on the ear, or internal. It is not less necessary to think in order to understand what is communicated to you, than it is in order to communicate what you wish some one else to understand. It is for this reason, among other consequences of this axiom, that a being unable to speak cannot of himself learn to speak. A bird, though his organs may be fitted to imitate the sounds of the human voice, does not therefore attain to language. Every child knows what is meant when he is told that he says his lesson like a parrot. As old Philo long since discerned, language is not only thought spoken, it is still more thought *thought*. If an animal cries and does not speak, it is because he has sensations to express, but beyond that he has nothing to say. In conclusion, if man learned to speak, it was because he was able to speak.

We are told, as a matter of experience, that man speaks only because he has heard others speak; thence, it is said, primitive man, who never heard speech, could never have arrived at language if the Creator had not taught it to him, and the example of deaf mutes is quoted.[1] Here is the same paradox which we noted above in connection with the human, natural character of religion. We suppose man in possession of his normal faculties, and we are met by examples drawn from exceptional infirmity. In the discussion in which we are engaged, we have a right to require that man shall be taken as he is normally, with ears that hear, with an organization rendering articulate language possible, with that instinct of imitation which we see reproduced in every child born into the world, with a tendency to derive from his organs and from nature all that can make life easier and more agreeable to him,—with, finally, that need, so marked in him, to realize, to represent to himself and to others, the impressions, desires, emotions, aspirations, which agitate him. For language is only one determination of the more general category of the sign. It belongs to the same family as gesture, posture, laughing, crying, grimace, adornment, and all possible manifestations of hidden thought. It is the most usual sign, because it is the most convenient and the clearest. Ah! the man whom we have to consider is not a deaf mute! He hears the sounds of nature, the roaring of the wind in the branches, the noise of the waterfall, the song of the brook, the rolling of the thunder, the pattering

---

[1] Appeal has been made also to the old history related by Herodotus of king Psammeticus of Egypt, who caused two nurslings to be shut up in a stable alone with the goat on whose milk they were fed. At the end of two years they were found, uttering only the word *be'kos, be'kos*. Thereupon the learned held a consultation, and gravely pronounced that, this word signifying *nourishment* in Armenia, the language of this country must have been the primordial language. Supposing the history authentic, we can only be astonished that none of these observers bethought himself of remarking that the poor babies articulated the only sound which their nurse had been able to let them hear.

of the rain, the innumerable voices of animated nature. Being what he is, we may be certain that he will imitate, whether for his pleasure, for his profit, or for his safety. His first speech will be composed of onomatopœia, just as his first writing will consist of rude drawings of the objects which he wishes to indicate. And just as the primitive hieroglyphy changes into ideography—that is to say, as the drawings take an abstract syllabic interpretation, and represent henceforth sounds, no longer objects—so will the earliest onomatopœias be changed into words corresponding to general ideas, and it is into this vessel that man insensibly pours the marvellous instinctive logic of his mind. Every formed tongue is in fact a marvel of unconscious logic. It is all very wonderful, but we do not see a single point in this development where it would be necessary to have recourse to supernatural action in order to pass to the next point.

But may it not be objected that the doctrine of a primitive revelation of religious truth has lost rather than gained by its association with the untenable theory of M. de Bonald as to the origin of language, and that it would be only just to deal with it by itself?

It is one of those theories which were in vogue for a certain time when historical studies, especially those concerning remote antiquity, were still in their infancy. It was then still believed that man is very recent on the earth. The proofs of his great antiquity on the globe had not yet been furnished. The earliest records told of a life rational, industrious, well-regulated, *quasi* idyllic. There did not seem any difficulty in attributing to the first men ideas, already very elevated, of the Divinity and his relations with them, nor any invincible objections against explanations of the supernatural order; so it was allowed that such a hypothesis as that of a primitive revelation was not out of harmony with what was believed to be known of the primitive world.[1]

[1] A curious specimen of this way of considering pre-historic times may be seen in the work of M. de Rougemont, *Le Peuple Primitif.*

But to-day, when we know that humanity has left traces of its existence in the epochs when the mammoth, the reindeer and the cave-bears still inhabited the central and southern regions of our country; when undoubted discoveries have revealed the state of barbarism, of extreme grossness, in which our ancestors lived for prolonged periods; when we have ascertained that the further back we go in the chain of time, so much the more does man approach the animal—we must confess that it is infinitely hard to imagine that in the beginning of this slow and painful development, man, yet plunged in absolute ignorance, was in possession of sublime religious doctrines such as the most pure inspiration has been able to offer to cultivated societies, rich in accumulated experience. Such a contention surprises and perplexes us. Analogy is wanting. What should we say to those who would claim that, in virtue of another supernatural intervention, the first men were in possession of an art such as that which produced the marvels of Greek architecture and sculpture? or, again, that they had, concerning the constitution of the world, the place of the earth in the universe, the nature of light, ideas identical with those which modern science has promulgated? We should certainly say that such contentions are in the highest degree unlikely; that nothing affords them either foundation or substance; that they are in contradiction to all that we know or can conjecture as to pre-historic times; and we should have the right of declining to discuss such hypotheses until the facts which they are reputed to explain are proved to us. It is absolutely the same with the hypothesis of a primitive revelation of religious truth. It is in contradiction to all that we know as to the extremely miserable and uncultured state of humanity anterior to history. We must come to facts, and when they are supplied to us we will discuss them.

But that is a demand in due form which other partizans of this doctrine would accept by founding it on the testimony of the Bible, a second mode of treating the question which we will examine in its turn.

Among the men of note who have maintained the reality of a primitive revelation against those who believe that this doctrine is clearly contradicted by the discoveries of historical science, we must quote Mr. Gladstone, the illustrious statesman, and at the same time an accomplished scholar, in the first rank. We could not choose a better qualified representative of the thesis of a primary religious revelation granted to man by the Creator.[1]

The mythologies are, according to Mr. Gladstone, the result of a systematic corruption of earlier doctrines of great sublimity and of great purity. They do not spring, as the modern school teaches, out of the direct deification of natural facts. They are at bottom only the old theistic, Messianic and biblical traditions sophistically re-clothed. God revealed himself in the beginning as powerful, holy and good. The corrupt sense of man retained only the idea of power, and grievously lowered the moral character of the Divinity. Hence the base tendencies which induced him to recognize this only in those phenomena of nature which most appealed to his imagination. The religion revealed in the beginning contained six great doctrines: 1st, the unity of God; 2nd, a divine Trinity, the three terms of which shared in the same dignity; 3rd, the promise of a Redeemer who should deliver man from the curse of sin; 4th, a divine personal Wisdom, creating and sustaining the world; 5th, the connection of the Redeemer with humanity by his miraculous birth of a woman; finally, 6th, the existence of a wicked being, of the *evil one*, exercising among men the power of a tempter and chief of the rebel angels.

Thereupon the Trinity is obliterated in polytheism, the foretold incarnation in anthropomorphism. Zeus, Hades and Poseidon are the caricature of the triune God. The notion of a Redeemer is reflected in the myths of Phebus Apollo, that of a divine

---

[1] The views of Mr. Gladstone on the religious origins of humanity may be found in three of his works: *Homer and the Homeric Age* (1860); *Address to the University of Edinburgh* (1865); *Juventus Mundi* (1868). They have been the subject of very profound criticism in the learned work on *Aryan Mythology*, by Mr. Cox.

Wisdom in those of Athene. Leto or Latona corresponds to the mother of the Redeemer. The devil and his following have as pendants the Titans and the monsters of fable, &c. All the Greek mythology can be thus disposed of.

Again we ask for the proof; for ultimately this Greek mythology is connected by ties of close relationship with that of the Vedas: it includes several elements having their origin in Egypt and in the Semitic East; and when we ascend to these various sources, we find ourselves face to face with a religion very simple, very rude, but very directly derived from nature, and we do not discover the least trace of systematic disfigurement of any anterior truth. Then it is that Mr. Gladstone and his partizans meet us with the authority of the Bible, and especially of the Book of Genesis.

We could clearly ask them why we are bound to accord to this sacred book a dictatorial authority which would oblige us to subordinate to it the results of purely scientific research. But we will rather descend to the ground on which they take refuge; we will simply open the Book of Genesis, and see if it contains all that they make it say.

It is generally agreed in these days that there are in this book two narratives of separate origin, one of which comprises the whole of the first chapter, is interrupted at the third verse of the second chapter, to be resumed only at the first verse of the fifth chapter.

This first narrative relates the beginning of the heavens and of the earth under that simple, majestic, we might say classic, form, too often spoiled by the efforts which have been made to found upon it modern cosmology and geology. It contains scientific errors on which we need not pause.[1] Then, when animals of all kinds have been created in their turn, God said, "*Let us*

---

[1] It speaks of the heaven, the firmament, as a solid vault, above which the waters are stored, of the creation of the stars after the formation of the earth and solely for its use, of the appearance of the entire vegetable kingdom before it could be subjected to the action of solar light.

make man in our image and after our likeness, and let him have dominion over all animals." It is in this expression, Let *us* make man, that accommodating interpreters have desired to trace the first revelation of the dogma of the Trinity, not recognizing that this expression is simply the royal plural used in Hebrew, as in many other languages, when kings are understood to speak in virtue of their sovereign power; or else, and more probably, it was an appeal to the *Bené Elohîm*, the sons of God, who later are called angels, and are supposed to have been present at the work of creation. Besides, there is not a word to tell us about this supposed revelation of the Trinity having been made to the human pair, who did not then exist, who were created immediately afterwards, and who received no other instructions than that they were to people the earth, to have dominion over the animals, and to feed on grains and fruits. Then the Creator, having finished his six days'[1] work, rests. Absolutely nothing indicates the revelation of any religious doctrine to the first human beings.

As we have said, the narrative breaks off (chap. ii. 3) to give place to another narrator, and is resumed in the fifth chapter only to record the genealogy from Adam, the first man, to Noah, in whose time, the earth being " corrupt and filled with violence," covered with crimes, God resolved to destroy the human race, with the exception of one family, by the deluge. It is then that he again meets the second narrator, without there being any more question than at first of a primitive orthodoxy revealed to the first men.

It is to the second narrator that we are indebted for the celebrated details concerning Eden, the first sin and its consequences. Much less concerned than the first with physical origins, he devotes himself in preference to the first evolutions of human life. He represents things in the beginning as though, before the appearance of man, there was neither rain nor vegetation.

---

[1] And not geologic periods. The proof of this is, that the Hebrew author connects with this divine repose on the seventh day the institution of the weekly Sabbath.

But Jahveh, having formed man of the dust of the ground, breathes his own breath into the nostrils of this clay statue, and man becomes a living person. Then he plants the Garden of Eden, where he establishes the man, who may eat of all fruits—among others, of that which ensures perpetuity of existence, but to whom he forbids the fruit which imparts the knowledge of good and of evil. For man, in a state of complete ignorance, and therefore of complete innocence, cannot yet distinguish good from evil. Man is to take care of and to cultivate this garden. There are the animals, which Jahveh, curious to hear how he will name them, causes to pass before him, which determines the birth of human language. Then, as alone of all living beings the first man had no companion, Jahveh took from his side, while he slept, the flesh with which he made the first woman. Old and venerable myth, the infantine crudity of which ought not to hide from us the deep feeling and exquisite delicacy, and which is certainly one of the pearls of Hebrew tradition! For the rest, our author takes special care to point out that the first pair are as yet strangers to the most elementary notions of morality, and he tells us that they were naked, without experiencing the least shame.

Then follows the famous scene of the transgression, thanks to which they attain to the conscious distinction of good and of evil; but not at all in consequence of a divine revelation; quite the reverse. For the promoter of the transgression, who is not at all the *evil one* of Mr. Gladstone, nor the devil of later theology, but neither more nor less than the serpent, the first serpent, in the literal sense of the word, insidiously leads the first woman to eat of the forbidden fruit; she draws her husband into her fault, and the consequences follow.[1] They are ashamed of their

---

[1] The proof that it is a question here of an animal serpent is furnished further on, when Jahveh punishes successively the three authors of the disobedience. The entire race of serpents are to undergo the punishment which has been drawn down upon them by their first ancestor. Let us say in passing that the characteristic trait of this Jahvist author (we call him so to distinguish him from the preceding one, who does not mention the divine name of Jahveh until the rise of Moses) consists in this, that

nakedness; they clothe themselves in leaves, and it is just this which betrays them to their irritated Master. The punishments which strike them are in the category of generic evils, always afflicting humanity, and denoting, according to the old Semitic point of view, an original fault, of which all men conjointly ought to bear the consequences. The serpent is condemned to the necessity of crawling painfully in the burning dust, and to the undying hatred of man henceforth. "The seed of the woman"—and it is in no way a question of individualizing this posterity in a single man, or the woman in any one woman—shall bruise the head of the serpent, which shall bruise him in the heel. This is the lasting conflict, while nothing indicates on which side shall be the final victory, and it required great goodwill on the part of the old exegetists to see in that a prediction of redemption. The generic punishment of the woman consists in the pains of parturition and in subordination to her husband. That of the man is summed up in the necessity of prolonged, irksome, ill-recompensed labour, with the dark prospect of that death which he would not have known (or foreseen) if he had remained in his primary ignorance.

And in order to prevent man from escaping this sentence, by continuing to eat of the fruit of the *tree of life* planted in the centre of Eden, Jahveh banishes both him and his companion from this garden of delights, and places at the entrance the terrible *Kerubim*,[1] monsters with flaming swords.

The narrative continues in the history of the first family of Cain and Abel, prototypes of two races always antagonistic, the sedentary agriculturist and the nomad shepherd. Thence results the first murder and its punishment. The mythic character of

he recognizes the tendency to progress and its successive realization in humanity, but that each step is accompanied by a moral fall and followed by disastrous consequences. In reality, in his narrative, the serpent had not lied, *the eyes* of Adam and Eve *were opened* as he had foretold, and they had acquired the knowledge of good and evil like divine beings. Jahveh is *jealous* of the progress of man, and takes care that he shall pay dearly for it.

[1] These are what Christian mythology has transformed into cherubim. Few words have undergone a more complete change of meaning.

the story is evident throughout. Cain, condemned to wander over the earth, is afraid of being put to death by those whom he may meet, as if there were other inhabitants of the world besides the Adamic family. He, his wife and his son build *a town*, which would seem to show that all these proper names have a collective rather than an individual meaning. Note also the mention of the first sacrifices, Cain and Abel offering to Jahveh, each on his own account, the produce of his labour, that which each esteems the most, evidently acting on the idea that the Divinity has the same wants and tastes as man. Nothing is said to indicate that the Divinity himself prescribed this kind of worship. For the rest, it is among the Cainites that the earliest civilization is developed, characterized especially by the employment of metals and the birth of the musical art. But at the same time arise two plagues, as attested by the old song of Lamech, polygamy and war. A third son of Adam, Seth, is the father of another race, and "then began men to call on the name of the Lord;" but not as the result of a recorded revelation. This narrative, like the preceding one, points out the state of corruption and wickedness of the human race; only it adds a touch, altogether mythological, of the love which the Bené Elohim, or sons of God, had conceived for the daughters of men. It was from this kind of union that the illustrious heroes of antiquity were born. It has been sought to find in this curious passage a sort of explanation of the formation of other mythologies. However that may be, we come to the deluge, which forms the first standpoint common to the two earliest narrators of the Book of Genesis.

The deluge is also related in double form, although with some variations, without interest in the question in debate. On leaving the ark, Noah and his family receive a revelation. But in what does it consist? In this: that man may henceforward eat the flesh of animals, always on condition of not eating the blood; that the blood of man shed by man shall be demanded again from the murderer; and that the rainbow, set it would seem for the first time in the heavens, shall be for all time a guarantee of the intentions of Jahveh, who will not again destroy the human race by a deluge. All this is full of poetry; but where do we find the primitive revelation of Mr. Gladstone?

Anything further which may be adduced from the Bible, as, for instance, the revelations made to the patriarchs, concern only the family of Abraham, and are consequently foreign to the hypothesis of a primitive religious teaching given by God to humanity. There is, then, absolutely nothing in the Book of Genesis to give substance to a claim which, if it had any foundation, would make religious history the reverse of all others. In admitting even the historical character of these details, in our view altogether mythical, in supposing that the first men really lived as the narrators in Genesis make them live, we must simply conclude that the first men knew that they had for their master a God powerful, formidable, of changeable will, creating man capable of a progress which he most frequently thwarts, but without anything to prevent man imagining other gods; indeed, his acquaintance with the Bené Elohim was not precisely calculated to draw him away from polytheism.

We have made a point, in order not to complicate a discussion already much prolonged and somewhat subtle, of abstaining from everything, in those numerous critical studies of which Genesis has been the subject, which was not indispensable to our argument. It remains to enforce a final consideration, which already has a place in this order of special researches, but which we will sum up as clearly as we can.

From a religious point of view, the traditions registered in Genesis certainly bear a Hebraic impress. The Israelitish authors, relating the beginning of the human race at a period when monotheism was for them an incontestable truth, could imagine only monotheists. But is the foundation itself of these traditions strictly Hebraic? We may question this, and regard them at least as springing from a source whence Chaldea and Persia drew more than one traditional notion. Some indeed maintain that the cosmogonic, Edenic and diluvian traditions were directly borrowed, modified only in the monotheistic sense, at a period relatively recent, by the narrators whose recitals have been combined in Genesis. But without entering on a discussion which will meet us later in our course, we may affirm that in every case the traditions of Genesis can apply only to a sufficiently limited group of peoples, those who, according to the Book of Genesis itself (chap. x.), can trace their origin to the three sons of Noah, Shem, Ham and Japhet. This deserves attention.

Let it be understood, however, that these names do not represent an ethnological division sanctioned by science. In admitting that the peoples descended from Japhet correspond to those whom we now call Indo-Europeans—and that greatly exceeds the limits assigned to the progeny of Japhet—we recognize the other peoples indicated in the same nomenclature as Semites and Chamites. But it is necessary that all the races of man shall be represented in the picture. Where are the Negroes, who have in reality nothing in common with the Chamites? Where are the Touranians, the Chinese, the Malays, the Polynesians, the American races, the Hyperboreans, &c.? This tenth chapter of Genesis, a very remarkable essay on ancient ethnology, and one of the most interesting in the Bible, while it supposes a great enlargement of the very narrow horizon which so long limited the gaze of the Israelites, does none the less indicate that the narrators of Genesis could only reproduce prevalent traditions concerning the beginnings of a fraction merely of humanity.

This observation, in our opinion, definitively settles the question. The hypothesis of a primitive revelation of religious truth to humanity, already so improbable, viewed in connection with all that we know of the remote past of our human species, finds no support in the book itself to which its partizans appeal; and this book, in turn, cannot pass as a document relating the beginnings of the whole human race.

We may thus, once for all, strike out this contention from the course of our discussions.

IV.

PRIMITIVE TRADITION.

We have, however, still to examine a kindred hypothesis which, without raising at first sight the same kind of objections as the preceding, will yet not the less cross the path of our researches in a way to compromise their independence, and will end, all things considered, by leading us into similar difficulties. The question now is no longer of a supernatural revelation, but of a tradition—that is to say, of a regular and continuous transmission of recollections going back to the beginnings of the species, which ought to serve us as a criterion for interpreting and utilizing parallel or divergent but less certain traditions. At bottom, and notwithstanding the apparent harmlessness of this new contention, it is once more the tradition recorded in Genesis that it is desired to set up as queen and mistress of all the others, without an immediate appeal to miracle. A little reflection will, however, suffice to discover that in reality this privilege of a unique tradition escaping from all the causes which have rendered the others untrustworthy or contradictory, presupposes a miraculous intervention of Providence quite as much as the doctrine of a primitive revelation.

We are required to admit that, prior to all which we call civilization, when men were still plunged in the densest ignorance, as yet strangers to the most elementary arts—when, destitute of metallic tools and incapable of cultivating the soil, they were obliged, like the animal, to depend for their daily food on the chances of the soil or of the chase, and were absorbed by the care of finding this in sufficient quantity, like the most backward savages of the present day—they took care to collect and to condense into short narratives, intentionally addressed to their descendants in future ages, their experiences, their impressions, their recollections of events of which they had been the witnesses or in which they had been the actors, and that they confided this kind of historic collection to the memory of their children, who in turn would do the same in regard to theirs. But this primitive tradition became obliterated, obscured and corrupted, among all fractions of the human race save one. One version alone remained free from adulteration, conscious or unconscious—one tradition only was preserved through the ages in incomparable conditions of authenticity and of purity, and it is in that exclusively that we must seek for what primitive humanity did, believed and thought.

Does not this mere statement produce upon us an effect just like that produced by those theories of the last century, in which our ancestors of pre-historic times were represented as assembled under the shade of virgin forests, to discuss with the gravity of old jurisconsults the principles of *le contrat social?*

Let us, however, disregard this impression. The first question which arises is this: Where must we seek this continuous tradition which will allow us to ascend uninterruptedly to the beginning of humanity? India, China, ancient Persia, Egypt, Syria, America, ancient Greece, the larger part of the nations who have made a mark in history, even certain savage tribes, have each their Genesis. Which shall we choose?

We shall be told that there are some points in common which will serve to mark out the line of direction. But that is not at all so simple as we might be tempted to think. There is a factor which would very well explain the greater part, if not all, of these points in common, without having recourse to the improbable hypothesis which we are examining. This factor, too much neglected, is the unity of the human mind applying itself to resolve the same questions with the same elements of solution. For example, many local traditions have in common the notion of a deluge. There are others which have not the least knowledge of it.

But if we take account of these two facts, that in all countries watered by great rivers and the scenes of devasting inundations, the same phenomenon has suggested the same idea, and since, to some extent, everywhere there has been a tendency to liken the creation to what occurs every year after the torrents of rain in the spring, or even each day after the morning mists are dispersed, can we still wonder to find the tradition of a deluge at the commencement of such a large number of mythologies? It is necessary to be very prudent when one introduces into religious history the elements of borrowing or of distortion. In virtue of the unity of the human mind working on like materials, the closest resemblances reveal themselves between religions and traditions which have never had any relations in history. Thus the religions of the Mexicans and of the Peruvians, before the arrival of Europeans in America, presented numerous analogies with the solar religions of the old world. There, however, there could be no question either of borrowing or of distortion. Sometimes, indeed, the religious or traditional resemblances between peoples who have never known each other extend to customs which seem to us very odd. Thus the *Couvade*, that strange usage which ordains that the father, as soon as his child is born, shall retire to bed and be cared for as a sick person—or, again, the tradition which commands those who have just lost a near relation to amputate a joint of the finger— has been ascertained to exist both formerly and in our own time among populations very remote from each other, quite different in race and manners, who could never have had any relations.

We have said that it is really the dictatorial authority of Genesis that it is proposed to save by this devious course. If the effort were limited to exalting all that the first chapters of the Pentateuch contain of just intuitions, of profound psychology, and of purity of sentiment, especially as compared with so many other cosmogonies or parallel legends, we should be very ready to subscribe to such eulogiums. But æsthetics and history are very different. The singularly high tone of Mosaicism has influenced the editorship of the narratives of Genesis; of that there is no doubt. But that does not prove their high antiquity. The labours of modern critics are far from favouring the idea that, in their present canonical form, their date is very remote. For example, it is difficult to understand why the serpent should have been with the Israelites, up to the time of Hezekiah, a symbol of deliverance and of safety, while their secular tradition made him the inspirer and promoter of evil.[1] In any case, these narratives are much later than Moses, whose death is recorded in the book which contains them.[2]

Besides, putting aside for the moment all such problems, the objection which we have already raised to the theory of a primitive revelation handed down in Genesis arises again in all its force; that is, the book of Genesis recognizes only a small number of races and of peoples, and wrongly regards them as constituting the whole of human kind.[3]

The point of view which we combat has nevertheless inspired many works which have had their day, and which professed to prove that all other traditions circumstantially confirmed the principal statements of Genesis—man made of the dust of the earth, the fall, the deluge, the ark of Noah, &c. One of the most celebrated was that published by Cardinal Wiseman, nearly fifty years ago, under the title, "The Connection between Science and Revealed Religion." Geology, still in its infancy, seemed to have been born only in order to illustrate the Mosaic account of

---

[1] Comp. Num. xxi. 8, 9; 2 Kings xviii. 4. We can, however, apply the same kind of observations to all the Old Testament (historical, prophetic, didactic books). We cannot but be struck by the silence which reigns throughout this literature, extending over several centuries, on the subject of the principal traditions of origin recorded in Genesis.

[2] We refer our readers who may be curious to know the most trustworthy results of criticism on the books commonly attributed to Moses, to the great work of Professor Reuss on the *Bible*, in course of publication by Sandoz and Fischbacher, Paris.

[3] We may point out on this occasion the common error which attributes the paternity of the Negro races to Cham. The families which the tenth chapter of Genesis connects with his name do not include the Negroes.

the creation, and comparative philology was simply the demonstration of the miracle of the confusion of tongues at the base of the Tower of Babel. This book, all the statements in which are contradicted in the present day, mainly followed the direction already indicated by the learned of the 17th century, such as Bochart and Jurieu, the pioneers who ventured to approach the religious history of humanity. The idea was that the Bible furnished a historical basis infallibly sure, of which the real or pretended analogies found in other mythologies were so many more or less unfaithful echoes.

In more recent years, the pre-historic studies which have been devoted to Chinese, Hindoo, American and other antiquities, no longer allow of ventures on such ground. From time to time, nevertheless, we still see the publication of well-meaning essays, the object of which is to demonstrate the antiquity and superior authenticity of the narratives in Genesis as compared with so-called pagan traditions. The most remarkable, as far as we know, is one which appeared in 1856, under the title of *Die Traditionen des Menschengeschlechts* (Traditions of the Human Race), by Herr Heinrich Lüken. We will quote only one specimen of the author's mode of proceeding, and this quotation will show its arbitrary character.

At p. 148, Herr Lüken examines the narrative of the murder of Abel, killed by Cain. In that, where we should see, by analogy with other myths of the same nature, the memorial of a sanguinary contest between a race of nomad shepherds and a race of agriculturists, in which the first succumbed, M. Lüken sees an event literally happening as recorded in Genesis; and thence all the murders related in Greek, Hindoo, Persian, Germanic and other mythologies, are in his view only variations from the first fratricide. Abel is the same as Apollo, the pure and the purifier, all the more that in Crete this god was named *Abelios*, the Hindoo Beli and the German Balder, the handsome young god killed at the instigation of the wicked Loki. He is also Osiris, killed by Typhon in Egypt, and Remus, killed by

Romulus in Italy. If it is objected that Apollo was not killed
at all in the Greek mythology, he replies that, according to his
arbitrary charts, Greek tradition has attributed to Abel-Apollo
certain features which belong to Cain. The latter ought rather
to have as pendant Hercules, the terrible slayer of oxen. He is
asked to notice that, in the Greek mythology, Hercules is a great
liberator and just judge. No matter. Hercules is a distorted
Cain, to whom the Greeks have given more than one characteristic belonging to Abel. With such a method, there is nothing
which cannot be proved.

The only rational method of studying religious history consists
in not assigning beforehand a separate place to any one of the
traditions which have prevailed, or which do prevail, among
divers races as the expression of their faith in regard to human
beginnings. The æsthetic superiority of the book of Genesis
has not yet conferred upon it the sovereign authority which is
claimed for it. Other religions may be inferior to it morally
and religiously, and may yet contain very interesting data which
are wanting to it. For example, there was a primitive invention
which more than any other changed the whole aspect of human
life, that of fire. The recollection, more or less vague, of a time
when man had no knowledge of this elementary art, is preserved
in several mythologies. Genesis says nothing about it. We can
see, on the contrary, in the myth of Prometheus, especially since
modern mythologists have traced its beginnings, what a strong
feeling in regard to this advance prevailed in Greece, where it
was considered that it had raised man near to the gods.

Let us add that it is found, as the result of a comparative
study of religious documents, that as a general rule the myths
relating to the first ages of the world are far from being the most
ancient. Infant races scarcely concerned themselves with their
own past, still less with that of mankind. It is in the age of reflection that questions are put to which the myths of origins are
the reply. It is natural that some very old recollections, which
seem to date back to the cradle of humanity, should then be

put on record. Not less natural is it that these recollections, and the ideas incorporated in them, should present themselves henceforth under a mythical form—that is to say, crystallized into a fact, or an event, or a personage—while in reality these ideas relate to permanent states, to periodical facts, or to communities of men.[1]

This work is done without method or rule; for it is rather the work of poetry and of the imagination than the result of rational research. This is why myths relating to origin are so easily inconsistent. We have a striking example of this in Genesis itself. We may remember that the first chapters of that book are the result of the combination of two distinct narrations, of which it is easy to indicate what we may call the points of suture. The first ignores the history of Eden and of the first sin, but affirms a fact of primary importance in the history of the antiquities of Israel. It is, that the name of Jahveh, or Jehovah, that which our versions render the Lord, and which corresponds to a notion of the Deity higher and more pure than that of Elohim, was not the name of the God of Israel until the time of Moses, who received the solemn revelation of it in the desert of Arabia. But according to the other narrator, there is nothing of this, and this name had been already invoked by man before the deluge.[2] There may be strong reasons for preferring one of these versions to the other, but we are yet far from this marvellously certain primitive tradition, not less marvellously preserved in a privileged race.

We have completely neglected until now a question which may be of great importance from the point of view of religious origins, that of the unity or of the diversity of the human race. The partizans of a single primitive tradition consider it as determined in favour of the unity. We beg leave to be less affirmative.

Not that we make any claim to solve the problem. We would

---

[1] See later on concerning the myth.
[2] Comp. Genesis iv. 26, and Exodus vi. 2, 3.

merely take into account two possibilities which open before us. There was a time, and it is not yet very remote, when specialists, emancipated from all extra-scientific authority, were generally of opinion that the theory of unity was not sustainable. Things have much changed since Mr. Darwin's theories have so greatly gained the ascendant, and the impassable voids which separated species are no longer believed in. Thereupon liberal thought has become much more willing to accept the idea of an original unity of all the races of mankind, and, matter for remark, the partizans of canonical tradition are little pleased with this.

It is now a question for us of taking up a position which will maintain at once the independence of the special science which we study, and its friendly relations with the sciences which so closely touch it. Admitting, what is not proved in such a way as to disarm all opposition, that according to the theory of evolution it might be possible to refer all the varieties of the human race to a single original type, it by no means follows that the same series of slow modifications which have determined the constitution of a human couple on a given point of the earth's surface has happened only at that point. It must be confessed that one is tempted to imagine that each of the great geographical divisions of the globe has witnessed the creation of its "own first man."

However, in regard to the formidable question which here presents itself, it is proper to start from a point of view which leaves the question of physical origin undecided. Whatever diversities of colour, of osseous structure, or of general development, may be observed in mankind, all the beings included in it have in common certain faculties of a psychic order peculiar to them alone, such as the art of supplying themselves with tools and arms which nature does not directly furnish, language, the religious faculty and a moral sense more or less delicate. This is what makes man. If a gorilla could make a stone implement, speak, exhibit anything resembling religion, even a grotesque superstition, though he were even more uncouth, more hideous than he is, we must yet class him among men. This is the true unity; we need not seek further. Have the ancestors of those whom we class under the denomination of men always possessed these faculties and aptitudes? We do not know. If they have not always had them, inasmuch as they have not had them, they were not men.

Now we know that human life, reduced to its primary rudiments, is of very ancient date on the earth, and that long ages rolled away before it could make any advance upon this very humble beginning of a life already higher than the purely animal life. It seems to us impossible, in the presence of such revelations of science, to continue to talk of traditions dating from the cradle of the human race, preserved intact by the pious care of certain families. A miracle would have been required for their formation, and another miracle for their preservation.

As, however, the original traditions of nations sprung up in an epoch less remote than our own from the primitive life, it is indispensable to consult them, to compare them, and to associate them with other sources of information which are available. From this point of view, the traditions recorded in Genesis possess, in addition to their own peculiar charm, a value of the highest order; but we cannot ultimately see in them more than a venerable fragment, well deserving attention, of the great genesis of mankind.

V.

OTHER *A PRIORI* THEORIES OF RELIGIOUS HISTORY.

The two hypotheses of which we have just shown the real worthlessness and untenable character, enable us to judge of the original and fatal injury which theories adopted *a priori*, without a methodical examination of facts, would inflict on our history. These are not the only prejudices which we have to remove. There are others, less serious, almost puerile, and which seem unworthy of discussion. Nevertheless, several hypotheses of this category of the second and third rank possess a certain popularity. We might cite as an example the prejudice which maintains that religions are merely the invention of the priests, as if religion had not necessarily and everywhere preceded the priest. We shall see this more clearly when we come to speak of the priesthood. No doubt it has frequently happened that the greatest enemy of religion has been the priest who has made trade and merchandize of it, who has used it as a means of satisfying his cupidity or his ambition, or even passions still more base. No doubt religious progress is achieved outside of the priests, without them and in spite of them. But that should not shut our eyes to the evidence that if there had not first been religion, there would never have been any priests. On what basis, in the name of what convictions or preliminary notions, would the first priest have established his authority? Does it require much historical knowledge to recognize that at certain epochs, the human mind having attained a certain level, the priest has responded to needs which he alone could satisfy; that examples of devotedness, of abnegation, and of moral purity, that eminent services rendered to civilization, are not at all exceptional in the history of priesthoods; and that in regard to this sacerdotal institution, as to so many others, it is necessary to guard against all passionate judgment? History is a great anodyne; but in order that it may take effect, it is necessary to free it from all prejudices derived from the controversies of the day and the hour. There are institutions, absolute monarchy for example, which we would not have to-day at any price, but of which, nevertheless, our spiritual ancestors, those who would now think and reason like we do, were quite sincerely zealous partizans.

There is another *a priori* theory of religious history, arising, it may be, from prejudices of education, it may be from the tendency which inclines us easily to believe that previously to the abuses and the errors from which we have actually to suffer, all went much better, and that the age of gold has always preceded the age of iron. This illusion is of ancient date. It is to some extent repeated in the case of each old man whose life is much prolonged. A venerable father of the Church, Cyprian, saw a sign of the approaching end of things in the diminished bloom and flavour of the fruits which he ate in his old age, as compared to those which he remembered having eaten when he was young, forgetting to ask himself whether this might not be the fault of his failing sight and of his worn-out palate. The Hebrew sage, whom we call Ecclesiastes, who had seen and thought much, said,[1] "Say not thou, What is the cause that the former days were better than these? for thou dost not inquire wisely concerning these."

In regard to religious history, this illusion has taken this form: There is an objection to believe that the dawn of religious faith was not of a radiant purity, and that mankind started with a childish polytheism. For example, there is a considerable number of historians who maintain absolutely that the primitive religion was monotheistic, and that polytheism is the corruption of an older and higher faith.

[1] Eccles. vii. 10.

On what is this contention based? It is difficult to see in it anything but the reflex action of preconceived ideas, the inaccuracy of which we have already shown. The monotheist idea does not naturally obtrude itself on the mind as yet uncultivated. It supposes reflection, experience, a notion of the world which is not primitive. It is not foreign to the human mind, and the proof of this is that in all mythologies we discern a certain tendency, sometimes very marked, to reduce the pantheons to unity. But from this more or less vague tendency to the conscious and deliberate notion of monotheism, there is a long step. The old thinkers of Greece, of whom it is often sought to make monotheists in the modern sense, do not deserve this honour. Plato, for example, stopped short at dualism. In the case of that very race which passes as the historical representative of monotheism, we clearly discern that a very long polytheistic period preceded the triumph of the faith in the absolute unity of the Divinity. Before being monotheistic, it was simply *monolatrous,* and even that for the religious leaders only, and its history consists chiefly in the obstinate resistance which it offered to the monotheistic idea. If, on the other hand, we consult the most ancient authentic record of religious beliefs which we possess, the Vedas, do we find there the least indication of a primitive monotheism?

What may have given the appearance of substance to this illusion is this: In the most distinctly polytheistic religions, most frequently at any given moment only one divinity is worshipped at once. The prayers and hymns which are addressed to him are all in his praise. When man worships, it is never by halves. He always attributes all power, all goodness, all perfections, to the object of his adoration at the moment. It is something like the village *curés* when they preach on the *fête* day of the patron saint. He is always the holiest saint in Paradise. In like manner, the worshipper of Indra or of Agni, of Phœbus Apollo or of Athene, of Diana with her silver bow, or of Aphrodite with her floating drapery, would never fail to confer on each the attributes of absolute sovereignty. It is this which has deceived those who, from hymns or prayers expressing sentiments which ought logically to have terminated in monotheism, have maintained the conclusion that those who used them recognized only one sole God. This was so little their meaning, that, on the morrow, when addressing themselves to another divinity, they offered him the same homage, without perceiving the contradiction.

It is this phenomenon which led M. Max Müller to consider that the question, Did mankind begin with monotheism or with polytheism? was an idle inquiry. Primitive humanity was incapable of making any such distinction. The primitive religious idea was hazy, indefinite, implying unity as well as plurality, but unconsciously monotheistic at the precise moment of worship.[1] Absolute sovereignty being thus attributed to each divinity successively, and all the divinities presenting characters in common (devas, Θεοι), there must result what the learned Professor calls *Kathenotheism*, or more briefly *Henotheism*, a term expressing the idea of the two tendencies which later diverged into polytheism and monotheism. There were several gods, but each in his turn was god.

We have nothing to object to this ingenious mode of presenting very real facts, unless it be that in the end all polytheisms, even the most developed, come under the definition. If the tendency of this henotheism has, as a logical consequence, future monotheism, it is nevertheless undeniable that polytheism is antecedent in fact. The successive transfer of the attributes of absolute sovereignty to several distinct divinities, is precisely what has always characterized polytheism; consequently we cannot deny the original polytheism. We shall see later how monolatry, required by a *jealous* God, was bound at length to engender conscious and reflecting monotheism.

Besides this, it would be an error to limit the *a priori* theories which we must challenge to those which spring only from the intellect. There are other prejudices which are blind from the beginning, and which come into the region of the moral sense.

[1] Comp. "Chips of a German Workshop," I. 27, 28.

Such is the *a priori* of men who study religious history only with the preconceived idea of deciding in favour of one or other of the forms of religion which divide mankind in the present day.

There is another of an absolutely opposite tendency, not less misleading. It is the *a priori* of men animated by a secret hatred against everything which is called religion, and who see in it only a prolonged aberration of the human mind. It seems to them that always and everywhere religion has been the auxiliary of covetousness, of furtive designs, and of despotisms. They forget that in religion, as in all else, there are two co-existing tendencies—that of the partizans of the past, whatever it may be, seeking in religion a pretext to colour their love of superstitions, of ignorance, of slavery; and that of the men of the future, who derive, on the contrary, from their religious feeling, not only the love of liberty and of progress, but also *faith* in this liberty, in this progress, that faith without which nothing great or lasting is ever done in the world, and which alone rises superior to deceptions and reverses. Do not let us deny the power of faith, that marvellous faculty which enables us to anticipate the realization of the ideal. We ought to be very unwilling to deny it, we who are now only just passing out of a period in our national history in which the only sentiment which made recovery from an apparently irremediable fall possible, was faith in the country. No doubt the history of religions is, in one sense, a history of errors engendered one upon another. In this long development there is no halting-place which does not show us man as the victim of illusions and of dreams. But is there nothing else? Is there not a truth which grows up in the midst of, we might even say by means of, these errors? Of what human ideal is not this the inseparable condition? If we have in the present day a social and political ideal of justice, of liberty and of philanthropy, do we not admit that the political history of the human race is full of errors and of miscalculations, which have, however, been necessary to the development of this ideal? Shall we suppress law because the history of legislation abounds with absurd, iniquitous or corrupt statutes? Shall we condemn natural science because up to a period comparatively near to our own it was full of false notions? Interrogate the history of chemistry, or of physiology, or of physics—through what a long course of errors has not the human mind passed, in order to arrive at the possession of that modicum of truth which we consider as having been acquired in these various domains?

It is, then, somewhat puerile to say, history proves that man is always deceived by religion, therefore religion is only a deception. The same history shows also the ascending line of religious sentiment, enlightened, purified and rectified continually. True, it took a long time. But what matter, provided it came to pass? And by what paradox of destiny can it happen that, of all the tendencies of the human mind, the religious tendency should be the only one doomed to end in nothing? Let us say rather, that there is a whole revelation in the very fact of the persistence with which the human mind, in spite of its demonstrated ignorance and of the consciousness of so many abortive essays, has maintained its direction towards the inaccessible object of its beliefs. To what odd notions the elementary phenomena of magnetism and electricity gave rise! But that did not prevent, formerly any more than now, every magnetized needle, pivoted on its axis, always turning towards the Pole. That was the nature of the needle. In like manner, through all its aberrations, the human mind always turns towards the Divinity. Efforts have been made from time to time to impress upon it a contrary tendency. It has always resisted, and taken again as soon as possible its constant direction. It also might say to us, This is my nature!

Religious history has not to record superstitions, follies, deformities only. It comprehends also noble and splendid elements. In it we find magnificent conceptions and sublime aspirations. In it we hear accents characterized by a purity, a justness, a charm so mysterious and so powerful, that we are involuntarily led to believe that they spring from a source much higher than earth. Religious inspiration in its supreme moments yields to no other in boldness and fertility. Morality has suffered from religion; it has also enormously gained; and in the present day that is its only solid support in the conscience of the immense majority. Art has for a long time owed its best works to it, and it is not saying too much to affirm that without it philosophy would never have been born.

Let us then pursue our history of religions without being astonished by the puerilities and the horrors we shall find in it, without setting ourselves beforehand against all that it contains that is great and noble. And perhaps, when we have conducted this study with impartiality, with independence and with loftiness of view, we may discern to which side the needle constantly turns, perhaps we may have found the compass. It is only when we are in possession of this wonderful instrument that we can venture in safety on the great ocean.

VI.

RELIGIOUS DEVELOPMENT.

A.—The Religious Sentiment.

Since we ought by this time to have cleared away all hypotheses which demand for religious history conditions of origin different from those which determine the beginnings of all other history, we have only to apply to it the principle which all analogies, all probabilities, already indicate, the *principle of development*, in virtue of which everything begins in the form of germ, of rudiments full of promise and of marvellous ductility, but as yet very incomplete and very crude, and in a state of rough outline.

This principle is indeed only the application to human history of the *principle of continuity* which is constantly being more and more triumphantly evolved by the conquests of modern science in all directions. It is increasingly evident that "everything hangs together;" that there is solution of continuity only where light fails us to discern the middle terms; that we find in the universe neither the immutability of eternal identity, nor the mechanical superposition of unconnected phenomena which a mysterious hand has been pleased to display arbitrarily, but a permanent, logical, internal connection between realities at first sight most dissimilar; and we have already so often observed this, that an irresistible induction compels us henceforth to affirm that this principle will find its verification even where we cannot at present prove it.

Continuity in history is not the identity of successive facts; it is their development.

But, on the other hand, all development supposes a primary germ, which unfolds, grows, develops forms, modifications and applications innumerable, finding the material for its ever-expanding manifestation and for its continuous amplification in a multitude of elements originally external or foreign to it. It is just the same with the tree which shoots up, swells out and grows tall by assimilating the carbon and the moisture with which the atmosphere furnishes it. But we must not consider the protomotor germ of this vegetable development as annihilated by the fact of germination and of the beginning of growth. It is that, always that, which is perpetuated in the organism which is the issue of its first operation. Without it, the organism could never have existed; without the elements which it could draw into the orbit of its attraction, it would have remained inert and unfruitful. But it is the initial fact and the guiding force; it constitutes the substantial element to which all the rest is subordinate.

In all development, then, it is necessary to distinguish two things: first, the substantial principle itself and its internal continuity, manifesting itself by successive growths, modifications and amplifications; then the external elements which render these modifications possible, and which may thence be considered as so many motive or exciting causes of development.

What is the substantial, vital element in religious history which represents its soul or permanent principle?

If reference be made to the definition which we proposed of Religion itself, the preponderating place there given to feeling or sentiment will be noticed. It is by that especially that religion is distinguished from science and from philosophy. These are subjects exclusively of the intellect; and although religion may be the object of a science and of a philosophy, it differs from both in its roots. It rests essentially on the awakening, on the calling into activity, of a sentiment *sui generis*, which impels the intellect to imagine the object of it under forms corresponding to its degree of knowledge, but which springs spontaneously in the soul when placed under certain conditions. This internal fact of the religious sentiment by no means implies that the forms with which it is furnished by the intellect answer exactly to the reality of the object. We can very well feel the effect of beings or of forces of which we are able to form only vague or false ideas. Man feels, for example, the heat and the light of the sun, even when he has no accurate idea of the nature of this light or of this heat, or of the celestial body which is their source. Feeling is in this case a spontaneous function of the living organism; a theory as to the nature of light and heat and of the sun could be a product of reason only. It is thus that the sensation caused by an object, only mysteriously defined, may be very lively, very real, and may yet be associated with very erroneous notions in regard to the object itself. Moreover, we must bear in mind—for this also is essential—that the sense of the bond which unites the human mind to the superior spirit (or spirits) whose sovereignty over the world and over himself he believes that he recognizes, is a source of secret, though it may be undefinable, comfort, of which those only can deny the reality who have never known it.

We have already noticed the error into which it is so easy to fall in the present day, when, for want of a sufficiently exact analysis of the religious sentiment, it is possible to see in it only a variety of the sentiment of fear. This last sentiment exists independently of all connection with the religious sentiment; it may be associated with it; in fact it is often and widely associated with it; but it is very far from exhausting it. It is very true that man seeks in religion the harmonious synthesis of his personal existence with this world which opposes itself to his egoism, whether as a whole, or by its destructive, alarming and painful phenomena. But why require that phenomena of this sinister order should have been the only ones to provoke in man, yet untaught, the sensations and emotions from which religion sprang? If we apply to the ages of entire ignorance the close analogy, already noted by Voltaire, which should exist between the infancy of humanity and the infancy of each one of us—an analogy which rests on so many verified conformities— we must conclude that the first impressions of mankind ought to present that mingled, confused character, where all is in all, which distinguishes the state of mind in infancy. The little child is at once timid and confiding. His impressions are very lively, and he easily carries every emotion to excess; he despairs of everything, and is delighted by the smallest trifle. Joy is with him as prompt as grief. Why, then, should it have been different with man, scarcely weaned from the breast of his foster-mother, Nature? Do not let us invent an unseasonable idyl. It is certain that, in comparison with civilized life, the still almost animal life of primitive man was frightful—or at least it would be to us. Was it so to him? Nothing authorizes us to think that he was inclined to suicide—rather the contrary. It is more probable that the awakening of the religious faculty was determined by the effect of the discovery which he believed he had made of the existence of superior spirits living and acting in the form of natural objects, and that the feeling which he had towards them was a mixture of uneasiness and of joy, of terror and of confidence. The phenomena favourable to, and the phenomena adverse to, his well-being—often the same phenomena, which might be sometimes favourable, sometimes the contrary— would inspire him simultaneously with the two orders of emotion. He felt both very intensely, as the child feels everything intensely, and we place ourselves in an inextricable difficulty when we refer to terror only the mingling of various feelings which gave to the religious sentiment its primary character.[1]

Especially let us avoid attributing to the origin of religion too much precision, too many rigorous definitions—in one word, too much dogma. The first religious notions must for a long

---

[1] We shall see in another and the next part of this course what we are to think of those savage nations who recognize two orders of divinities, one good, the other wicked, who forget or neglect the first, and assiduously worship only the second. We only say beforehand, that other facts of an opposite significance can be pointed out, and especially that we must be careful of extending to all humanity conclusions which are valid in regard to certain regions and certain races only. It might well be that we are here in the presence of a primordial difference ranking among those which would explain why some races are so worthily developed in the sense of civilization, while some have remained stationary.

time have been variable, fugitive, indefinable. It may be asked, for instance, what must have been the object of the first worship of mankind? We answer willingly: Probably any, not all—for of that he had no idea—but any phenomena which had the effect of revealing to him a spirit in relation with his own. As with our little children, the phenomena of food and of light, as well as their contraries, must be counted among the first which would suggest this course of ideas to him. The tree which bore nourishing fruit in abundance, and the return of daylight after each night, must very early have given him the impression of beneficent powers; then that which moved, that which stirred, that which seemed to live, the clouds and the rivers, coming he knew not whence, and going he knew not whither; the mountain which never moved, but which looked sternly from its inaccessible heights across its white sheet of snow, and on the sides of which were heard voices echoing with mocking or melodious vibrations; and then the darkness, the storm, the thunderbolt, the inundation, the glacial cold, the devouring heat, everything which seemed to pursue man with the intention of injuring him and of causing him to perish; the animal, to whom as yet man still felt himself so near, whom he loved or whom he dreaded, but whose proportions, or instincts, or physical faculties, he admired —all this would be the object of that feeling apart which gives rise to the recognition of one spirit by another spirit. The difficulty is not to say what man could adore in nature; it would rather be to point out what he could not.

But let us never forget that, whatever might be the notion which he formed in his own mind of the divinity, man has always experienced and cherished a special sense of comfort in being in normal relation with it, and that even when this divinity presented itself to him under terrifying aspects, even when from our point of view it could have provoked in him only feelings of horror. We are struck with astonishment in presence of those terrible divinities who feast on human flesh, who tear the first-born from their parents in order to gratify their ogre-like appetites or their insatiable wrath. We may, however, remark, that certain notions of the divinity consecrated by certain Christian traditions are scarcely higher. But we may rest assured that while faith in these repulsive divinities endured, man enjoyed, often even at the cost of the heaviest sacrifices, a state of comfort and of inward enjoyment resulting from the worship which he offered them.

We have already spoken of the relation which exists between this phenomenon of a religious kind and the taste of mankind for the tragic. This deserves some further explanation.

What is tragedy? It is the exhibition by the setting forth of an event, or of a situation, or of a human destiny, of a superior order of things, overwhelming in its irresistible course our petty calculations, our limited previsions, our vulgar wisdom, advancing imperturbably towards its goal without concerning itself with these spiders' webs, and attaining its ends with the fixity, the regularity and the certainty of a planetary movement. Take any, no matter what, example in history or in art of stirring tragedy, and this definition will be justified.

Most of those who are the spectators of a tragic event or catastrophe, are unable clearly to describe the profound impression which they receive from it. Their imaginations, their consciences, are stirred, but they do not think of analyzing the signification of this; they see only the terrible or the grandiose side of tragic things. Nevertheless, there are terrible things which we cannot call tragic—the hurricane, for example, when it passes over without causing great misfortunes: and there are grand things, such as the sea when calm, but which again are not tragic. The terrible as such, and the grand as such, are not enough to constitute the tragic element. It is necessary that there should be, in addition to those, the revelation of a law, or of a superior direction of things. The ancient drama for a long time confined itself to the external side of tragedy, showing in it little more than fatality. The oracular utterance of a god, the curse of a father, the punishment of a crime, would sooner or later receive their accomplishment by means, if necessary, of a supernatural intervention. In the present day we require that tragedy shall be logical also; and we are right; for it is so. But to-day, as in the old times, it is really the manifestation of the superior law of things which constitutes its value and its true character. A powerful empire which falls, undermined by internal vices long concealed under brilliant appearances; a benefactor of humanity, who, at first received with acclamation, perishes, the victim of human wickedness; a catastrophe which engulfs the most legitimate hopes, the most tender affections, all that recalls the inalienable sovereignty of the moral order, or the frailty of our best-combined plans, or the necessity of aspiring after eternal spheres as the only region in which the supreme sentence of destiny is pronounced—all this is tragic, and deserves the name.

Well! if he is assured of not suffering from it personally, man is led by a secret tendency of his being to love the tragic and to find pleasure in its contemplation. The proof of this is in those masterpieces which have always counted among the highest and the most admired productions of the human mind. This is because there is a mysterious affinity between that mind and this superior order of things which tragedy reveals; and the more the human mind is developed, the more it is sensible of this emotion which stirs it to its depths. There are many religious ceremonies which are only understood as so many tragedies periodically represented.

We should not, consequently, be surprised at the charm, at first sight so strange, which may for a long time retain man in his fidelity to religions of terror and of blood. It is not fear alone which gives rise to these; it is not fear alone which maintains them. There is, in the beginning and afterwards, the special attraction of the tragic, the enjoyment resulting from the union of the spirit within with the spirit without. All these terrorist conditions claim to realize the conditions and the means of safety. Such are the ceremonies, or the offerings, or the prayers, or the voluntary sacrifices, or the sanguinary immolations, which may appease the fury of the terrible god; and the believer feels himself happy in thinking that he is henceforth united to a spirit whom he dreads; he has nothing more to fear from his wrath, but is able, on the contrary, to imagine to himself that he is under the protection of his power.

Schleiermacher was right in recognizing the sentiment of dependence as forming an integral part of the religious sentiment. In effect, the spirit with which man desires to know himself to be united must be superior to him. Otherwise he could not find in union with him that victorious synthesis of the world and of destiny which constitutes the very essence of religion under all its forms. For the sake of historical truth, we confine ourselves to the idea of superiority. In its development, the religious sentiment raises this superiority to absolute sovereignty. It is under this condition only that the synthesis is legitimate. But this is true only of advanced religions, many contenting themselves with simple superiority. Nevertheless, we discover here one of the great reasons why the object of human adoration has always been conceived of as a conscious and personal being. It is one of the causes of variety in religion. In proportion as the dense ignorance of early days is dissipated, man discovers that many objects which he took for persons are in reality only things. From the moment in which he is assured of this, he no longer adores them. For the man who feels, who thinks and who desires, will always know himself to be superior to that which has neither feeling, nor thought, nor will. It is the commentary on that grand thought of Pascal on the superior nobility of man in the presence of an unconscious universe, even when that universe can overwhelm him; man "knows that he must die, and the advantage which the universe has over him, the universe knows nothing of." We see thence that the sense of dependence is religious only when it has relation to a spirit. We depend constantly on forces and on inanimate phenomena which escape our free action—inclemencies of weather, for instance, or diseases. We do not dream of making gods of them. When they were worshipped, it was because they had been personified.

Schleiermacher's error is in not having seen, or at least in not having taken into account, that in the religious sentiment the sentiment of dependence is intimately mingled with the sentiment of union, of reciprocity and of mutuality, which is no less essential to religion than the former. It is the mysterious *Dein mein* inscribed on the horn of Charlemagne at Aix-la-Chapelle. The analysis of the religious sentiment is complete only when we put on the same line these two primary factors, the sentiment of dependence in relation to the religious object, and the sentiment of union, real or to become real, between this object and the subject.

In fact, the religious sentiment possesses a savour of its own which can be compared only with itself, like the sentiment of the beautiful or of the true. Definition pauses here as before an element irreducible and without analogy. But it is composed ultimately of other heterogeneous elements which it brings into unity, by which it is nourished, and which it stamps with its impress. We may see here a double gamut, or a double series of sentiments, which we may enumerate in their ascending order of intensity.

There is the gamut which relates to the sentiment of dependence, and which we may arrange thus:

Respect, veneration, fear, dismay, terror.

There is then the series relating to the sentiment of reciprocal union:

Admiration, joy, confidence, love, ecstacy.

We set down ecstacy as the supreme moment of the second series, because the religious sentiment, over-excited in a very impressionable soul, goes to the point of ecstacy, which is one of the religious phenomena the most worthy of notice.

We may here remark that these two gamuts, one of which has *fear* for its fundamental tone, and the other *confidence*, are most frequently mingled in reality. It is sometimes one which prevails and sometimes the other, but with an infinite variety of shades, of half-tones, and, if we may say so, of quarter-tones. There is a religion of which fear occupies the centre; another of which the central element is confidence.

We contend, however, that by means of a careful analysis we can always find something of the one intermingled with the other.

Take, for example, a devotee of narrow mind, but whom we suppose to be sincere. His religion has for its principal motive a terrible fear of hell, that is, of the devil, who may probably await him there, with all the demons under his command, preparing for him all tortures imaginable and unimaginable. This is not a religion of a high order; it is in our eyes lamentable, we admit. To this man, religion is a terror. Nevertheless, in the earnest fervour with which he performs the rites and the works which his faith dictates as possessing undoubted efficacy, observe an indescribable expression of satisfaction pervading his whole demeanour, and repaying him for all the torments to which he deliberately submits. Do not pity him. It is he who may pity you. Given his state of mind, there is satisfaction and joy in the innumerable exercises the painful burden of which he lays upon himself.

Observe, on the other hand, a Christian spiritualist whose faith raises him above these miserable superstitions, who believes with his whole heart in the promises of the gospel, who fully enjoys the conviction that he is in personal and direct communion with the infinite Father whose essential attribute is love, while his whole life is filled with the calm, the moral purity and the charity, which such persuasions inspire. We are here at the other pole of the religious sentiment, and yet it would be an exaggeration to say that fear, at least in the attenuated form of veneration, does not enter into the religion of this man.

We have also already remarked that there must necessarily always be something mysterious in the object of the religious sentiment. Man becomes religious under the feeling of an intelligent power superior to himself, but he at the same time recognizes that an impenetrable shade envelopes this power on all sides. Mystery, the unknown which perplexes and defies our thirst for knowledge, characterizes the religious object quite as much as his revealed existence. To us, with our education permeated by rationalism, mystery is not always religious. In history there are mysteries which arouse our curiosity, but that is all. An old castle long uninhabited, the rooms in which have not been opened since times immemorial, and where the good people pretend that the former possessors "walk," inspires us simply with the desire to go and see it. But we are not in reality differently constituted from our ancestors, and when, from those mysteries which excite a smile, we rise to those which shape our destiny, to those which surround the great problems of life and of death,—to those, finally, which, no matter in what system of philosophy or of faith, end always by checking our reason and our researches, we comprehend the close affinity which binds the religious sentiment to that of mystery. If we penetrate into a forest of large trees, where the domes of foliage succeed one another till they are lost to view, where only the sound of our footsteps on the dry leaves disturbs the silence of the depths, are we not seized by that same sentiment of mystery which made the forest in remote times, and notably in our ancient Gaul, the habitual residence of the most august divinities? It is thus that the religious sentiment associates itself with that of the infinite, charms away its dull vacuity by filling it with a positive reality, and derives new strength from this association. A mystery defined, circumscribed, is only half a mystery; but religion has for its object undefinable mystery. This sentiment gives a special colour to the religious sentiment, and is inseparable from it.

On the other hand, man never resigns himself to worship the purely unknown. Even when the only affirmation which he ventures to make as to the object of his worship is that of actual existence, it is already another thing than, and beyond, absolute ignorance. The object of human religion is necessarily a spirit. Otherwise it would fail of all point of contact; it would be a link uniting nothing; it would be nothing. Man, then, with more or less simplicity, with more or less philosophic severity, endows this spirit with characteristics borrowed from his own spirit. This is the inevitable anthropomorphism of which we have already spoken, resulting from the affinity for which man stipulates between his own spirit and the spirit which he worships. We find there the common reason of the grossest errors and of the most elevated notions in religious matters. The same spontaneous postulate which leads the ignorant man to personify trees, stones, rivers, mountains, fire, stars,—the same impulse which transforms a log of wood or a flint pebble into directors of human destiny,—has also caused a Plato, a Seneca, a Leibnitz, or a Hegel, to proclaim the co-essentiality of man and of God. The gospel owes its power to its fundamental principle of the potential kinship between man and the celestial Father.

Religious development, though starting thus low, has yet not lost its substantial element in the midst of its secular evolution. Supposing that we could have been enlightened and thoughtful witnesses of its first manifestations, it would have been as difficult for us to predict what would spring from it, as it would be for us now, if daily experience had not taught us, to foresee how the earliest lispings of the nursling who tries to articulate his first syllables should become the clear, full and rich language of the adult.

We are not on that account the less in possession of the lever which shall raise the world. The religious sentiment, however indeterminate, fugitive, fluctuating, it may have been in the beginning, is now established and fixed; it has unfolded its varied contents, seeking its satisfaction constantly higher. It has not always remained imprisoned in visible and connected nature. It has not always spent itself on ridiculous or paltry objects. It has brought arts, morals, all society, within the sphere of its attraction. It has raised itself to the level of the great forces and phenomena which overawe the world. It has even surpassed them, in placing over them a sovereign spirit which dominates them all. It has assumed a thousand forms; it has created masterpieces; it has been the source of magnificent inspirations; it has produced systems, and peoples have lived for ages under their shelter. Its history will be that of its revolutions, of its variations, of its modifications ceaselessly renewed. We must now consider the determining causes of these historical changes.

B.—Active Causes of Religious Development.

An historical development is ordinarily produced through the action of causes foreign to its principle, but entering into relation with it and determining new phases and more or less serious modifications. We can satisfy ourselves of this by considering the course of political history or of the history of art. Causes, which had in themselves nothing either political or artistic, influence in the most powerful manner the direction which politics and art shall take, and the transformations which both shall undergo. The same rule applies to religious history.

The first in date, and perhaps the first also in importance, of these active causes of religious development, is the increasing knowledge of surrounding nature, and later of the world itself in its real greatness and constitution.

It is clear that at the period of this prodigious ignorance, of which we can scarcely form any idea, man was not, could not be, sensible of that which we call the universal order or harmony of things. In the beginning, man would act like the child, who takes as much interest in a detail as in the whole. It is true that to him this detail which strikes and attracts him is something very important, which hides from him all the rest. In the objects of small importance in our eyes which provoked the awakening of the religious sentiment, primitive man discovered a whole Olympus. A tree, a water-course, a rock of strange form, a mysterious cave, an animal dreadful in aspect, or a very clever hunter, would induce in him the idea of one or of several animated beings much stronger, more intelligent and more powerful than himself. To understand this state of mind, we must as much as possible free ourselves from all that the accumulated experience of ages has taught us in "lessons on things." Before we are out of the cradle, we inherit from our parents, from our nurses even, however ignorant they may be, a mass of knowledge which seems to us to be immediate, to be acquired by ourselves alone, and to demand, for its possession, only eyes to see and ears to hear. Sometimes, by observing closely, we succeed in finding in our children something of this first innocence of mind, especially at the age at which they wonder that water wets, and they run to see if they cannot outrun their shadows. One evening in the winter, passing along a road edged with trees, through the bare branches of which the moon might from time to time be seen struggling through the clouds, we overheard a conversation between a mother, a woman of the people, and her little boy, who was bent upon knowing what had become of the other moon which he remembered having seen in another shape, and which was gone. The mother had to repeat to him several times that there was only one moon, and that it was always the same which sometimes appeared, sometimes disappeared. The child was still in the mythological age. Let us suppose a group of men as ignorant as this child, having no one to correct their ideas, and nothing to prevent them from imagining that each new moon is a fresh moon.

Another analogy which it is important to notice. The child avows a deep affection for some damaged toy, for an armless doll, for a wooden horse which has still three legs, but only one ear and one nostril. He often prefers this to those superb toys which the skill of our manufacturers constantly tends to bring nearer and nearer to works of art properly so called. It is evident that children see things, forms, colours, with eyes different from ours. They idealize their toys, they lend them all sorts of beauties and of charms which we do not perceive. This is the secret of the passionate attachment which they experience for a stick wrapped in rags, out of which they make a little girl, and for a block of wood badly shaped and mounted on four sticks, which has to them the effect of a splendid race-horse.

Just so, in the primitive epochs, the human imagination was disturbed, over-excited even, by phenomena in which it is impossible for us to discover what it was which gave them such a power. When we think of the log which for ages represented to peoples already very highly cultivated and very powerful the Lady Hera, Queen of the shining Heaven, we say to ourselves that it was no doubt protected by the veneration of ages, by the most august traditions. But in the beginning, when some one first bethought himself of setting this log in the sun and of presenting it to the homage of his contemporaries, it is evident that this piece of wood spoke to their imagination quite a different language from that which it speaks to ours. Nevertheless, this rude symbol is far from dating from primitive times; it is already part of an organized mythology.

It is this which renders it so difficult to determine with precision what were the objects of the first religion. No human family, even among the most backward, can be found at the present day in the original conditions of human life. We shall speak further on of the direction which his first observation of his own nature, and of the nature of the things which surrounded him, impressed on the religious notions of man in the sense of animism (the worship of spirits) and of fetichism. Let us continue here to indicate the earliest modifications of this worship of visible nature, which must in all cases have preceded them, and which analysis discovers underlying the faiths which have supplanted it in practice.

A little more experience, a little more knowledge of the visible world, will impart a certain notion of the whole in place of exclusive pre-occupation with details.

Man had not, so far, ceased to attribute conscience and will to material existences, but at any rate those that he endowed with these faculties were more worthy of being accounted as masters of destiny. The sky, the sun, the dawn, the stars, the wind, the earth, the sea—all these he had hitherto chosen to personify. Here is the beginning of the great mythologies. But, as the principle remains the same, he does not deny what he has previously believed. Only he subordinates primary objects of adoration to the grand phenomena, the superior importance of which he henceforth recognizes. At this stage of general development, beliefs already greatly differ, according to the climates and the regions in which men live. In India, in Greece, in the countries of radiant brightness, of blue sky, the dazzling azure of light which is over everything and dominates everything, becomes the supreme god. In such countries as Syria, Arabia and Egypt, where the sun is the visible master of all nature, he becomes the centre of worship. In Middle and Southern Europe, the wind would be a very great god. Dwellers on the sea-shore would naturally have different divinities from those populations who did not even know that the sea exists.

This is also the moment at which, among peoples endowed with a lively imagination, there will be formed, by way of analogy, types and figurative conceptions, which will be gathered up later by developed mythologies. For example, the sky, with its single round sun, produces the impression of a great face pierced by a single eye opening and shutting: it is this which later gave us the Cyclops. Again, the moon, in the form of a crescent, suggests the idea of a pair of horns: nothing more was wanted to make a grand celestial cow, and this conception, so odd to us, will be the initial germ of the myth of Io, the young girl loved by Jupiter and changed into a heifer. In like manner, the stormy cloud became the shield of Jupiter or of Minerva; but a shield of goat's skin, fringed, only allowing its outer threads to float in the wind, the ægis.[1] The waves of the sea, with their rounded backs, have for marine populations the effect of horses or of sheep throwing themselves tumultuously one upon another.

---

[1] Αἴξ, αἴγος, goat.

Even at the present day, while the sailors of our shores call the foamy breaking of the waves in the offing sheep (*moutons*), the Italian sailors call it horses (*cavalloni*), and those of the Ægean Sea goats. This explains why in certain maritime regions the god of the liquid element, Poseidon or Neptune, is the breeder, protector and trainer of horses.

Once arrived thus far, the human mind soon began to dramatize nature, to see in it, by analogy with human life, all sorts of scenes, graceful or terrible, lively or melancholy. We may here mention a factor the effect of which has been already indicated in the preceding pages, that is, the special genius of races. There are races which have little imagination, and whose mythology consequently will always remain very poor —the Kaffirs, for example. There are others, like the Semites, who have no dramatic genius, and among whom consequently the dramatization of nature will always be very much restricted. It is possible to establish a relation of the same kind, although with a much less marked difference, between the old Italian mythology and that of Greece, which so beguiled Italy by its seductive charm that the latter adopted it, as it were, unconsciously. The Celtic and Gallic legend has something dreamy, passionate and tender, mingled with paroxysms of jovial or cruel coarseness, as we see in the curious history of Melusina, in the stories of the White Ladies, and in the popular legend of Gargantua. The Chinese religion is saturated with ritualism, with monotonous regularity, with practical good sense, and with doting nonsense; while the German mythology presents that mixture of idealism, of vigour and of sturdiness, with which its last great product, the *Nibelungen*, is so strongly penetrated. In a word, it is at the moment in which the dramatization of nature begins, that the special genius of the race also begins most powerfully to influence the formation of beliefs and of myths.

But the knowledge of nature is continually extending. The idea of that which the Greeks called the Kosmos, the idea of the world regularly organized, submitted to a constant order

always victorious over the attacks of which it may be the object
on the part of hostile powers, such as winter, storm, earthquake,
&c.,—this idea spreads, especially among the most intelligent
nations. Immigration, commerce and travels, bring the human
families and their traditions more closely together. It is then,
also, that the great mythologies begin to be organized. A history
of the divinities is elaborated. Their numbers and relations,
finally a hierarchy, are assigned to them. A distinction is made
between the greater and the smaller gods. In virtue of the conservative principle of which we have spoken, no previous beliefs
are eliminated, but they are more or less harmonized with the new
notions. The worship of Zeus or Jupiter having acquired in all
the Greek countries a sort of catholicity, but many cities assigning to him some other companion than Juno or Hera, who was
recognized as his lawful wife, the difficulty was got over by
transforming Danaë, Leda, Semele, Alcmena, Latona, Europa and
many others, into the mistresses of the king of the gods. Mythic
theology is easy of composition.

Finally, the knowledge of nature still further increasing, its
scientific study commences, and the most advanced begin to ask
themselves if all this dramatization of nature is anything else
than an illusion. Then begins the great bifurcation between the
East and the West. The extreme East comes to believe that
not only is the dramatization purely imaginary, but that Nature
herself is, if not an illusion, at least a wrong or an evil; it
denies its legitimacy, and desires to achieve its negation even
in man himself. Thence Buddhism and its frightful asceticism.
It is the religion of death. In the West, a germ of new life
springs up in the bosom of a small and profoundly original
people, which began by adoring simply a national god, whose
original physical nature it may one day be possible to determine, who should be absolutely invisible to every living eye,
and this people, as a result of worshipping him only, has been
more readily open than all other peoples to the idea that only
their god is God. The idea of nature, of its reality, of its fun-

damental goodness, is maintained; but nothing in nature is any longer worshipped; the object of adoration is henceforth *super-natural*. We have already pointed out, and we shall not need again to return to it, how, from the beginning of the fifteenth century, a more and more complete knowledge of the world modified anew all traditional beliefs.

The progressive knowledge of nature is, then, one of the most active motors in religious development.

We find another in the progress of reason. We have already somewhat anticipated this new order of considerations when we spoke of the organization of divinities and of mythological traditions. Reason is essentially the friend of unity, of generalization, of system and of symmetry. True, its part in religious history is subordinate, or, to speak more correctly, it is very slow in action. The most irrational religious beliefs may for a very long time resist the most formidable assaults of reason. This is because the religious sentiment still finds satisfaction in them; and it is difficult to exaggerate the degree of subtlety which it can impart to those who feel the weight of arguments against traditional doctrine, but who also feel the need of escaping from them. At length, however, this satisfaction begins to diminish. The religions which have exhausted their principle, or which cannot derive from it the means of transformation, are doomed to perish after a certain time, unless, indeed, the mind of those who profess them remains stationary. But the day that it gets beyond them, they are virtually condemned. Thus philosophic education by the force of reason undermined the Greco-Roman polytheism, without being able to substitute a religion for it; but it prepared the mind to receive willingly that which emanated from the anti-polytheistic principle. The reactionary romanticism of Julian and his friends was itself permeated by monotheism. In our day, endeavours are made to restore, at least in form, a religious condition irrevocably passed away. But we might challenge the promoters of this restoration to re-establish certain institutions, or to re-organize certain public ceremonies, in which, at the time of that simple fervour the disappearance of which they regret, pious souls took delight.

The progress of the moral conscience is, again, a powerful motor of religious transformation.

Religious and moral development are distinct, and are far from being always on an equality. Sometimes morality is in advance of religion, sometimes the reverse. Mythologies, as a whole, demonstrate that little care was taken that the divinities should be of irreproachable morality. In the Old Testament, notwithstanding the inculcation of a morality relatively very pure, sentiments and desires are attributed to Jahveh, the Eternal, which are not in any way edifying. But this dualism does not always prevail. Morality seeks a support in religion, and religion finds its principal application in morality. Notwithstanding the defects of character imputed to the divinities, the chief laws of social order, hospitality, the sanctity of an oath and household chastity, are placed under divine patronage. Plato complained of fables which brought discredit on the divinity. Man does not easily tolerate the idea that the spirit whom he worships does not possess moral perfection. The favourite argument of the apologists of Christianity consists in the enumeration of the vices and faults of the gods of paganism. Christianity itself derives its chief strength from the beauty of its morality. In principle, moreover, it does not allow that communion with God is possible outside the pale of that morality. It is thus one of the most powerful agents of dissolution which can precipitate the fall of religions. The generality of men, so often inaccessible to pure reason, are very easily moved by moral arguments. From the moment in which the hidden bond uniting religion and morality is recognized and felt, any notion of God which wounds the conscience is rejected. We do not think, at least if we understand the meaning of words, that morality can, without suffering much thereby, dispense with all religious principle; but in any case, if morality can dispense with religion, we may certainly affirm that religion cannot dispense with morality.

Events of a political order must also be reckoned among the active causes of religious development. We do not speak merely of the circumstances in which a conquering or despotic power desires suddenly to change the religion of its subjects. There are results of great political changes the effect of which on religious beliefs is even more certain.

When we study the religions of antiquity, we are struck with their close connection with the national life. Each city has its patron gods. If it is invaded or conquered, it thence concludes either that its gods have forsaken it, or that they are less powerful than those of the victorious nation, and they adopt these latter. The reverse may also happen, at least if the victorious nation is inferior in civilization to the vanquished nation, and finds the religion of the latter more beautiful and more attractive. This is not a contradiction; apparently victorious, it is in this case morally conquered. Sometimes the change of religion arises simply from transplantation, as in the case of the colonists led by the kings of Syria into the depopulated territory of the kingdom of Israel, who thought it prudent to adopt the religion and the god "of the land" (Samaritans).[1] Political events may also decide the final victory of one religious tendency over another with which it has long struggled in the midst of the same people. Thus the Jews became permanently monotheists only in consequence of the catastrophe which doomed their nation to fall under the yoke of the victorious Babylonian. If some weakness showed itself for a moment under the domination of the kings of Syria, it was the occasion of an accession of energy and of strength for the national monotheism. On the other hand, conquering Rome, in whose midst the Hellenic religion and the Italian religion had already united, carried this combination to the peoples which she subdued; and thence new combinations resulted, notably in our own Gaul, where the old Celtic divinities were surprised to find themselves identified with those of Latium and of Greece. We know how considerably the barbarian inva-

[1] Comp. 2 Kings xvii. 24—28.

sions augmented the number of the Christian populations. The Roman empire itself, by the very fact of its creation, had singularly opened out the way for Christianity. It had shattered the nationalities, that is to say, the essential forms of the old religions. A sort of amalgamation of the most heterogeneous beliefs was formed. The West was all at once fascinated by religions of Eastern origin. The idea of humanity gained by all which the narrow patriotism of earlier times had lost. There were, in truth, no longer Gauls, Spaniards, Egyptians, Africans, &c.; but everywhere there remained men. So many circumstances were favourable to the progress of a religion proclaiming itself superior to national distinctions, and by preference sustaining itself on the general needs and the universal tendencies of the human being. When we study more closely the many causes which have won for Christianity its victory over the old anterior religions, we find nothing miraculous in them; history resumes all her rights; and we end by feeling surprised, not that paganism was vanquished, but at the obstinate resistance which, all moribund as it was, it offered to the invading power, and at the extent of the revenge which, in spite of its official death, it knew how to take at the expense of the victorious religion. Moreover, we must not regard the establishment of international religions as having suppressed the influence of national character. When we compare the Buddhism of Ceylon with that of Thibet, Persian Islamism with Arab Islamism, Christianity of the North with that of the South, and even without going outside of Catholicism, the most at one with itself and the most centralized of the international churches, that of France with that of Sicily or of Brazil, we can perceive that the nation, and all that which precedes or which constitutes it—region, climate, historical antecedents, collective intelligence, &c.—are always great causes of religious modification.

It remains for us to point out a last order of facts, counting also among the most influential in regard to the course and the variations of the religious idea. We would speak of the personal action—very powerful and very intense—of men who could have done nothing without the concurrence of the other moving causes which we have enumerated, but in regard to whom it would be contrary to all evidence to deny their immense part in history. These are the men whom the ages and millions of men revere as prophets, revealers and founders of religions.

The oldest religions are anonymous. The work of their elaboration is collective. But it is to be presumed that from all time, in the midst of the most uncultured populations, there were individuals endowed with more imagination, of a more subtle religious sense, of a more fertile poetic faculty, than the mass of their contemporaries, and who contributed, by their relative superiority, to determine the beliefs and the religious life of their kind. Already the mythologies make mention of names themselves more or less mythic—Orpheus, Numa, Tiresias, Calchas, &c.—which suppose a personal action of this kind. But, as a general rule, it is not indissolubly connected with proper names.

It is otherwise in this respect with a certain number of other religions, precisely the most remarkable for the number of their adherents or for their rank in history. Judaism is connected with the person of Moses, the ancient Masdeism with that of Zaratustra or Zoroaster, Buddhism with that of Buddha, Christianity with that of Jesus Christ, Islamism with that of Mahomet. The importance of the bond which joins these various religions to their personal founders is attested by the fact, that the faithful of each of these great religious forms attribute to a quite special revelation, individually received and conveyed by him, that which each of these founders has bequeathed to them of new beliefs, and rest on this contention their legitimacy and exclusive truth.

Formerly it would have appeared scandalous to place thus on the same line of observation the individual founders of the most important religions which divide humanity. There was a time when Mahomet was never called anything but "the false Prophet." From the strictly historic point of view at which we place ourselves, we cannot thus prejudge matters. We can only distinguish these revealers as together forming a class apart, and worthy of a quite special interest. That does not mean that after examination we shall not have to set forth the differences which will enable us to decree the palm to him who merits it. But, at the moment, we must keep within the terms of the most severe objectivity. There are anonymous religions; there are religions founded by revealers whose names are known to us; they are inseparable from their persons—that is enough to cause us to divide them into two distinct groups.

Now, in each case, the revealer ought to possess in a very high degree *religious genius*, independently of knowledge, properly so called, and of philosophy. Each revealer was the bearer of a principle incarnate in himself. This principle and its immediate consequences embody themselves in certain forms which are confounded with him in the eyes of peoples who are guided more by feeling than by reflection; they spread, they unfold, they mingle themselves with everything and penetrate everywhere—and there is another great religion in the world.

This is because, like all else which springs from sentiment, like art, like morality, like poetry, like patriotism—we may say, indeed, like science herself when she is guided by intuitive perceptions—Religion has its *inspired ones*, men endowed in such sort that the religious sentiment common to all acquires in their case an extraordinary intensity, joined to a great and marvellous clearness of expression, and that they reveal, in the natural sense of that word, that which the multitude suspected, perhaps sometimes murmured, but that which no one before them had known how to say in a loud and intelligible voice. By their side and below them, there are men who also act very powerfully on their kind—reformers, prophets, religious orators. They also come into the category of inspiration. But their part, like their genius, is not to be compared with that of those powerful arousers of consciences which we have enumerated.

VII.

CLASSIFICATION OF RELIGIONS.

The active causes of religious development are then: 1st, increasing knowledge of nature; 2nd, the genius of races; 3rd, the progress of reason; 4th, that of the moral conscience; 5th, social and political events; 6th, the personal action of religious geniuses (revealers, reformers, &c.). We shall now proceed to the classification of historic religions; but in order to justify the order in which we range them, we must first note the principal phases through which Religion passes in its development.

We need not retract what we have said as to the fluctuating, fugitive character of primary religious intuitions. Probably many centuries rolled away before they were fixed in such a way as to be able to be made the object of a description. We must leave to the pre-historic sciences the care of deciding whether, in the *débris* which the palæoutological races have left in testimony of their existence on the earth, any traces of belief or of worship are found. The most significant of the discoveries which we may place in this order is probably a kind of amulet unearthed in the grotto of the Gourdan, and dating from the age of the reindeer and the mammoth. It is a plate of bone pierced in the centre, probably in order to be worn. From the central hole rays diverge, which make this object look like an image of the sun. The same symbol is engraved three times on a staff of office, or kind of sceptre, on which it seems to confer a sort of consecration. There is reason to believe, also, that the custom of trepanning skulls, either living or dead, may be traced to the same prodigious antiquity, and by analogy with a similar custom still in vogue in historic times, it would seem to be connected with *animist* beliefs. The evil spirit dwelling inside a sick man was to be cast out, or the soul of the dead was to be allowed a way of escape, just as the Iroquois take care to arrange a small outlet to each grave with the same end in view.[1]

This leads us to speak of a subject for a long time relegated to the background in the history of religions, but to which we must henceforth assign a leading place. We refer to *animism*, or the worship of spirits, of which fetichism itself is only a modification.

Man, we have seen, adores only that which he personifies, that is to say, the beings to whom he attributes a conscience and a will analogous to his own. From a very early date he was able to distinguish—not in the sense of an abstract spiritualism, of which he could not have any idea, but in the most concrete manner—mind and body in all the personal beings whom he knew or thought he knew. The sight of a dead body suggested to him the feeling that that which had desired, spoken, acted, a few hours previously, was no longer there, but still could not have been annihilated. His own experience, founded especially on the phenomenon of dreaming, led him in the direction of an analogous conclusion. Savage races attach great importance to dreams. The savage who is transported in a dream to a distant country, in which he meets persons dead or absent, firmly believes that his soul has really travelled far from his body, that it has seen real beings—in a word, the subjective character of the dream entirely escapes him. Thence this double consequence: the soul can detach itself from the body and live its own life without it, and although of a much more subtle and aerial nature,

---

[1] Comp. M. Joly, *L'Homme avant les Metaux*, Paris: Germer Bailliere, 1879, p. 306 and onwards.—We need only remark that we have nothing to alter in this statement, whether humanity had only one stem or several. If it dates back to a single primitive stock, the awakening of the religious sentiment must have occurred in more than one place in regions where the descendants of the first human couple swarmed. If we must admit several—if, as has been said, each continent produced its man—the religious faculty was born, if not simultaneously, at least in parallel lines, in each of the primordial races; and this parallelism, like the fact of religion itself, enters among the characteristic traits of humanity as much as distinct unity.

since on awaking one does not see it go and come, it yet has all the form and appearance of doing this. Almost everywhere the breath furnishes the least material analogy possible by which to indicate the nature of this invisible soul. Also the greater number of the words which serve actually to designate it—*âme, anima, ψύχη, spiritus, πνεῦμα*; Hebrew, *rouach, nephesch*, &c.— were originally formed on the basis of this analogy; and our word *spirit*, which denotes the system of which the soul forms a part, has no other meaning. It thence results to the man given up to the illusions of ignorance, that not only his own soul and body, but also the soul and body of all the natural beings personified by him, can detach itself the one from the other; that, for example, the invisible spirit of the river, or of the tree, or of the animal, or of the sun, which he adores, can quit its visible form and traverse space in all directions. And as the objects of adoration continually increase in number, it is not surprising that very soon his preponderating religious practice consists in the worship of spirits which people the air. The dead which have become spirits, especially if they are ancestors, are joined to this mysterious army. In fact, almost everywhere the worship of the dead is closely connected with that of elementary spirits. Soon the remembrance of the link which connects the latter with natural objects is effaced, and it frequently happens with very backward tribes, such as Negroes, Hottentots, the Red Indians of North America, &c., that the worship of nature may be, so to speak, supplanted by that of spirits. The religions in which this predominates were formerly arranged under the category of *shamanism*, because the shamans are the priest-sorcerers of the Finns and of the Tartars, whose religion is in practice almost entirely concentrated in the worship of spirits. But it is proved that this worship holds a scarcely inferior place in the religions of many other uncivilized peoples, who are neither Finns nor Tartars, and the more general denomination of animism is to be preferred.

Fetichism, which we shall have the task of studying more

closely elsewhere, is a particular form of animism; it is, in fact, its grossest form. This word has indeed been quite wrongly applied to the adoration of very simple natural objects, such as a tree or an animal. The *fetich*, a word of Portuguese origin, which comes from the Latin *factitius*, must, as its essential characteristic, be transportable at will, must belong corporeally to the man, who has usually chosen it, and who attributes to it the power of influencing his destiny. Fetichism is distinguished from pure animism in this, that there is no question of a possible separation between the soul or spirit of the fetich and its visible form. The only approach to that is this, that the fetich has power only because it is considered as the dwelling of a spirit. It is in reality an animated amulet. The spirit of the fetich has no necessary connection with those natural objects whence have proceeded the spirits preferably adored by animism; it comes rather into the class of anonymous spirits, or those become such.

But it is an error to consider fetichism, and even animism, as the primordial religion. They suppose too much reflection for that. They are evidently secondary phenomena, such as, in Christianity, the worship of saints, of the Virgin Mary and of the Sacred Heart. Seeing the Christianity of certain peoples, if we did not know its history, we could believe that Christianity consists in those adorations which are in reality only applications of or deviations from (according to the point of view at which we are placed) the doctrines of the gospel. In order that a belief in the independent spirits of nature should be induced, a certain number of observations and of reflections on human nature itself, which denote something quite different from primitive simplicity, are necessary. In order to believe that spirits or fetiches influence the course of things and modify their order, it is necessary to be alive to the sentiment that there is a course of things, that there exists a natural series, and that we can interrupt it through the intervention of a power higher and stronger than it. All that could not be primitive. There must have been first a worship of nature or of natural objects personified; thence came animism, which among certain races, and especially among Negroes, was condensed into fetichism.

This view is confirmed by the fact that we discern more and more clearly the *naturist* basis of beliefs which flourish among peoples the most given up to animism or fetichism. We can no longer doubt it in the case of the Finns since the great work of M. de Castren.[1] We may say the same as to the North-American Indians, and we shall show it elsewhere in regard to Negroes, Kaffirs and Hottentots.

What is true is this, that the extension and the absorbing nature of this kind of religion has proved injurious to the development of a natural mythology among races the least endowed with generalizing imagination. Although we discover traces of fetichism, and especially of animism, in all religions, it cannot be denied that they are passed by and left in the background in those which have prepared and followed the upward movement of the human mind among races the most apt for civilization.

No doubt, there also, in India, in Persia and in Greece, the natural object personified, in assuming personal form and life in this dramatization of nature which produced the great mythologies, acquired an independence of action which made it impossible that it should be any longer identified simply with its visible appearance. When, for example, the Greeks recounted the prowess of solar heroes, such as Heracles or Perseus, it is abundantly certain that they did not absolutely confound them with the sun shining above their heads. But when we examine their legends more nearly, we see that these heroes always maintain a very close relation with the sun. The separation is never absolute. The exploits assigned to them, the romance of which they occupy the central place, their mode of birth, of growth, of fighting, of loving and of dying, all recal their solar origin. The animism here is not self-evident; it is rather the personification and the dramatization of the natural phenomenon which are implied. It is this

[1] *Vorlesungen über die Finnische Mythologie*, 2 vols.: St. Petersburg, 1853—1862.

which has made myths so varied and so rich in meaning. Animism, from an æsthetic and poetical point of view, is very barren.

Among the Chinese, animism and the deification of the great phenomena of nature, notably of the earth and of the heaven, are developed, so to speak, in parallel lines. It is especially under the form of the worship of ancestors that animism has taken root among this people so obstinately attached to its past. But it has never destroyed what we may call official mythology, of which the very constitution of the vast empire is a chapter.

Polynesia presents the very rare spectacle of a race remaining in the lowest state of civilization and social growth, who yet nevertheless possess a mythology of a certain richness, and often of great poetical power.

What is interesting in this new stage of religious history is the very distinct physiognomy which the genius of each people impresses on the religion of nature. That of the Vedas, in which the worship of grand natural phenomena still exists in all its primitive fervour and simplicity; that of Egypt, in which, on the same fundamental but infinitely varied idea, that of the antagonism of life and death, a superior and remarkably endowed race enshrines in sublime surroundings those most degrading superstitions of which Africa has never ceased to be the prolific source; those of Nineveh and of Babylon, military and imperial mythologies, which, like their sisters of Tyre, of Syria and of Arabia, sacrifice even paternal love, even woman's chastity, to the sovereign power; those of countries once unknown, where Europe was to find in full vigour a solar religion not less bloody nor less despotic; that of Italy, where we must distinguish between the religion of that mysterious Etruscan race, whose origin it is so difficult to determine, and the as yet very simple religion of the Latin centre; those, finally, of Gaul, of Germany, of the Scandinavian countries, not to speak of others less known—here are the fields which spread themselves out beyond the confines of our vision on the height which we have gained; and yet just above us another presents itself, more limited in its circumference, but as rich as, if not richer than, all the others put together—the field of Greek mythology.

All the mythologies which we have just enumerated are autochthonous, springing from the soil. Greek mythology also has this character, but it more than any other incorporates with itself numerous elements borrowed from Egypt and the Semitic East. It so well impresses its seal upon them, that at first sight it is difficult to perceive their foreign origin. What a difference there is, for example, between the Tyrian and Carthaginian Melkart, this brazen god, the devourer of children, the terror of men, and the Greek Hercules, the great lawgiver, the tamer of monsters, the peacemaker, the liberator! Nevertheless, it is in fact the same god. But that which has most contributed to give to Greek mythology its character of mythology *par excellence* is precisely this, next to the incomparable superiority of the Greek mind itself, this power of assimilation, which has enabled it to blend traditions of different origin into one homogeneous whole. When later the Italian mythology was absorbed into its elastic framework, Greek mythology gave proof of the same ductility, and received its poorer sister without doing itself the least violence.

In proportion as we rise in the religious scale, the relation between religion and morality comes into operation. The Egyptian, Latin and Greek mythologies, present very remarkable aspects from a moral point of view. Readers of the learned work of M. Alfred Maury, on *Les Religions de la Grèce antique*, will assuredly not have forgotten the chapter in which the sublime maxims of the religious wisdom of the Hellenes are collected. We could imagine ourselves on the propylæum of the gospel. Nevertheless, we must bear in mind that among the Greeks morality was never digested into a body of doctrines systematized and recognized as an integral part of religious teaching. We shall see elsewhere to what this deficiency is to be attributed; but we discern already the point of departure of a new class of religions which are distinguished from the others in this, that the emphasis of the religious life falls on the conduct of the believer, and that they impose upon him, as an essential condition of union with the sovereign Spirit, the observance of a law moral as much as religious. It is this character which serves to define this class of religions as *religions of law* or *legalistic*.

They are six in number, and may be reduced to four.

We ought to count among them two Chinese religions, that which is connected with the name of Kon-fou-tzeu, and that which springs from Lao-tzeu. We may unite them, in spite of their divergences, under the common denomination of *Chinese legalism*. Then comes *Brahmanism*, the very rich and complicated mythology which arose on the basis of the Vedas, but which, systematized and taught in India by the sacerdotal caste of the Brahmans, became a religious, ritualistic and moral law, with sacred books to explain and comment upon it (Brahmanas, laws of Manou). Mazdeism, or the religion of Zoroaster and of Iran (Persia), is a mythology dominated by the principle of *dualism*; that is to say, that its organic principle is the separation of the world and of divine beings into two hostile camps, each commanded by a superior god,—Ahura Mazdâo or Ormuzd for the good, Anromaïnyus or Ahriman for the bad. Moral obligation is comprehended in the sense that man should be the ally of Ormuzd in his lasting struggle with Ahriman. Thence came a religious, moral and ritualistic legislation, laid down in the Zend Avesta, and especially in its first part, the Vendidâd—the Mosaism of the eighth century before our era, and the Judaism which is the codification of it, enriched and systematized, or, if you will, its definitive evolution, determined by the effects of Babylonian, Persian and Greek conquests. We do not need to recal its eminently legalistic character. But this character is not the only one which distinguishes it. Mazdeism, in its repugnance to Ahriman, physical and moral evil, in its almost exclusive adoration of Ormuzd, practically approaches very nearly to monotheism, without setting it up as an absolute principle. With Judaism the monotheistic principle made its first appearance in history as the basis of a popular religion, and the Jewish law is rigorously governed by the requirements of this new principle.

We should consider Islamism as the younger brother of Judaism, with which it presents closer analogies than with Christianity itself, although Judaism was the historical cradle of the latter religion. Like Judaism, Islamism rigorously maintains the principle of the divine unity, and makes that its foundation-stone, but takes away from it the purely national character which Judaism had impressed upon it, in order to make it the principle of a universal or international religion founded by the Arab prophet Mahomet. Nevertheless, like Judaism, it is essentially legalistic, and it makes adhesion to its principle, and observance of its ritual and moral precepts, the condition of the supremacy of believers on earth as well as of their happiness in another life.

We may no doubt regard it as favourable to the general progress that a religious law should be at the same time a moral law, and sanction by its promises and by its threats the fulfilment of duties. But there arises a new point of view which determines a new direction of religious thought. Not only do these legalistic religions, by making as much of rites often puerile as of duties, and by ritualizing morality, impose on man a painful yoke which his reason cannot always approve, but they also arouse in him the sorrowful, despairing feeling of his own insufficiency and of theirs also. The legalistic practice does not procure for him the security which it promised, and experience shows him that, judged according to the rigour of the religious law, he will infallibly be condemned. The need of synthesis or of harmony which is at the bottom of the religious tendency of man requires, then, a new satisfaction, and thence the appearance of two great international religions which have this common character of being religions of *redemption* or of *deliverance*. The earliest in date is Buddhism, the second is Christianity.

Buddhism offers us this phenomenon, at first sight very strange, that, differing absolutely from Christianity in its point of departure and in its tendency, it not the less presents us with

H

the most curious resemblances to it. We shall elsewhere give
the key to these profound differences and close analogies. At
present we have to point out this character in common, whence it
is that historically we must place them in certain respects in the
same class of religions. Both start from the fact that the condition of man is unhappy through his own fault, and teach him
the means of attaining safety, that is, perfect happiness. Both,
consequently, are eminently propagandist, not only from love of
truth, but also from love of humanity, which they seek to save
from its misery.[1] It is very well known that Buddhism, the
origin of which dates back to five centuries before our era, is the
veritable international religion of Eastern Asia, as Islamism is
that of Western Asia and of Africa, as Christianity is that of
Europe and of America, whither it was carried by Europeans.
Two points, however, widely distinguish Christianity and Buddhism, one having reference to their respective points of departure, the other to their different religious principle. Buddhism,
born on the domain of polytheism, has fought against it, not by
rising above nature in subordinating it to a single sovereign
spirit, but by reproving nature in principle, and condemning life
itself as an evil and a misfortune. It may be asked whether the
original Buddhism was anything more than an ascetic morality
without religion. In the result, in order to become a religion,
it has been obliged to amalgamate with the polytheisms in the
midst of which it was propagated, without possessing in itself a
power of reaction against the intermixtures which have caused
it to lose its true character. The destiny of Christianity has
been, and must be, different in this sense, that, being the supreme
evolution of an anterior monotheism, in place of suppressing
nature and life, it tends, at least in its first principles, to transform the one and to intensify the other.

It is, however, a law of religious history, to which we have

[1] Islamism is so in a lesser degree, in the sense that it is voluntarily more conquering
than missionary. It accommodates itself very well to a state of things which allows
other monotheistic religions to exist on the sole condition that territory and power
belong to the true believers.

already made allusion, that every new and higher principle is established only on the condition of accepting more or less completely the heritage of the past still existing under other forms. There are in the highest polytheisms evident traces of animism and of fetichism. We find them even in the most pronounced monotheisms and international religions, precisely because these extend among more numerous and more diverse classes of men and are more liable than others to include beliefs, traditions and superstitions,[1] foreign to their principles.

But we see from all this how difficult it is to make a logically correct and methodic classification of religions. There are intercrossings of principles and of claims which render this operation impossible, and we must content ourselves with an approximation. A religion, elevated in its principle—Judaism, for example—remains confined to the class of strictly national religions. Mazdeism, which is really polytheist, is in practice much nearer to Judaism than it is to the Greek religion. Buddhism is, in truth, a polytheism, and nevertheless it presents a number of characters in common with Christianity, being, like it, a religion of redemption. Whatever may be the principle of classification adopted, we see ourselves reduced to bringing together in theory that which is in fact very distant, or which represents other principles very important and reciprocally hostile. How can we rank in the same historic category Brahmanism, with its florid mythology, and Islamism, with its very severe monotheism? Nevertheless, these two religions are both legalistic.

From the historical point of view, that which guides all our study, we think it convenient to maintain the fundamental division, although it is criticised in the present day, between *polytheistic* and *monotheistic* religions. There is no question here of necessary or of possible superiority. Historically, monotheistic religions govern the modern world; their history can be written only on

---

[1] Superstition means that which survives, persists, and is superfluous, because belonging to a state of mind which the intellectual and moral aristocracy of any given time have passed beyond. It most frequently consists in an application of the principle of causality, erroneous and contradicted by experience.

condition of a continual parallelism between their destinies and
their reciprocal evolutions. It would be quite impossible to
detach the history of Christianity from that of Judaism, or the
history of Islamism from that of the other two religions. They
thus form a group clearly distinct from all the others, the study
of which should be pursued separately. We may characterize
them by applying to them categories like those which serve to
distinguish the religions forming the polytheistic group from one
another.

This, then, is the general view which we propose:

I. Polytheistic Religions.

1. The *primitive religion of nature*, the simple worship of
natural objects, which man represents to himself as animated,
conscious, powerful, and influencing human destiny.

2. The *animist and fetichist religions*, developed on the basis
of the preceding, and peculiar to races in a so-called savage
state—Negroes, other African tribes, Esquimaux, Finns, Tartars,
American Indians, Polynesians, &c.; always possessing the beginnings of mythology, and especially remarkable among the Finns
and Polynesians.

3. The great *national mythologies*, founded on the dramatization
of nature, imagining relations between divine beings in accordance with those which prevail in human life, and collecting the
primitive creeds and myths into one vast whole—the religions
of China, of Egypt, of Nineveh, of Babylon, of Germany, of Gaul,
of Italy, of Greece, &c.; a class of religions of which the Vedic
mythology presents the simplest form, the Grecian mythology the
most refined and indisputably the most beautiful. Probably we
ought to place in the same class the ancient mythology of Japan,
as yet so little understood; certainly the mythologies of the
peoples of the New World, such as they were discovered in
Mexico and Peru, belong to it.

4. The *polytheistic-legalistic* religions—Brahmanism, Mazde-

ism, and the two philosophical Chinese religions of Kon-fou-tzeu and of Lao-tzeu.

5. *Buddhism*, the religion of redemption, universalist or international : in principle opposed to polytheism, but in practice irremediably blending with local polytheisms.

II. Monotheistic Religions.

1. *Judaism*, the descendant of Mosaism, legalistic and national.
2. *Islamism*, legalistic and international.
3. *Christianity*, the religion of redemption, international.

Second Part.

I.

THE MYTH.

It is through the *myth* that we approach a group of intellectual forces and of special facts in close relation with the religious development of man, and we shall meet with it more or less everywhere in the course of our history.

The myth has been the object of special study only within a comparatively recent period. For a long time it was confounded with the fable. The seventeenth century knew nothing about it; the eighteenth, not much. Nevertheless, we there find glimpses denoting that light was beginning to break. We may quote the lines of the *Emile*, where J. J. Rousseau says that "man began by animating all the beings whose action he felt," and that thus the universe "was filled with material gods." It is just also to mention the now almost forgotten work of Bergier, Principal of the College of Besançon, on the *Origin of the Gods of Paganism* (Paris, 1767), which somewhat learnedly develops the idea that mythology is a tissue of romances received as real by the imagination which invented them. Some memoirs of Fréret and of Bougainville also contain indications of a truly scientific notion in regard to the innumerable narratives of mythology. But it was reserved for Germany, much less absorbed than France in political and social questions, to throw light on a subject the difficulty of which consists entirely in this, that, in order to understand it thoroughly, it is necessary to transport oneself into a state of mind very different from ours.

It was not that no one previously had ever asked whence sprang this rich harvest of narratives, which, however, were scarcely known except through the Greek and Latin mythology. The middle ages had their answer quite ready: It was the work of the devil.

This answer could not satisfy the inquiring and not very credulous spirit of modern times, which fell back upon an explanation which appeared so much the more acceptable since it was found to have been already admitted in pagan antiquity. It is what is called *evhemerism*, from the name of its author, Evhemerus, a wit of the Cyrenaic school, who lived at the court of the Macedonian king Cassander in the second half of the fourth century before our era. Before his time, certain philosophers of the Ionian school had already traced some lines of the system to which his name is attached. Its tendency was to bring all histories concerning gods, goddesses and deified heroes, to the proportions of real but terrestial and common events. The gods were formerly only men who had powerfully impressed the imagination by their strength, or by their conquests, or by their superior wisdom, and after their death they had been deified. Thus Jupiter was an ancient king of Crete, and the proof of this is, that they show in that island his cradle and his tomb. The same method was applied to all the Hellenic gods, and nothing seemed more simple than to submit all the mythologies of the world to this convenient rationalism.

Among the moderns, also, evhemerism counted its partizans, especially in the eighteenth century, and even since. Certain mental affinities explain this momentary success. Evhemerus is to us one of the ancients; to his contemporaries he was a free thinker, emancipated from vulgar superstitions; in reality, his was one of those too ingenious minds who understand everything except the simplicity of those ages which were governed by spontaneity. If he had had more knowledge of religions, he would have known that the Cretan Jupiter, born and dying, is in the same category with many other divinities of Western Asia, whose worshippers in no way concerned themselves with the kings who may have reigned in Crete. He would have known that this Jupiter, bearing everywhere almost the same name, is found in Italy, in Asia Minor, in Germany, even on the banks of the Indus. And what a paradox to explain the origin of gods by the deification of men! As if, in deifying a conqueror, a hero, a sovereign, it was not done with the idea of making him equal to existing gods! In reality, this explanation explains nothing, and it has, moreover, the misfortune of being extremely commonplace. Æsthetics, no less than science and reason, protest against it.

As this system, although banished from serious mythological science, has yet some partizans, conscious and unconscious, we will show, by an example easy of comprehension, what becomes of the most tragic myths when the method of Evhemerus is applied to them.

All the world has heard of the miserable Ixion, who perpetually revolves in the depths of Tartarus on his burning wheel. He endures this frightful fate, says the Greek mythology, as a punishment for the sacrilege he committed in aspiring to the favours of Juno (Hera), the wife of the king of the gods. Jupiter, who sought to prove him, created the phantom Nephele (cloud), giving her a likeness to Juno. Blinded by his passion, Ixion fell into the snare, and thus drew upon himself his terrible chastisement. To us, through comparison with other analogous myths, the sense of this myth is transparent. Wherever in mythology it is a question of a burning wheel which turns, it is certain that it has to do with the sun. This sun is often understood, in the myths which concern him, as a great criminal, because he appears to be so very unfortunate. According to a certain set of ideas, he must indeed have committed a great fault to have deserved the punishment which consists in revolving perpetually, without knowing a day's respite. Later, these representations of an unhappy, guilty and punished sun, were transferred to Tartarus. But that in no way changes the original meaning of the myth. Ixion, the sun, passionately loves the cloud which he gilds, which he embraces with his rays, which he would bear away with him to his nocturnal retreat. But this cloud is only a vapour, which is dissipated under his embrace, and he remains in the presence of angry heaven, which condemns him to turn and to burn for ever. Quite a tragic poem might be disentangled from this old dramatization of a natural phenomenon.

Let us now see what this becomes in one of the latest works, written from the evhemerist point of view, *Le Dictionnaire de la Fable*, by Fréd. Noël (1823, fourth edition):

"It is not difficult here to separate the historical from the fabulous. A king, surnamed Jupiter, generously accorded hospitality to Ixion, who ungratefully returned this benefit by black perfidy, and fell in love with the queen. But the king put a slave named Nephele in his wife's place, and was no longer in doubt as to the criminal intentions of his guest. Ixion, having subsequently boasted of having rendered the queen susceptible of his desires, was banished from the court, and led afterwards a wandering, sad, restless life, hated and despised by all the world." Here is one of the most tragic conceptions of Greek mythology transformed into a petty story in the style of the Decameron.

Evhemerism is a system of absurd explanations, and we must resolutely reject its principles if we would understand anything of the old mythologies. It was after its absurdity and emptiness had been guaged that attention was turned to another explanation, which had at least this in its favour, that it supposed as much simplicity as imagination on the part of the inventors of myths.

Let us imagine a period in the history of the human mind in which the imagination shall be sufficiently lively, and general ignorance sufficiently great, for the phenomena of nature to produce the effect of animated scenes: nothing more is needed for myths to appear. If, for example, the sun appears like some being, the red clouds of evening like a herd of great red oxen, and the spring vegetation like a lovely young girl, does it require an extraordinary effort of imagination to fancy things thus: the sun is a herdsman, for he has a drove of oxen which he feeds in the evening; at the same time he loves the fresh spring, and he prospers in his love; but this love is fatal to the poor child, who dies under the caresses of her celestial lover? Here is the central idea of a complete solar myth.

Or, again, if we know a large rock named Actæon, which the dog-days, like so many devouring animals, despoil of its verdure, burn and destroy, and if this great rock projects its shadow across the trees over the neighbouring river at the hour when the moon, Diana, with her silver bow, refreshes herself in the clear waters far from indiscreet gazers, shall we have great difficulty in picturing to ourselves the mythological scene which shows us the too curious Actæon torn by the dogs which the enraged Diana urged against the bold youth who had surprised her

Le soir, un pied dans l'eau?[1]

The whole question is reduced, then, to knowing if there was, in fact, an epoch of the human mind in which things could present themselves to it in this manner,—in which it could see in nature so many little and great dramas, which were at bottom only poetic interpretations of nature, but which it took for so many positive realities.

Such a question is solved beforehand by the very existence of myths; only it must be understood that they are not born all at once and complete. The developed and complete myths were preceded by *simple mythic elements* going back to the primary intuitions of the imagination. A somewhat complicated geometrical theorem is demonstrated by means of anterior simpler theorems; these, in their turn, are only the methodical applications of definitions and of axioms previously laid down. It is the same with myths. In each of them we discover the elements of which it

[1] Alfred de Musset, *Ballade à la Lune*.

is composed. Primitive humanity, reducing all visible phenomena to the analogy of animal or human life, translated its impressions into the forms which experience suggested. To it the lightning was sometimes the coils of a gigantic fiery serpent, sometimes the spear, or the hammer, or the sword, which a celestial warrior, hidden behind the storm-cloud, brandished. In the thunder it heard the war-cry or the terrible anger of the hero, or the sound of his chariot and horses, or the roaring of a lion, or the bellowing of a colossal bull. In the sounds of the wind it recognized the howling of a pack of hounds, urged on by mysterious huntsmen; while, according to the populations and their chief occupation, the clouds which passed across the distant sky were milch cows or lambs, grazing under the care of their shepherd, the sun, or the boats of the celestial fishermen, or even fish, or swans, or aërial dragons. According as the storm and its floods were looked upon as fertilizing or devastating, they suggested either the idea of the marriage of heaven and earth, or of war between the bright and beneficent heaven and the monsters of darkness issuing from black depths. These are so many simple mythical elements.[1]

There is as yet nothing specifically religious in these poetic imaginations; but they hasten the moment in which the spirit of man will feel itself in the presence of celestial spirits analogous to itself, its superiors in power and masters of its destiny. Man is led by that means to think that there exists a relation between these spirits and himself, and to behave himself in the way which the feeling of this relation would suggest. A lively interest induces him to concentrate his curious attention on their manifestations. He associates them, he groups them, he sees those who seek his favour or those who oppose him, those who love him or those who hate him; and he is henceforth in the presence of dramas, joyful or sad, which he amplifies indefinitely. If especially this spontaneous work goes on in the midst of a race of lively, ingenious, poetical spirit, stories of

[1] Comp. Pfleiderer, *Religionsphilosophie:* Berlin, 1878.

divinities of every kind will be innumerable. Many will relate to the same natural object understood in different ways. The sun may be described as beautiful, bright, devouring; as a purifier, a warrior, a conqueror of monsters, as irresistible, a great traveller, &c. Thus we discover him in all the myths of which Phœbus, Helios, Phaëton, Esculapius, Perseus, Bellerophon, Hercules, Theseus and many others are the heroes. The moon, in the same mythology, is simultaneously presented to us as Artemis, Selene, Hecate, Io, Pasiphaë, Europa, each of whom has her history. Uranos, Kronos, Jupiter, are all three heaven, but heaven differently understood, as sheltering, or as ripening, or as shining. The distinction between the visible object and the personal spirit, which it is believed may be discerned in it by detaching at a certain point this spirit from its base material, opens a still larger field for dramatic invention.[1]

But this detachment leads to another very important result. Logically, the dramatic representation ought to begin again each time that the phenomenon which gives rise to it recurs. It is not so. It becomes the description of an event which has happened once, at a certain moment of time, on a point of space, and which will not happen again. In reality, Hercules ought to die each time that the sun disappears amid the flames of his setting, as though he would force himself away from the black tunic of clouds which obscure him.

But in the mythology it is only once that the sun, the vanquisher of monsters and the liberator, consumes himself in order to escape from the tortures which the tunic of Dejanira causes him to endure. Each time that in the freshening breeze which precedes the dawn the thousand stars of the firmament grow pale

[1] As an example, the well-known myth of Pallas Athene associates a certain number of elements accepted beforehand : the dark sky is a sick man ; the clap of thunder is a blow from a hatchet or hammer dealt by a divine blacksmith ; the pure light which follows the storm comes from the face of heaven looking like a bright young virgin ; the shield which she like her father bears is the fringed cloud by which she is preceded ; light is the spear with which the divine virgin victoriously repels the monster, &c. See how, from this association of simple elements, a dramatic myth may arise.

and seem like so many closing eyes, Hermes with his lyre lulls to sleep Argus with his thousand eyes watching the moon Io, too well loved by the shining heaven. Each time that the purple heaven sends down its golden rain on the gloomy earth which it fertilizes, the king of the gods has found his beloved Danaë. But no: mythologically all this happened only once, and this is one of the laws of frequent application in the history of religious ideas, this condensation in one fact, accomplished once for all, of things or of experiences which in reality recur very often.

That being granted, we can understand that the myth may lend itself to ideas other than those which are furnished by visible nature considered as animated. A natural form, at one moment of the history of the human mind, and of representative and theoretic thought, it will serve also for the expression of ideas, of principles and of observations suggested by other experiences than those derived from visible nature, and of moral truths already become philosophical. Thence a second class of myths, less ancient than the first, inasmuch as they denote more experience and reflection. This is why we see them appear specially in monotheistic religions which have a tendency to banish the mythology of nature. The Old Testament contains several, notably the myth of Eden, which brings together and reduces to one single event the general conditions of the development of the moral nature of man. The myth of the mysterious wrestling of Jacob with God belongs to the same category. Others have in view the explanation of a fact bearing upon human destiny, like the narrative of the Tower of Babel, which seeks to account for the diversity of languages; or the justification of a reform or of a religious prescription, like the myth of the sacrifice of Abraham, which clearly tends to destroy the custom of the immolation of the first-born. These myths also evidently present the character of reduction to a single incident of that which is continually occurring. We find this always. The purpose which inspires them is didactic rather than representative, and they may serve as the transition between the myth properly so called and history. The Greek mythology also includes myths of this kind. The most celebrated is that of Prometheus, the inventor of fire, the promoter of civilization and of human progress, the object therefore of celestial anger, and tortured by a fearful punishment. Prometheus is the personification of the *pramantha*, that instrument which dates from such high antiquity, and which is still in the present day used in India to obtain the sacred fire.[1] But personified, the myth expresses just the same idea which we have already remarked in Genesis, that human progress is a usurpation of the divine province, and that he who promotes it pays by new tortures for the almost sacrilegious boldness of which he has been guilty.

These are the considerations which lead us to give this definition of the myth:

The myth is either the description of a natural phenomenon considered as the exponent of a divine drama, or else the incorporation of a moral idea in a dramatic narrative. In both cases, that which is permanent or frequent in nature and in humanity is brought together into one event accomplished once for all, and the drama, although invented, is looked upon as real.

This last characteristic, the attribution of the character of reality to narratives of pure imagination, is that which is essential to the myth. It is that which chiefly distinguishes it from the fable and the allegory. The fable is also a dramatic narrative, in which a moral idea, a truth derived from experience, is found incorporated; but it is invented with a purpose, and propounded without any claim to pass as a reality. When Lafontaine relates the dialogue of the Fox and the Crow, it does not occur to his mind, any more than to that of his readers, that fox and crow have ever really held such discourse. The allegory is also a work of methodic reflection, composed in full consciousness of its imaginary character. By using prolonged and connected analogies, it explains other things than those which it

---

[1] This is a block of wood pierced with a hole, into which a stick is introduced; a thong round the stick allows it to turn rapidly perpendicularly to this hole. The friction disengages great heat, and the wood lights.

narrates. The parable is itself a kind of allegory, and neither the author nor the hearer is the dupe of this method. The myth, on the contrary, is a work of credulous simplicity, of which the shell and the kernel are inseparable in the minds of those who relate it, as in the minds of those who hear it. It is we moderns who, in our need of analyzing everything, distinguish in it idea and form. In remote antiquity this idea and this form were one.

We must not be astonished if we come across myths which surprise us by their ingenious direction or even by their profound philosophy. This is often the character of spontaneous products of the human mind. The language which we speak is a philosophic marvel, and we can scarcely surmise the period in which we began to lisp it; no more could our ancestors who bequeathed it to us. The human mind when it works thus spontaneously is a philosopher, just as the bee is a mathematician when it constructs its cells, as the beaver is an architect when he builds his hut. We must, it is true, distrust any tendency to see in myths anything but what is there, and to transform them into depths of wisdom. The charm which is peculiarly their own belongs precisely to their simplicity, to the absence of critical reflection. It was a gross error of the learned to imagine, as they too often did, that the myths had been methodically composed by judicious priests, wise men, or primitive philosophers, who sought to teach the multitude that which otherwise they could not have understood. The unknown authors of the myths were the first believers in them. They were more poetic than the rest; that is all the difference.

When once the general idea of myth had been grasped by science, people became infatuated by it. Soon nothing but myths were seen from one end of history to the other. It sufficed that a narrative presented mythical elements or parts in order to find in it only a myth from the beginning to the end. Thus, though Strauss never committed this extravagance, the forlorn-hope of the Hegelian Left went so far as to deny any kind of reality to the evangelical history, and contended that the very person of Jesus Christ was simply the fruit of mythological imagination. This kind of exaggeration was very suitably met by the witty pamphlet which undertook to demonstrate that the application of the mythic theory to the history of the First Empire resulted in proving that Napoleon I. never existed. In fact, it said, all this history is only a solar myth. The conqueror comes from an island—that is to say, from the sea—disappears in another island in the far West. His mother is named Lætitia, a symbolic name which may designate the dawn. He had twelve marshals, who are the twelve signs of the Zodiac. Setting out very low, he rapidly rose to his zenith. In his character of solar hero, he fought great battles, accomplished wonders, gained the most splendid victories; but, finally, he came to an unfortunate end. In one word, this pamphlet is the caricature of an exaggeration; but it warns us that it is well to determine the signs by which the mythic character of a narrative may be recognized.

There are some myths which immediately declare themselves as such. When a narrative, formed in a time in which there were no historical documents, is composed of things evidently impossible, absurd, and contrary to all experience—when, nevertheless, it has for ages been a part of a whole body of beliefs, and it is possible to interpret it by connecting it with some phenomenon of visible or moral observation—we cannot hesitate as to its nature.

In the second place, a narrative apparently mythic must be received as something other than a myth, when we possess documents or monuments contemporaneous, or nearly so, which attest its historical reality. This does not indicate that all that it contains is historical; but it is the business of criticism to distinguish that which bears the impress of reality from that which does not bear it.

In the third place, myths form a very numerous family, spread over the entire globe, but presenting everywhere many analogies. When, for example, in Greece, in Italy, in Gaul, in Germany, in India, in Mesopotamia, in America, in Polynesia, &c., we find at least one traditional narrative which makes the moon the sister, or the betrothed, or the jealous lover, or the victim, or the rival, of the sun, it would certainly be lost labour to seek the prince and princess whose history could give birth to this way of looking at the two stars. There is a sort of mythic language which is very quickly learned, and the modifications of which we can follow through space just as the philologer follows with his eye the transformations of a root reproduced in a whole group of languages.

The most difficult cases are evidently those of narratives of mythic appearance, which come to us even in the midst of historical epochs and of communities in which the mythological genius was, we might say, extinct. The best method to follow in such a case is to assure ourselves of the reality of facts antecedent and consequent to that the character of which is doubtful; then to see whether, the latter being admitted, we can pass logically, by a natural transition, from these antecedents to these consequents. It is the internal logic of history which serves in such cases as a touchstone. For example, the moral and religious state of the Jewish people in the times which immediately precede the evangelic history is well known. The formation of the Christian Church in the years which follow it—a formation proceeding from the simultaneous, sometimes mutually hostile, labours of the direct apostles of Jesus on the one hand, and of the apostle Paul on the other—is also an incontestable and documentary fact. Now it is easy to show that, in order to go from one to the other, it is necessary to pass through a series of intermediate points which confirm, not the details (these are a separate study), but the main outlines, the essential features, of the history of Jesus. This history may thus contain mythic parts, but as a whole it is real.

We might offer the counter-proof by asking ourselves what degree of reality ought to be attributed to the narrative of the Acts, according to which the first disciples were unexpectedly invested on the day of Pentecost with the faculty of speaking all the languages of the world without having learned them. Nothing which precedes and nothing which follows the event related is of a nature to confirm its historical reality.

The *myth* and the *legend* are often confounded, and, in fact, they touch each other very nearly. The primary sense of the word *legend* is, "that which may be read." It was thus that in the middle ages they preferred to designate the lives of the saints, several compilations of which existed. The most celebrated is the *Golden Legend* of Jacques de Voragine. Then, and not without cause, the legend came to mean a history, traditional, popular, marvellous, but more or less imaginary, and having no serious title to the acceptance of enlightened men. In this sense we may say that the legend contains the myth. The latter is in its nature legendary. But the legend properly so called seeks, above all, to interest, to astonish; it is not necessarily dictated, like the myth, by the unconscious desire of interpreting a natural phenomenon, or of giving expression to a moral truth. There are mythic legends containing mythic elements which they have picked up by the way. Thus the legend of the house of Lusignan has been incorporated with the poetic myth of the fairy Melusina, a lunar myth which dates from high antiquity.

There are, in like manner, "mythic histories"—that is to say, histories relating a veritable fact, but joining to it mythic elements or even entire myths. Thus the history of the emancipation of primitive Switzerland is enriched with the incident of William Tell, the skilful archer, who is no other than a solar hero. It is surprising to find this romance in Scandinavian countries, whence in all probability it came to Helvetia, brought by an immigration from the North.

Let us remark, finally, that the faculty of mythic production is sure to decrease in proportion as reflection and a spirit of generalization are strengthened. Modern races are as barren as can possibly be imagined in mythology. As, however, the difference is enormous between the intellectual processes of the instructed few and those of the ignorant masses, we can establish the existence, even in epochs relatively modern, of the outlines of myth, if not of entire myths. The Wandering Jew and Pope Joan may serve as examples—one personifying the lamentable destiny of the Jewish people, the other giving satirical expression to the sense of scandal aroused by the learned corruption of the Pontifical court. It is not only Germany who believes in her emperor Barbarossa, asleep with his knights in a cavern, whence he shall one day come to restore his empire. In our own campaigns, the immortality and the certain return of the first Napoleon were for a long time believed in. In 1848, it was not impossible to find peasants who still had faith in them.

II.

THE SYMBOL AND THE RITE.

WHAT we have said as to the myth shows that it owes its appearance to that faculty which distinguishes the human mind, and which we designate as the *analogical intuition*.

Analogy is the relation which allows the association of two things distinct, irreducible the one into the other, resembling each other very remotely, often even not resembling each other at all, and which nevertheless produce upon us impressions so similar that the sight or the idea of the one immediately arouses a thought of the other. *Analogical intuition* is the faculty of perceiving this kind of relation. Animals do not appear to possess it. They may be sensible of resemblances; and many implements of the chase—not to speak of the artifices of the savage, who so well imitates the gait and appearance of certain animals that he glides into the midst of them without their perceiving him—are founded on this possibility. But the analogy escapes them. Never, for example, does a stream suggest to them the idea of a serpent, nor a ray of sunshine that of an arrow.[1]

Man, on the contrary, never ceases to discern analogies between the most dissimilar things. His language is full of them; and all those expressions which rhetoricians have classed under the name of *tropes* or *figures of speech* rest solely on analogical intuition. A "heart of stone," a "honeyed tongue," the "collision of interests," the "torrent of passions," &c., are some examples taken by chance which could be indefinitely multiplied.

---

[1] If the dog bays at the moon, is it not simply because he takes it for a person, from its likeness to a human head, and that he deems it a great impertinence on the part of the moon thus to wander through the dwellings and the grounds of which he has charge? This is an illusion of resemblance, and not of analogy.

It must even be admitted that this facility of perceiving analogies may go too far. There are some which have struck the human mind only at certain periods and in certain countries, and which are very difficult to comprehend. When, for example, the poet of Canticles likens, with a view to compliment her, the nose of the Shulamite woman to a tower which overlooks the way to Damascus, it is difficult for us to see the relationship which may exist between the two terms of the comparison.[1]

It is analogy, we have seen, which has furnished the mythic elements, the grouping and association of which under a dramatized form have made complete myths. It is analogy also which gives rise to the *symbol*, undeniably akin to the myth, always distinct and capable even of surviving it. For there are purified religions whence the myth has disappeared; while there are none, and we can scarcely conceive of any, which could dispense with the symbol.

A symbol is an act or a thing which represents by analogy either an object of faith or the various shades of religious sentiment.

Thus the act of kneeling to pray, or of striking the breast when confessing sin, or of crowning oneself with flowers in order to present to the deities sacrifices of thank-offerings—these all are symbols corresponding to certain religious dispositions or expressing them. In like manner, a serpent gnawing its tail, the image of the infinite, which has neither beginning nor end; a statue of Ganesa with an elephant's trunk, the elephant being the wisest of animals, as Ganesa is the wisest of deities; the fetich of the Negro, which he paints white on the day when he commemorates the deceased, because, in the belief of the Negro, white is the colour of departed spirits,—are all so many symbols expressing beliefs or representing their object.

---

[1] We may observe here that the language of gallantry is an old offender, and that the woman whose attractions accurately reproduced the descriptions given of them in its refined style (the figure of a wasp, a brow like ivory, a neck like a swan, &c.) would be a perfect monster. In Greece, if we may believe certain epithets, it was a point of beauty to have eyes like an ox, and the young Arabs gallantly compare their mistresses to a "camel."

What is the psychological origin of the religious symbol? It is connected with the need which man experiences of materializing and of expressing his impressions, his sentiments and his convictions. We have already seen that it is to this tendency, joined to the physical conformation of man and to his social aptitudes, that the faculty of language is due. In fact, language is a sign, and forms part of the same family as gesture, expression of feature, screaming, crying, laughing, the posture of the body, &c. Man, by nature, is expansive. If prudence does not forbid him —often, indeed, when it does—he finds pleasure in giving to his feelings a corresponding external form, or that which seems to him such. It is to that end that he sings, that he dances, that he draws, and that he adorns himself; and the more nearly he approaches the state of nature, the more imperious is this need. It is also intensified by social life. Man delights in showing himself before others and among others. He loves to propagate in their souls the sentiments by which he is moved, and to feel in himself the sympathetic propagation of sentiments which animate them. The enthusiasm of crowds when they are under the influence of a common emotion; the contagious effect of feeling entertained by a group hitherto under much restraint; the lively pleasure which we experience at the sight of a spectacle of which a great number of our kind are witnesses with us— these are so many consequences and confirmations of this law of our nature.

Therefore, given the religious sentiment, with its diverse shades, with its intense vividness, it was certain to engender signs of manifestation, either individual or collective. It must seek to find vent in, and to strengthen itself by, sympathy. This it is which has produced symbols.

The word symbol has its history.[1] In ancient Greece, the words and agreed signs by which those initiated into the mys-

---

[1] From the Greek σύμβολον, from σύν, with, and βάλλειν, to throw, to throw together, and, by extension of meaning, that which is admitted by a group or an association, and that which represents their unity.

teries recognized each other were thus called. Later, the same word served to designate the dogmatic formularies recognized by the adherents of the same religious society (Apostolic symbol, Nicæan symbol, Lutheran and Reformed symbols). In actual language, it designates any act or any object in which we agree to recognize a religious or moral signification.

Religion must naturally give scope for a great number of symbols. We know that it is essentially synthetic. It seeks to reconcile the human mind with the *non-ego* which is opposed to it, by means of its union with the higher Mind which it discerns in things; and man loves to cherish the consciousness of this union. Thence, that which gives it substance, a sort of visible and tangible reality, that which helps man to realize its certainty, ought equally to give him pleasure. By symbol, man gains the assurance that he is in harmony with the Being whom he worships. In a foreign land, do we not dearly love to see the flag of our own country waving? Nevertheless, this strip of cloth adds nothing to the liveliness of our patriotism. No matter. These colours of the absent country, by means of all with which they are associated in our hearts, bring her before our eyes, and awaken the feeling of our union with her. The simple shaking of hands is a symbol of mutual goodwill, frequently a deceptive symbol, as all symbols may be. But that is neither its fault nor theirs. In its original intention the symbol is always sincere.

There will thus be in religion symbols of submission, such as the act of bowing, of uncovering the head, of kneeling, of prostration, &c., all attitudes expressing with more or less energy the dependence which the being worshipping recognizes as defining his relation with the Being worshipped. Before him, he becomes small, humble, grovelling in the dust.

There will also be symbols of religious grief, such as would cause him to clothe himself in mourning garments, or to cover himself with sordid vestments, or to put ashes on his head, in accordance with the experience that the man who is a prey to violent grief neglects himself, and pays no attention to the manner in which he is clothed. It is this which secures to fasting also a great place in religious symbolism; at least, among the associations of ideas which have led to the adoption of this widely-diffused symbol, one of the most frequent, perhaps the most general, has been the desire to express sorrow. A man absorbed by grief disdains nourishment.

There are, on the contrary, symbols of religious joy. Thus in many religions we see the worshippers deck themselves with leaves or flowers, wreathe the sacred places, and abandon themselves to joyous dances. There were many of these symbols in the great mythological fêtes celebrating the return of the sun above the horizon, or that of spring. In those times especially in which morality and religion were yet quite distinct things, these outbursts of sympathetic communion with resuscitated nature extended even to orgies, revels, and the letting loose of the grossest appetites.

We ought to mention also the symbols of purity or of purification. The water of baptism, which was administered in early times by immersion, and not as now, except among the Baptists, by simple aspersion, represented the complete purification of the neophyte. In the same category, again, we may mention the light of lamps or of wax tapers, fire in general, white vestments and white flowers, such as the lily, the orange-flower, and yet again the sheep, with its white fleece newly washed, &c.

Let us further notice the symbolism which seeks to express the sentiment of mystery, of the unknown, of the incomprehensible. In ancient initiations this was very prominent. In certain religions, the worshipper approached the divinity only with his head enveloped in linen many times folded, in order to express that he knew himself to be incapable of fathoming the unfathomable, and that he abandoned all pretence of submitting to human reason the august and terrible power whose protection he solicited. We find a feeble echo of this order of ideas in the preference which is accorded in the present day to religious edifices in which a mysterious obscure light reigns, and in which the coloured glass windows at once diminish and idealize the light of day.

There are a large number of animal and vegetable symbols which occupy a great place in mythological religions. The trees which remain green throughout the year, which thus triumph over the causes of destruction and of death to which the others succumb—the ivy, the myrtle, the box, the mistletoe, the laurel, &c.—seemed to reveal a divine power, or to be specially favoured by the gods. Thence the idea of revering them at first as divine beings, then simply as symbols and attributes of those who were regarded as the source or the patrons of the natural life—Dyonisius, Helios, Aphrodite, &c. The Israelite, rebellious against monotheism, preferred to sacrifice "under the green trees." By a close analogy, the pomegranate was consecrated to Hera, or Juno, as a symbol of fecundity, and the crown of oak-leaves to Mars as a symbol of vigour. We know the part which the mistletoe played in the religion of our ancestors. As the depositary of vital or divine force, it was in their eyes a sort of panacea, a remedy for all evils. We know also that there were animals placed in relation to certain divinities. There is even ground for supposing that before representing the gods under human form, the ancients had attributed to them animal forms. Thus the fish-gods of Syria and of Babylon are the gods of fecundity and of multiplication. If the owl is the bird of Athene, it is because, with its round, glaucous, glistening eyes, enabling it to see clearly in the dark, this bird is associated with the idea of penetrating light like that of the dawn, or that which shines again after a storm. If Hera, or Juno, the spouse of Heaven, has for her symbol the peacock, with its starry tail, it is because an analogy was seen between this appendage of the beautiful blue bird and the sky which at night, hiding its body of blue, displays its constellated orbs in infinity.

But of all symbols, the most interesting are those which we shall call *symbols of imitation*, by which the worshipper seeks to imitate the divinity in order the better to unite himself to it, by living, so to speak, as the divinity himself lives. This is the beginning of a very special and very important chapter of religious history. We see already appearing in the distance those identifications with the divinity of which the communions, differing in name as well as in meaning, Mexican, Buddhist, Christian, are the various forms. Here the symbol begins to lose its character of a representative sign, in order to become the means of the realization of the union desired and enjoyed by the religious sentiment.

For example, in certain mythologies it has been observed that all the stars move, turning round the earth and following their regular courses. Nothing more is wanted for these movements of the stars to be likened to a rhythmic and complicated dance. The consequence will be a religious dance in honour of "the army of the heavens." The dance will develop in a manner apparently entangled, but nevertheless methodical. There were several sacred dances having this character of imitation of the movements of the stars; among others, that of the Labyrinth, which was danced in Crete and at Delos. The labyrinth itself, with its thousand circuits, was a symbol of the starry heaven, and the dance of the same name must have been a sort of animated representation of it. Elsewhere the sun is likened to a burning wheel, which revolves and travels from one end to the other of the heavens and of the year. It is while revolving thus that he diffuses over the earth life and fertility. Well, in many places they have tried to imitate the sun. A common wheel, wrapped in straw, has been set on fire and made to roll all burning across the country in order to increase its fruitfulness. It is not very long since this custom was still practised in the plains of Poitou, and a yet shorter time since, each year in the spring, the vine-dressers on the banks of the Mosel made a wheel of this kind to roll from the top to the bottom of their vineyards in the direction of the river. If it reached the water, and the flame was there extinguished, that was the presage of an abundant vintage, as if the sun had promised to shine that year throughout the course of the fine season.

In other places we find in full paganism an obscure and rude tendency to monotheism. It is maintained that the divinity is not in reality either masculine or feminine, that it is of both sexes or of neither. Thence arise monstrous symbols, mutilations, or indescribable impurities.

We might prolong this list of symbols of imitation indefinitely. If in the creed we find something which resembles a divine drama, we may expect that the worship will reproduce some indications of this drama which may even pass for its repetition. On the anniversary of the death of Adonis, loved by Venus, who was no other than the beautiful young sun of Spring put to death by the fierce wild boar of Winter, the women, in their grief, tore their hair before the emblem of the young god prematurely taken away; they imitated Venus, and were ready to frolic in the following spring, roving through the country like mad creatures, when they had the certainty that he had come to life again. In an order of ideas infinitely more elevated and purer, we find an analogous phenomenon in the *stigmatists*, like Francis d'Assisi, who bore on their bodies the bleeding marks of the crucifixion. In the last century, in those communities in which Jansenism was dying out after a paroxysm of exaltation, one of the most highly appreciated devotions was to have oneself crucified like Christ.

The symbol, then, may lose its nature of emblem or of simple analogy, and pretend to all the reality of that which at first it only signified. It is this which engenders *idolatry*, which must not be confounded, as it so often is, with polytheism, from which it is very distinct. Idolatry consists essentially in the adoration of the image as if it was the divine person itself. It is clear that in the beginning every divine image of recent fabrication was understood only as a symbol. It was little by little, on the strength of rendering it divine honours, that the ignorant people identified it with the real object of their worship. When we think of the innumerable relics of which so many religions claim to be in possession, it is inadmissible that bad faith, speculation, silly credulity, could have succeeded in so many places in propagating the absurd. We, at least, incline strongly to the belief that many of these relics have been figurative representations or symbols, and that, by the aid of ignorance, they have passed later for realities.

Symbolism is, then, quite a language, as rich as it is varied, of which we must learn in some sort the vocabulary and the grammar if we would understand religions. Christianity has quite as many symbols, especially under its Latin and Oriental forms, as any other religion. If we had to analyze the Mass, we should see that, with the exception of the sacrifice which occupies the centre, everything in this ceremony is a succession of symbols, from the vestment of the priest to the waving of the censer by the children of the choir.

It is the symbol which has produced the form of worship, because it is that which has made the *rite.*

A rite is an assemblage of symbols grouped round a religious idea or a religious act, intended to enhance its solemn character or to develop its meaning. Just as a myth is the grouping of mythic elements associated under a dramatic form, in like manner a rite is the grouping of several symbols converging towards one central idea. Thus we have the rite of baptism, funereal rites, sacrificial rites. Ritualism is that tendency which consists in attaching a very high value to the accomplishment of symbolic ceremonies; while the opposite tendency, Puritanism, or Spiritualism, seeks to re-act against this importance easily becoming superstitious attributed to material symbols. Both tendencies are equally natural. This explains why two men, both sincerely religious, may entertain the most opposite opinions in regard to the value of a form of worship. The pious Catholic will find his edification, his religious nourishment, in the opulent symbolism of his Church; while the Calvinist turns away from it with a sense of painful repulsion, as if it were a profanation.

Let us take, from the manner in which sacrifices were celebrated in ancient Rome, an example serving to show us how a collection of symbols may form a rite. We leave on one side the idea of sacrifice itself, which was not at all symbolical. But all the externals with which it was surrounded were only symbols. Thus the sacrificer was to be clothed in white—symbol of purity. He was to be crowned with the leaves of a tree consecrated to the divinity to whom the victim was to be offered—symbol of union with it. If the sacrifice was offered to obtain some divine favour, the priest must go with his hair dishevelled, his girdle untied, his feet naked, because he ought to present himself as a suppliant. The animals offered must be of fine quality, healthy and freshly washed—symbol of deference and of decorum. They were ordinarily chosen from among those which the divinity preferred, or which were consecrated to him, so that at least, in order to enter by another way into his favour, these animals may not be of those which he would immolate in his anger. A herald commanded silence—a mark of deference and of respect. The profane—that is to say, those who were not in the ritual condition required in order to be present at the ceremony without invalidating its efficacy—were ordered to withdraw. The priest threw over the victim a salt dough; for salt is a symbol of union, it prevents dissolution, and the dough is the bread which is eaten with the flesh. It was necessary also to offer drink, and a cup of wine was brought; of this the officiating priest drank and made his assistants drink; the rest he poured on the head of the victim. That done, the fire was lighted —symbol of purification. The victim was placed in front of the altar, and the *cultrarius*, servant of the priest, killed it with one blow of the axe. It was desirable that the victim should not make any resistance when he was led up, otherwise his repugnance to approach the altar might have the appearance of revolt against the divinity; and for the same reason it was wished that he should die without uttering any cry. His throat was immediately cut; his blood was received in cups, which were poured out on the altar; for the blood was the life properly so called. Then they stretched the victim on the sacred table; they skinned it, they cut it up; and that done, they either burned the whole, in the idea that, ascending to heaven with the smoke, it was transformed into celestial food, or they burned a part only, sharing the rest between the sacrificer and his assistants. It was thus a repast which they imagined themselves to be sharing with the divinity. Finally came ablutions, liturgical formulæ, and dismission in due form.

We omit many other details. On this general canvas, many other special symbolical ceremonies might be sketched, according to the nature of the sacrifice or that of the god to whom it was offered. We have said enough to show how a great number of simple symbols have formed a whole, an organic whole—in one word, a rite. If religious symbolism is a language, if simple symbols correspond to the vocabulary and the grammar, we may say that the rite is its syntax.

But we have seen how the symbol at length loses its purely analogical character to become a positive reality, a means of realizing the unity between man and the divinity. On the other hand, there are objects and acts at first invested with an intrinsic and concrete value, later preserved only as symbols. We now proceed to study the origins and the meaning of that which has too often been considered as a pure symbol,—of that which, on the contrary, in the greater number of religions constitutes the practical centre of the form of worship, and the means pre-eminently of that union to which all religion aspires.

III.

THE SACRIFICE.

ALL religions consider sacrifice, more or less transformed, as pre-eminently the means of realizing the union of man with the divinity. The only exceptions to this are the philosophical and rationalistic religions, which place it in the same category as the symbol; but they count for very little in religious history. In all polytheistic religions, the universality of sacrifice is as unquestionable as its preponderance. In monotheistic religions it is transformed, but it remains. Islamism, which perhaps of all the monotheistic religions accords it the smallest place, has yet its sacrifices in connection with the pilgrimage to Mecca and the yearly feast of Bairam. Among the Israelites, we know with what luxuriance of details the law determined the number, the kind, the dates and the celebration of sacrifices. If, after the destruction of the temple at Jerusalem, the Israelites no longer sacrificed, it was because the same law strictly interdicted any celebration of sacrifice elsewhere than in the temple; but, in theory, sacrifice always formed a part of the Jewish religion, and in fact the Jewish Easter, the immolation of the Paschal lamb, is a family sacrifice. Among Christians, the belief is general in the sacrifice of Calvary, with which is connected the redemption of the human race. Catholics think that they repeat it in each Mass; and Protestants, who reject the idea of sacrifice in the Mass, insist with redoubled zeal on the sacrificial Redemption which forms in some sort the *nucleus* of the Protestant orthodox theory.

Under all its forms, sacrifice is the offering to the divinity of that which is considered likely to dispose him favourably towards the offerer, or towards those to whom the offerer desires that good should be done.

If we refer to our definition of religion, we may remember that the human mind is religious through the feeling of a bond which unites it to the divine spirit, and of which it loves to feel the consciousness.

But man is not always sensible nor certain of this union, and he likes to think that he may draw it closer. He may find that it is weak—he seeks to fortify it; that it is destroyed—he desires to re-establish it. Already adoration, homage and prayer, meet these various desires. But, in primitive times especially, man, judging his divinities by himself, considered that words alone did not merit a good gift from them. Thence, and very naturally, he determined to make them presents.

What shall he give to his divinities? That which he likes the best himself. And as in primitive life, as with the savage of the present day, the great pre-occupation, the fixed idea, is to have something to eat—and next, good things to eat—the offerings which man makes to his god are always fine fruit, cakes, honey, wine, milk, butter, oil; finally and specially, the flesh of animals. It is thus that Genesis affords us a glimpse of the first offerings. This is the point of departure of sacrifices; and naturally, in virtue of the same ideas, man will add to his alimentary gifts offerings belonging to the domain of the other senses, such as ornaments, flowers and perfumes. The Red Indian, before setting out for the chase or for war, lights his pipe, and blows his first whiffs towards heaven, because, being a great lover of tobacco, he believes that he is making himself agreeable to the great Spirit by allowing him to inhale its vapours. For the same reason elsewhere odorous resins, incense, myrrh, are burned. But these offerings of perfumes are merely accessories beside the offering of food, which is the principal. Euripides and Plato had already remarked that the way to insinuate oneself into divine favour was the same method which succeeded so well with the great ones of the earth, Δῶρα Θεοὺς πείθει, δῶρα αἰδοίους βασιλῆας.[1] We find the same idea in the verses of Ovid on the similarity of the mode of gaining favours in heaven and on earth:

> Numera, crede mihi, capiunt hominesque deosque
> Placatur donis Jupiter ipse datis.[2]

But these satirical remarks belong, in Greece as in Rome, to an age of reflection and of rationalism. It would be a misconception to attribute them to the primitive age, in the depths of which the institution of sacrifice has its roots. In the beginning, sincerity walked hand in hand with simplicity.

It is important to distinguish two elements of a moral kind, fundamentally distinct, which are associated in this old custom. The first is the perfect egotism of calculation. Man gives to his god only in order that he may receive, and reckons upon receiving much more than he has given. That would go far towards the material development of sacrifice. The other sentiment which manifests itself, and which also would lead towards the ideas which were later entertained in regard to sacrifice, is that man definitively despoils himself, deprives himself, and imposes a sacrifice upon himself—in one word, renounces that which pleases him—even if it does not at once result in pleasing his god.

This is in no way contrary to that view which makes him also immolate to his adored divinities that which he regards as the object of their hatred. If, for example, he sacrifices horses to Poseidon or Neptune, the god of the sea, because the waves resemble horses galloping one after the other, he will put to death before the altar of the sun-god the animals which the latter seems to hate because he cannot endure the sight of them, which he seems to pursue, because they flee from the light, such as the wolf, seen chiefly at night and in winter; rats and mice, the

---

[1] Plato, *De Rep.* iii. 399; comp. Euripides, *Medea*, v. 934.
[2] *Ars Am.* iii. 653.

friends of darkness; or the devastating wild boar, in honour of goddesses personifying the fertilizing sun. It is always some immolation which is supposed to be acceptable to the deities, or some repast worthy of being offered to them. For it is supposed that they have no objection to feed on the flesh of beings abhorred by them when living. The altar itself is in reality a table, the table of the divine banquet.[1]

On this simple base arose numerous diversities of application. The sacrifice may be simple and frequent, a comb of honey, a bowl of milk, a libation, that is, some drops of the liquid which one is about to drink, and of which one gives a part to the gods; or on certain solemn occasions it may attain to frightful proportions, as in the *hecatomb*, in which the blood of a hundred oxen flowed. There are besides motives of various kinds which determine the sacrifice. If the object be to render the divinity favourable to some enterprize, a sacrifice of *propitiation* is offered. If it be desired to express gratitude, there is the sacrifice of *thanksgiving*. Further, as it is known that there are terrible gods, destroyers, jealous of the life and of the happiness of men, there is the sacrifice of *appeasement*. It is here that cruelty and simplicity closely touch; and it is to these religious terrors that we must specially attribute the prolonged maintenance of human sacrifices which as we ascend to remote antiquity we find everywhere, and which were long considered the most efficacious safeguard of peoples and of families. They played in some sort the part of fire.

Here arises a question which has been very often discussed in the present day. Anthropophagy seems to have been, if not universal, at least endemic in the beginning of all races. This odious custom is preserved, as we know, among the most backward races, those most nearly approaching animalism. Among many of them it is always associated with religious rites and occurs only exceptionally, without relation to the ordinary cus-

---

[1] It is in connection with this idea of a repast offered to the divinity and shared with him that sacrifice became the sanction of treaties of alliance between individuals, families and peoples, or, as with the Hebrews, of the national alliance with Jahveh. The divinity was thus at once witness and contracting party.

toms. Thereupon it has been said that anthropophagy never was anything but a religious rite. But the question is only transferred. How came man to imagine that the flesh of his kind could be agreeable to the divinity? That could happen only because he himself considered it as a great luxury. To resolve such questions, we must strip ourselves of all our hereditary antipathies. Experience shows that man, assured of sufficient food, is horrified at the idea of feeding on human flesh. But it shows us also—the history of shipwrecks, of famines, and of prolonged sieges is evidence of this—that, goaded on by furious hunger, man, even when civilized, can reconcile himself to this terrible extremity. Now under the conditions of primitive life, as still in the present day among savages, periods of famine were frequent. Necessity must often have compelled beings who had not our profound repugnance; and competent observers have learned, by interrogating anthropophagists in various places, that to one who is unprejudiced, human flesh is of all the most savoury.[1]

If, then, we affirm the close relation which unites cannibalism to religious sacrifices and rites, we do not err; but the immolation of human victims would never have been invented if it had not been believed that they were meat worthy of being offered to the gods.[2] The religious custom supposes the physical custom, and it is natural that it should be preserved as a religious custom long after it had disappeared from manners and tastes. It is the property of religious customs, which have become traditional, to perpetuate themselves even when they no longer answer to contemporaneous ideas.

---

[1] We have been privately informed by a captain in the Dutch navy, that having had occasion to converse with some aged natives of certain islands of Malaysia, in which cannibalism was not abolished until within a date relatively recent, he had received from them the declaration that they remembered with delight the repasts of human flesh which they had eaten in their youth.

[2] It is in virtue of another set of ideas, in no way contradictory to the first, that the custom was established of immolating domestic animals, slaves and women, in order that they might join their defunct master or husband, and continue to serve him in another existence.

Here, again, even in this monstrous aberration, we may discern the double element of sacrifice, a revolting egotism and a renunciation which the offerer imposes on himself. Such at least is always the case when a human sacrifice, full of sadness for those who accomplish it, is in question. They may say to themselves that the more the sacrifice costs the offerer, the more certain is its efficacy. It is this sentiment which underlies the phrase which is attributed to Louis XIV., overwhelmed by reverses, "After all that I have done for God!" It is thus that, notably among the Semites, they have come to place above all others the sacrifice which parents make of their own children, and especially of the first-born. Mosaicism had great difficulty in extirpating this horrible custom among the Israelites. We know that at Carthage and in the Phœnician towns, in time of calamity, they took the children of the chief families in order to sacrifice them to the national gods. Evidently, if the prejudice had not been stronger than all objections, rich and powerful families, wielding authority in ordinary times, would not themselves have enacted such laws. We must put in connection with this set of ideas the tragic episode of the war which the combined kings of Israel, of Judah and of Edom, made against Mesa, king of Moab.[1] It is this Mesa of whom the Museum of the Louvre possesses an extremely curious stela. When this Moabite king, driven back into his capital, saw his affairs in a desperate state, he took his eldest son and sacrificed him on the ramparts in sight of the enemy. "Then," we are told, "there arose great terror among the children of Israel, who withdrew into their own country;"[2] that is to say, they considered the divinity as conjured by such a terrible sacrifice, and forced, as it were, to declare himself for the king Mesa.

Among all the nations who advanced in civilization, human sacrifice ended by becoming the object of reprobation. In more than one religion, compensations, a kind of succedanea, were found for it. Circumcision is one of these. Among our Gallic

---

[1] 2 Kings iii. 26, 27.   [2] According to the true rendering of this passage.

ancestors, who preserved human sacrifice until the Roman conquest, it had been already modified so far that they sacrificed criminals, and added innocent people to them only when their number was insufficient. Later, instead of complete immolation, they confined themselves to making an incision sufficient for blood to flow. This was substituting the symbol for the reality. Among the Greeks, myths such as those of Atreus and of Thyestis, of Lycaon and of Iphigenia, suppose at once human sacrifices and the repulsion which caused them at length to be abolished. We may connect with the same transmutation the bloody flagellation of the young Spartans before the altar of Artemis. In the biblical tradition, the narrative of the sacrifice of Abraham derives all its interest from the substitution which it legitimatizes of an animal for a human sacrifice.[1] At Rome, the emperor Augustus was obliged to enact laws for entirely abolishing human sacrifice, and it was necessary to renew them under Trajan.

But already, long before, especially where religion had been penetrated by morality, sacrifice had received a new signification. In the beginning, man sought simply to satisfy the appetites of divinities supposed to be sensual, or to turn away the fury of gods given to destruction. But when he represented to himself the divinity no longer as distributing only physical good or evil, but also as the guardian and the avenger of the moral law, the divine anger, the reflex of the remorse which smote the conscience, could be appeased only by a special sacrifice, the sacrifice called *expiatory*, the idea of which survived the disappearance of all the others and bequeathed a dogma to Christianity.

There was already an idea of substitution in the sacrifices of appeasement of which we spoke previously. The divinity was

---

[1] Assuredly we have great difficulty in representing to ourselves the state of mind of parents able to believe themselves religiously bound to sacrifice their children. And yet is there any radical difference between that state of mind and that of parents in a time still less remote who, taking no account of the repugnance or of the despair of their children, condemned them to the slow suicide of the cloistral life under the pretext of thus expiating their own faults?

animated by murderous designs against a tribe, a city or a nation; then victims were substituted for the tribe, the city, or the nation menaced, and it was thought that the divinity, satisfied, would spare it. Analogous reasoning prevailed in the domain of the moral law. It was considered that it did not essentially concern divine justice that the punishment of faults committed should fall precisely on the guilty; what did concern it was that it should fall on some one, that it should have its accomplishment. That is the common foundation of expiatory sacrifices, of which the *lustral* sacrifice, or sacrifice of purification, is only one variety. Such ideas might be accepted in a time when the personal character of faults committed was still very ill understood, and when there was no objection seen to the idea of making innocent beings perish in order to spare the guilty from merited punishment.

It is true that certain experiences may give to this point of view a sort of superficial justification. The fact is that, in virtue of the solidarity which links together human destinies, the consequences of faults committed descend at each moment on others than their authors. Human imperfection has also very often this sad issue, that the best men, those who dominate others by their sanctity and their genius, are exposed to the attacks of prejudice, of narrowness, of superstition, of egotistic interests menaced by their generous enterprize. Plato has already made this melancholy remark in his wonderful passage on the just man misunderstood and persecuted. He no doubt thought of Socrates. The anonymous prophet who preached hope to the captive Jews on the banks of the Euphrates, and whose prophecies our canonical Bible joins with those of his predecessor Isaiah, consoled himself for the sufferings endured by the group of faithful Israelites, by seeing in it the condition of the redemption of the whole nation and its future restoration. In this sense these faithful ones were the expiatory victims of the sins of the people; their sufferings paid the ransom of all. Finally, it is easy to show that Jesus himself, when the prospect of persecution and of a violent death not far off presented itself to his mind, understood in like manner their necessity, and consequently their conformity to that mysterious order of things to which he religiously bowed.

This it is which will transform sacrifice by raising it into another sphere, more tragic, more ideal, than that in which ordinary sacrifices remained confined. Upon this was grafted the dogma of redemption, the history of which we shall take in its turn; for it has a history, and a very curious one, which often descends from the height on which it should have remained in order to assimilate itself to the ancient sacrifices, but which, taken according to its primary idea, easily comes into the philosophy of history.[1]

On such ground as this, we are very far from the vulgar sacrifices consisting of material offerings made to the gods in order to conciliate their goodwill, and it is difficult to explain their continued existence into epochs in which the intellectual level on which such a belief could arise had been left behind. In Greece and elsewhere there were protests against the traditional custom. In the Old Testament we are struck with the number of passages which formally dispute the necessity or the efficacy of sacrifices.[2] But for a long time these protests had no appreciable effect. Sacrifice remained as before the centre of public and private worship. Not only have religious traditions a very persistent life, even when the general belief no longer sustains them,[3] but

---

[1] It is to be regretted that the Christian Church has not adopted the view put forth by Origen, who saw in the sacrifice of Christ the divine type and, so to speak, the culminating point of all that devotion and unmerited persecution to which humanity owes its deliverance and its progress of all sorts.

[2] Comp. Isaiah i. 11—13, lxvi. 1—3; Jeremiah vi. 20 and following verses, vii. 21 and following verses; Hosea vi. 6; Amos v. 21, 22; Micah vi. 6—8; Psalms l. 8—14, li. 16, 17; Proverbs xxi. 3.

[3] We may, for example, assure ourselves of this, by seeing how funereal rites are long preserved among peoples who have become absolute strangers to the ideas which determined their first institution. In many places, notably among the Jews, stone continued to be the obligatory material for instruments dedicated to religious use long after the use of metals had become general. The spruce-fir, always green in December, and the box-tree of the octave before Easter, continue to play their parts in the midst of innumerable Christian families who do not suspect their absolutely pagan origin.

also, in default of any other expression as popular and as universally accepted, of sentiments of adoration, there was in favour of sacrifice the prejudice that it was the normal, regular form of religious worship. Enlightened men of the classical ages considered sacrifice as the *sacrum* properly so called, which they must respect and observe under pain of impiety. Thus, even in our day, scepticism and even rational incredulity do not prevent many of our contemporaries from celebrating traditional rites in the efficacy of which they do not believe.

It is especially in reference to sacrifices that we may maintain that law of transformation which, from a strange ignorance of history, it is contended is foreign to religion. What a change of ideas must have taken place for that which formed the centre of practical faith to have become so completely alien to our turn of mind that, if it was suggested to restore among us these rites so long sacred, we should have difficulty in repressing our laughter, or still more our repugnance! Can we imagine ourselves obliged to be present advisedly at the slaughter of a sheep or of a pair of pigeons, with the idea that the most august of religious acts was being accomplished before us? Sacrifice continues theoretically, as we have said, greatly honoured in Judaism; but it is only theoretically, because the Mosaic law which ordains and regulates it, always interdicts its celebration elsewhere than in the temple of Jerusalem. But if the Israelitish nation again recovered possession of the land of Canaan, and if they for a third time rebuilt the temple at Jerusalem, how hard it would be in the present day to restore the daily celebration of ancient sacrifices ordained by the law, and to impress them with a religious character! If we could see oxen and cows, rams and lambs, continually entering the sacred precinct in order to be put to death there, would it produce on us the effect of a temple or of a slaughter-house?

Note that the people who have taught us to suppress sacrifices under their ancient form in the religious life, are precisely the Jewish people. It is they who first instituted in their synagogues a popular worship, very graceful and without sacrifices. This innovation, one of the most remarkable and the least remarked in history, took place during the Babylonish captivity, at a time when the pious Jews, deprived of their temple, and consequently of the possibility of celebrating the legal sacrifices, must either abstain from all worship or invent a form which could dispense with them. It was thus that they invented the *synagogues*, where they could be edified by the Word, by instruction, singing and collective prayer, but where they did not sacrifice. Those who, profiting by the liberating edicts of the Persian kings, returned to the country of their fathers, no doubt rebuilt the temple and re-established sacrifices; but they brought back also the worship of the synagogues, which had become a necessity. These multiplied throughout the Jewish territory. The most humble village had its own. And when other events or the desire of gain dispersed numerous swarms of Jews throughout a great number of countries, the synagogues were opened at the same time as their counting-houses. The ancient world had never seen such a thing. The Christian Church is the daughter of the synagogue. The gospel could never have been conceived by the sacerdotal spirit which dominated the temple and which celebrated sacrifices. It was in the synagogues—and thanks to their more elastic and more liberal forms—that it was propagated. The first Christian churches are only dissenting synagogues. Their organization is founded on that of the Jewish communities. Indirectly, the mosque proceeds from the same source.

Sacrifice has thus become something quite different from what it was in the beginning. Mysterious and supernatural fact, the object of faith and no longer of sight, whether with Catholics or Protestants, accomplishing itself henceforward in a transcendent sphere, it has no longer anything but a historical descent and a moral bond in common with sacrifices such as were known in ancient times. But yet it occupies a central place in orthodox Christianity.

IV.

THE PRIESTHOOD.

Religious development has not only led man to seek guarantees and reparative means of union with the Divine Being in acts determined and calculated to secure his goodwill—it has also led to the constitution of the priesthood, or the selection of a certain number of men, invested with special religious functions, alone capable of fulfilling them, and without whose ministry the desired union is considered impossible. The word *sacerdote*, sometimes proposed in order to designate these functionaries under a general term, not having been adopted, we have only the word *priest* answering to the same idea.

This word, etymologically, is not happy. It comes from the Greek *presbuteros*, which has nothing sacerdotal about it, and means simply *ancient, aged*. In the Jewish synagogues, as in the first Christian churches, the *presbuteroi*, or elders, designated by their co-religionists to direct the spiritual and temporal interests of the community, presided over the assembly of the faithful, but they derived their powers only from the delegation which the community conferred upon them. They were not at all priests in the modern sense of the word. They were called also *episcopoi*, overseers, whence the French word *évêque*, and the English word *bishop*. Towards the middle of the second century of our era, the title of *episcopos*, or bishop, in the singular, became that of the president or sole chief of the *presbuteroi*. Hence the superiority of the bishop over the simple *presbuteros*, or priest. But the development of dogma and of Christian worship more and more introduced into the Christian Church a very characteristic sacerdotal element; the word *priest* signified thenceforward something else than *elder*, and included the possession of sacerdotal dignity. It is under this acceptation that the term has remained in our language. All priests are not bishops, but all bishops are priests. Sacerdotalism is thus the function, the priest is the functionary.

What is the definition of sacerdotalism?

It is the religious institution in virtue of which the union of the ordinary man, of the *laity*, with the Divinity can be effected only by the intermediate agency of other men invested with a special character, which places them in immediate relation with it and allows them to connect others with it. Sacerdotalism is essentially a mediation, a necessary mediation, and a mediation which cannot be effected except by those who are invested with it.[1] It is this double character of necessity and of monopoly which we must endeavour to understand before entering upon the history of sacerdotalism.

The greater number of historical religions have a priesthood—that is to say, the greater number set apart a class of men whose intervention is supposed to be necessary for the establishment of normal relations between man and the Divinity. But however general may be this institution, we cannot say that it has the same title to be considered primitive as, for example, sacrifice. It is to sacrifice especially that it owes its establishment, although other causes also have concurred in forming it. But wherever we can go back to the primitive conditions of societies, we see that the priesthood properly so called was as yet unknown. Each one, or preferably the father of the family or the chief of the tribe, sacrificed at first on his own account and for the benefit of those belonging to him. This can be shown in the case of the Greeks and of Semitic and Vedic antiquity. The history of the patriarchs and the book of Job furnish us with proofs of the

---

[1] For this reason it is an abuse of terms to apply the designation of *priests*, or necessary intermediaries between man and God, to *ministers* or simple officers of non-sacerdotal religions, such as Protestant ministers, Jewish rabbis, &c. In Judaism there was the Aaronite, the Levite, the sacrificer, who was priest or necessary intermediary. The rabbi can be only teacher, adviser, helper. It is the same with the Protestant minister.

same thing within the reach of all. We may see also that, as the petty clans or tribes of remote ages united to form peoples and nations, this function of sacrificer was attached to the chief or the king who personified the city or nation. The king-priests are a common feature of early antiquity. Nevertheless, very early also, and even in some places in the very dawn of history, we find priesthoods distinct from the political or military power, forming and succeeding in concentrating in their hands, along with religious authority, all the essential functions of worship.

How can we explain this phenomenon?

In the lower stages of religion, even in our own day among peoples strangers to civilization, we may remark the frequency of the tendency to consider certain individuals more highly endowed than others, of a more lively imagination and of a more subtle religious sense, as more nearly related to the Divinity, better qualified consequently to interpret his will, to predict his designs and to indicate what must be done in order to be in the desired relationship to him. It may even happen that what would be in our eyes a proof of physical and mental inferiority may pass with these men, still profoundly ignorant, for a sign of superiority and of divine vocation. Thus ecstacy arising from a nervous paroxysm, hallucination, certain kinds of madness, produce on men remaining at this level the effect of possession by a superior spirit. Even without descending so low, we may remark how the least superiority imposes on a community deprived of culture. He who, by chance or by tradition, knows the curative virtue of some simples, can speak in picturesque and flowing language, without being embarrassed in finding expressions—he who is familiar with charms, incantations, mysterious formulæ, &c.—immediately acquires great authority over his kind. It is thus that, not only among the Finns and Tartars, to whom this commencement of sacerdotalism has too long been exclusively attributed, but among all uncivilized nations, there exist sorcerers, conjurors, magicians and diviners; and we know too well that the race is by no means extinct in the lower depths of our own civilized society. But, at least among savages, charlatanism alone would not account for the frequency or the permanence of the phenomenon. It is more probable that the sorcerer himself was the first to believe in his own supernatural powers. Much more were ignorant populations disposed to resort to his ministry in order to approach the gods, to deprecate the effects of their ill-will, or to secure their favours.

This is, however, not yet sacerdotalism properly so called, with its exclusive pretensions and its character of necessary mediation. We might say that the singing sorcerer of primitive epochs and religions represents the type as yet confused, the amalgam as yet unformed, of what will be later the priest or the prophet, the poet or the scholar, the artist or the physician. Out of this will come the priest.

Men for the most part seek union with the Divinity, but they regard it rather as a thing which ought to be than as a thing that is. Either they feel too ignorant to know how they can realize it, or they feel morally unworthy to place themselves in immediate relation with the Divine Spirit. Those who appear to them bolder and more confident, especially if they justify this assurance by superior knowledge (pretended or real), seem to them to be the object of the marked preference of the gods. They find, then, the security which they need by leaning in some sort upon these favourites of the Divinity, who will shield their insufficiency and their unworthiness. It is in this sentiment of timidity, of apprehensive weakness, that in all time and everywhere the great power of sacerdotalism will reside.

More than that. We have just seen the leading place which sacrifice occupies in religious history, and how almost everywhere it is held to be pre-eminently the means of union or of re-union with the Divinity. We know how it became the centre of a very complicated ritual. The mode of sacrifice, the presages to be derived from the immolated victims, the hymns, the formulæ and the special prayers—all that was much too difficult for the ordinary sort of men. Nevertheless, it was believed that if things were not done punctually and regularly, the sacrifice would lose its efficacy. Hence the desire, the necessity, of having sacrificers knowing the ritual and neglecting nothing, so that all may be done in conformity to rules. In the ancient commentaries on the Vedas, we see clearly that the sacerdotalism of the Brahmans arose out of the necessity of having a professional class able to celebrate the sacrifices, which had been considerably amplified since the times of innocence in which Arya each morning threw butter on her hearth in order to regale the powerful Indra or the pure Agni. This prepossession in favour of ritual, joined to the idea that the present could be agreeable to the Divinity only if it were offered by the hands of those whom he specially favoured with his preference, ended in constituting the priesthood by establishing a class of men who alone were considered qualified to sacrifice, so much so that every sacrifice accomplished without them was held to be an invalid act, and soon, indeed, a sacrilege.

Naturally this class of men, owing to their distinguished functions, were greatly venerated. They received honours, privileges and exemptions. They lived a separate life; they had their own interests; and it is easy to conceive that in remote epochs—thanks to their superior position, to their leisure, to the praiseworthy ambition of their principle of justifying these advantages by a real superiority—this class consecrated itself more willingly than any other to what was already called science, to collecting the old traditions, digesting annals, determining dates, the divisions of the year, and that enormous source of influence, the popular calendar. Thus it was that in so many places the priesthood were the first depositaries of all the higher knowledge. We see this in India, in Egypt, in Chaldea, in Persia and in old Gaul. Something analogous was reproduced in our own middle ages. Finally, in those religions in which moral prepossessions were closely united to religious thought properly so called, the clergy were considered not only as the sole authority who knew how to enlighten and direct the conscience, but also, and above all, as the only one who could grant divine absolution. It is this last

THE PRIESTHOOD.

privilege especially which rendered them so powerful wherever they could exercise it, even in those periods in which they possessed no marked intellectual superiority.

To sum up: on the basis of a simple superiority, native, or acquired by certain men in the midst of their fellows who were still profoundly ignorant, these are the three elements of that which constitutes sacerdotalism: 1st, the sentiment of fear, of uncertainty, or of unworthiness, general among the mass; 2nd, the extreme importance attached to sacrifice and to the ritual conditions of its celebration; 3rd, the prestige vested in this class, who for a longer or shorter time concentrated and monopolized the higher knowledge, the want of which was felt, but which no one else possessed.

As a final analysis, that which produced sacerdotalism is the sentiment of the incapacity of ordinary man, who does not believe himself capable of being or of doing what is necessary to realize union with the Divinity.

See also why in all time and in every country, the autonomy of conscience, the progress of general knowledge, the growing sentiment of human dignity, have been followed by a diminution of sacerdotal authority and power.

Let us add, that according to the manner in which it has been constituted, the priesthood has developed its characteristic features in an extreme form, or has presented only an enfeebled image of them.

Thus we have *hereditary* priesthoods, privileges of race, of tribe, of family. The Hindu Brahmans, the Levites and the Aaronides, come into this category. Every Brahman is born a priest. No doubt, in order to exercise his sacerdotal functions, he must pass through schools and initiations; but the fundamental quality required is to be the son of a Brahman. The priesthood in such a case forms a caste. Ordinarily the origin of this kind of priesthood dates from some warlike struggle, invasion or civil war, terminated by the destruction of the vanquished, and procuring, either for a fraction or for the whole of the victors, a religious ascendancy of which the possession of the priesthood is the consequence. Time effaces the memory of this origin, and the religious prestige is henceforth enhanced and maintains its position in the popular belief. Among the Israelites it was a long time before the sacerdotal privilege was recognized. In the most ancient times—that is to say, after the establishment of the tribes of Israel in Canaan—there was a tribe of sacrificers named from Levi, and they probably owed this distinction to the preponderating part which they had acted by the side of Moses the liberator. But for a long time this priesthood had nothing exclusive. Whoever would might sacrifice. Samuel, Saul, David, who are not Levites, sacrifice when it pleases them. It is only later, and owing to the persistent efforts of the Jahvist party, that the Levites attain to a monopoly of sacrifice. Later still, the high-priesthood is confined to a part of this tribe, that which was supposed to descend directly from Aaron. The priesthood in Israel was thenceforward an essentially aristocratic institution, and remained to the end true to that character.

Elsewhere, on the contrary—among the Romans, for example—the priesthood was a magistrature of the city conferred by popular election. Such was at least the mode used in Rome to designate the pontiffs and the priests of highest rank. The hereditary feature, so marked in the two preceding examples, appears again in the fact that the priesthood at Rome was for a long time accessible only to patricians. It is easy to understand that in ancient times, and when the priesthood owed its prestige specially to its superior knowledge, consequently to transmitted traditions, heredity might pass for the natural condition of their scrupulous preservation; to which was joined the idea, then so easily accepted, of superiority of blood being proved by social superiority. It was only after a severe struggle that the plebeians ended by gaining on this point, as on so many others, equality with the patricians. In every case the fundamental idea of this system is, that the city chooses within itself those whom it believes the most worthy to represent it before the gods.

In other places, again, the priesthood is open to all; but in order to be invested with it, it is necessary to submit to a certain number of preliminary tests, to receive a special education, to bind oneself down to a regular life; and after all that, the predecessors of the new member confer upon him the powers of which they themselves are in possession. To the idea of heredity succeeds that of continuous transmission. As examples, we may cite in ancient times the Egyptian priests and the Gallic druids; and in modern times the priests which Christian churches have admitted to the priesthood.

Of all the countries of high civilization, Greece least felt the influence of the priesthood. She owed this, in the first instance, to the absence of political centralization; afterwards, to the variety in the forms of her priesthoods, which could never constitute a caste, or one of the great powers of the state. We find, in fact, in the priesthoods of ancient Greece the various types which we have just noticed. In the beginning, it is the heads of families or of tribes who are the sacrificers. Later, the dignity of priest and of king is united. The monarchies disappear, the royal priesthood disappears with them; but in many places the priesthood remained a privilege of the local aristocracy; and as a religious memorial of the ancient state of things, there were priests who joined to their name the honorary title of king, Βασιλεύς. At Athens, the archon-king had only the second rank among the archons, but he was charged with all that concerned religion. His wife even received on that account the title of queen, Βασίλισσα, and presided in that quality at certain ceremonies. Analogous facts are found in other Greek cities. But there were also priesthoods instituted for the worship of certain divinities, which remained a patrimony of certain families. Thus the descendants of king Codrus retained the high-priesthood of the sanctuary of Eleusis. The Eumolpides and the Boutades are also sacerdotal families.[1] For the rest, at Athens as at Rome, sacerdotal functions could devolve only on the *eupatrides* or

---

[1] Comp. *Religions de la Grèce Antique*, par M. Alfred Maury, Vol. II. ch. xii.

descendants of the old families. The plebeians did not succeed, as in Rome, in sharing this distinction with the patricians, but they got special priesthoods created on their own account. There were, finally, in the neighbourhood of several sanctuaries—notably at Olympus—sacerdotal schools in which novices were instructed in order to prepare them for the functions of sacrificer. They had to acquire an accurate knowledge of the preparation of the victims; the Athenians, indeed, satirically compared them with cooks. But other studies also were imposed on the future priests. All this demonstrates that in Greece there were priesthoods of all kinds, and explains to us why the Greek priesthood never attained to that unity of organization, of doctrine and of interests, which made priesthoods elsewhere such a formidable power.

It is especially through priesthoods that the history of religion and that of civilization touch. We need not discuss theologically the principle and the primary idea of the priesthood. Some regard the priest and his indispensable mediation as forming an integral part of all religion worthy of the name; others, on the contrary, think that the priesthood represents an inferior stage of religion, and that by right, as in fact, every man ought to be in direct immediate relations of union with God. From the strictly historical point of view, the relative legitimacy of the priesthood depends altogether on the need which there is of it, and it is thus that its action, sometimes beneficent, sometimes pernicious, is explained.

It is to the sacerdotal corporations, or to that which resembled them, that the first great discoveries which have rendered civilization possible—the first astronomical observations, writing, the first calculations and the first annals—are due. Their utility is especially manifest when we think of all the risks of loss and of oblivion which these elementary inventions ran in the midst of peoples as yet destitute of culture. How many things could be discovered and perpetuated only under the shadow of the sanctuary! We moderns know how much our civilization owes to the clergy of the first centuries of the middle ages. We might very well say that in epochs of extreme rudeness the very existence of men who continually represent a certain ideal of knowledge, of religion and of sentiments superior to the dense vulgarity of material life, is something. Art is not less indebted to them. Those old clergy loved it; they made use of it in their own interest; but not the less did they call forth those great works which posterity contemplates with admiration and despairs of imitating.

But we must not forget that all sacerdotalism rests on the feeling which the mass have of their own incapacity. And if this sentiment goes on diminishing, if the progress of knowledge and the evolutions of religious thought cause men to rise above their former level, then from the constitution of the priesthood—if it, essentially conservative, becomes stationary and ends by being overtaken and passed by—an inevitable conflict ensues. The priesthood, by its conservative instinct, by fidelity to the faith of which it is the guardian and which it sees menaced by the movement of mind, remains attached to another social ideal than that which is forming around it. It tries to suppress this, to stifle it at its birth, to limit its application. An ever-growing quarrel arises between it and the society of which it forms part; and as, although weakened, it has still at its disposal a formidable force, the strife between it and the new spirit becomes desperate and often degenerates into war to the death.

Sacerdotalism is an institution very tenacious and very resistant; but there are two things which have a more vigorous life than even it, although it contends that their existence depends upon its preservation, and those are human society and religion. Experience has already more than once proved that both the one and the other can very well dispense with it. It too often forgets that even in the religious order it has a competitor in prophetism, the origin and transformations of which we are about in turn to study. Sacerdotalism has its origin in the sentiment that it was necessary. It must, then, take care not to become useless. On the day when it so acts as to be hurtful, it will have signed its own death-warrant. Such is the lesson of history, and the only one which it belongs to us here to point out.

V.

PROPHETISM.

The title which we give to this Chapter is justified by the rule, *A potiori denominatio*. We rank under this name all which comes into the phenomena of individual inspiration; and among these phenomena, prophetism, in ancient times, is the most original and the most worthy of being studied. In addition to this, we shall see that it belongs also to contemporary facts. If it has lost its ancient name, it has spread itself out into several distinct branches which represent to the modern mind the same number of constituent features as formerly.

It is always necessary to agree as to the sense of the words *prophetism* and *prophecy*. In the common acceptation, a prophecy is a prediction; prophetism is the art or the gift of predicting the future with certainty and even in detail. In reality, prophetism goes far beyond this mean definition. It is essentially the individual religious conviction expressing itself under the influence of exalted religious feeling.

Popular error is never destitute of all foundation. At first, when speaking of the prophets, we think of the Biblical writers who bear that name, and we are accustomed to regard them as men who received supernatural light in order to announce beforehand the coming of a Redeemer, his incarnation, and even the details of the evangelical history. It must be confessed that the Jewish commentators have always had great reason to protest against this mode of interpreting their prophets. The fact is, that there is not a shadow of a miraculous prediction in the books called prophetic; there are previsions, which are not at all the same thing—previsions some of which were very exact, others which have not been confirmed by the event.

But the illusion dates from long ago. The beginnings of prophetism, rude like all religious origins, show us that the first phenomena which could come into the category of individual religious inspiration were specially utilized as serving to unveil the future, a thing to which man in ancient times attached great importance. This is one of the most notable differences which may be observed between the religious tendencies of antiquity and those of modern times. We have ideas, forms and religious ceremonies, which antiquity had also. That which we absolutely lack in the present day, even in those churches the most nearly related to the past, is the oracle, the augur and the prediction. At least, that which sets up a claim to resemble it is relegated by every sensible man into the class of idle puerilities, and no contemporaneous clergy patronize divination.

In the beginning it was otherwise. In that need of synthesis which is at the bottom of the religious sentiment, man, influenced by the desire of reconciliation between the course of things and his individual destiny, sought and believed he had found in certain phenomena of an order at once physical and psychical, the means of charming the unknown future into revealing beforehand what it would unfold.

Here, in fact, physiology and psychology have each a word to say. We know that there are certain physiological conditions which give rise to a certain exaltation of feeling, and that, reciprocally, this great exaltation of feeling brings about those physiological conditions in which the individual more or less loses all control over himself, and finds himself taken possession of and subjugated by that state of feeling. Then either he is plunged into a comatose state, into a sort of mute ecstacy; he remains indifferent to the reality which surrounds him, seeing things which we cannot see, hearing sounds which we do not hear, without anything which he experiences finding any external interpretation; we perceive at least nothing of his extraordinary condition except the rigidity of his limbs, a certain contraction of features, his eyes lost in space or turned inwards as if they were following an internal vision; or, on the contrary, his tongue is free, his power of speech is increased tenfold, and a man who in his ordinary state speaks with difficulty, begins to speak with a facility, a fluency, often even with a poetic eloquence, which enchants the listeners.

That there is in such a state an element of unhealthy overexcitement is incontestable, since all self-control is suppressed or at least weakened. But do not despise the humble beginnings of great things. When exaltation of thought does not go beyond the point at which man can command himself and knowingly guide himself, it becomes the source of the finest productions of the mind. The manifestation of genius in art, in poetry, in eloquence, and the enthusiasm which makes heroes and martyrs, and inspires sublime acts of devotedness, all spring from it.

It is true that this source may for a long time send forth turbid waters, before being purified by reflection and moral feeling. In religion, as in other domains, the primitive phenomena of individual inspiration are to some extent violent, excessive, and consequently morbid. It may be supposed that in remote antiquity they were less rare than in the present day. Among many savage races they are even now very frequent. As it grows older, humanity increases in reflective power and in self-possession. The accumulative experience of ages has rendered us distrustful of all unreflecting impulse. We allow ourselves to be governed by the emotions of the moment less readily than the ancients did. We may remark, however, that this is true only of the class to which we belong. If we penetrate into the lower strata of our population, we still meet with phenomena of the ecstatic order.

Religious enthusiasm was much stirred up by such phenomena in ancient times, and, reciprocally, corresponding physiological conditions were attributed to a religious cause. A sort of momentary delirium was supposed to be the divine power taking possession of the patient. It was discovered that there were physical means, such as fasting, for inducing this state of exaltation; and this is why we so often see fasting held to be a preliminary condition of divination. The oracle of Delphi owed its foundation to the discovery that those who for some time inhaled the vapours ascending from a certain natural spring were soon found to be in a state of over-excitement, which made them utter words listened to as mysterious, because they were believed to be dictated by a divine being. *Prophetic furore* was the expression used to designate this state of nervous and intellectual paroxysm. Racine well understood this side of ancient prophetism:

> Entre les deux partis Calchas s'est avancé,
> L'œil farouche, l'air sombre, et le poil hérissé,
> Terrible, et plein du dieu qui l'agitait sans doute.

From the mouths of those thus inspired there issued more than once in very ancient times discourses characterized by picturesque eloquence, tragic poetry, or passionate admiration of nature. In these was sought some revelation of the future.

In order to entertain this idea, it sufficed to believe in the divine origin of this exalted language. Moreover, it often happens that, in these exaltations of thought and feeling, the inspired person rises to a certain clear-sightedness which has nothing supernatural in it, but which leads him to announce catastrophes or deliverances in general terms, which his audience immediately makes specific. He speaks with a complete conviction which overawes, without enumerating the middle terms through which his thought passes before coming to a conclusion, something like the young mathematical prodigies who solve by intuition very complicated problems. Among ignorant races, prevision easily passes for miraculous divination, and, as so many other analogies prove to us, the previsions falsified by the event are more quickly forgotten than those which are confirmed by it.

Among the Greeks, tradition has preserved the names of some illustrious diviners—Amphiaraüs, Tiresias, Amphictyon, Cassandra—and, historical or not, they show the importance attached in primitive times to this gift of divination. They were the μάντεις, whose professional name is derived from μαίνομαι, to be in a rage, to be delirious. They had raised divination to the height of an art. It was this perhaps which slowly killed it, just as rhetoric at length extinguished eloquence. The Greek diviners acquired a great reputation even beyond Greece. Their influence was still powerful in the epochs in which the most enlightened class were undeceived in regard to them. The art of divination extended also to presages, to auguries which could be drawn from accidental phenomena, a singular application of the idea that there exists an order of things which determines details as well as the whole. They believed themselves able to divine the direction which this order would take by interpreting the meaning of trivial incidents, just as we can calculate the range of a projectile by measuring a fraction of the curve which it describes. It was the divine language of things which it was necessary to try to decipher. It was thus that at Dodona they predicted the future by listening to what was said by the venerable oaks, whose leaves rustled in the wind, at the entrance to the sanctuary; and that everywhere they imagined that they could discern the hidden meaning of things by interrogating the entrails of animals who had been sacrificed. As might be expected, in proportion as it departed from its primitive simplicity, artifice and charlatanism increasingly mingled with this pretended science. However, it did not always fail in good faith. The principle of divination was long admitted, even by men very superior to the common herd. "Delirium (μανία) is not always an evil," said Plato;[1] "on the contrary, the greatest benefits come to us through delirium inspired by the gods." "It must be," said Diodorus of Sicily,[2] "that human souls possess something of divinity; for it sometimes happens that they predict the future, and that by the phantoms

---

[1] Phædre, 547, ed. Bekker.
[2] Liv. xxxvii. Fragm. 15; comp. Liv. xviii. c. 1.

which the imagination creates they see beforehand what is about to take place." The Latin, not less superstitious, but less imaginative and more sober in idea than the Greek, never had any diviners as remarkable or as loquacious. He knew only unskilled augurs who could not answer questions except by Yes or No, without fine phrases; while the Greek soothsayers predicted the future in beautiful verses and copiously. Collections were made of their predictions. The famous Sybilline Books, so carefully preserved at Rome, appear simply to have contained the centos of old Greek oracles, which the Romans revered as a revelation concerning the destiny of their republic.

Often also it happened, and this was the case with the Pythia of Delphi, that the words pronounced in the artificial or spontaneous delirium of exaltation were incoherent, presented no consecutive meaning, and had need of interpretation. This was in Greece the office of the *prophet* so called. Thus was the priest designated who was charged with arranging and explaining the incomprehensible oracle. It was thence that the word passed into the religious vocabulary of the Hellenist Jews and into the Septuagint version.

We see in Greece what became of individual inspiration utilized solely by curiosity concerning the future. It descended to the rank of a trade; and if prophetism had never risen above this superstitious level, it would no more have recommended itself to our favour than the astrology with which so many people in the sixteenth century were infected. But it was destined among another race to rise much higher, to originate the reforming tendency in religion, and to open the way of progress in the sense of spiritualism and moral purity. Thence it became one of the great forces of the human mind.

Developed mythology, or the systematic dramatization of nature, is essentially Aryan; ancient prophetism is essentially Semitic. This belongs to the same tendency of race which has given birth to great epics and great dramas among the Aryan nations, whilst the Semites are in the highest degree lyrical.

That is to say that, influenced by a very lively sense of his personal independence, the Semite likes to express what he feels, what he believes, what he prefers, without taking into account that he himself may thus displease the traditional authorities or the social powers under whose régime he has to live. The *ego* predominates in him. Prophetism is in the religious order that which lyrism is in poetry. It depends, before all, on the individual, on his disposition, and on his personal emotions. The prophet is not a priest tied to a sanctuary, the slave of a tradition. He is an individuality.

We have the advantage of possessing numerous documents, bequeathed by the most remarkable, from the point of view of religious history, of the Semitic nations, which enable us to follow the successive transformations of prophetism from its origin to its complete development. As everywhere else, it begins by this kind of spasm, at once nervous and psychic, combining enthusiasm and delirium. We cannot furnish a more evident proof of this than by quoting the words which, as a preliminary refrain, introduce the prophecies of Balaam, the renowned prophet summoned to the banks of the Euphrates by the king of Moab to curse or to bewitch the tribes of Israel who had invaded his territory: "Balaam the son of Beor hath said, and the man whose eyes are open hath said: he hath said, which knew the ways of God and knew the knowledge of the Most High, which saw the vision of the Almighty, falling into a trance, but having his eyes open."[1]

Here we have the language of a visionary; and if the sacred tradition of Israel represents Balaam as animated by evil intentions, we must not forget that it in no way disputes his character of prophet, and that it even makes him the passive instrument of the will of Jahveh, who puts into his mouth blessing when he desired to utter curses.

The prophetic state is, then, according to this old narrative, an ecstatic state of second sight, independent of the will of the

[1] Comp. Numbers xxii.—xxiv. 15, 16.

prophet. Also the ancient name of the prophet in Israel is the *seer*, the man who sees in his moments of inspiration that which escapes the view of the vulgar. One thing may be noted, and it is confirmed elsewhere by numerous experiences extending to the present day, that there is something contagious in these special states of body and of mind. The same Israelitish tradition has recorded, in connection with king Saul, an incident which a knowledge of the character of this prince, who had nothing at all of the prophet in him, would lead us to consider as very rare in his life. Saul having come into the midst of a group of seers, all of whom had abandoned themselves to prophetic ecstacy, was seized by the contagion and began to *prophesy* with the rest. And as a result, this saying remained in the memory of the people, "Is Saul also among the prophets?"

We see then that, in its origin, the prophetism of Israel was not distinguished from phenomena of the same kind which we have been able elsewhere to verify. The difference which manifested itself later consists in this, that prophetism did not degenerate among the Israelites, as among the Greeks, into a mere trade, destined to fall more and more into charlatanism. Individual inspiration, under the influence of religious principles and of higher morals, was purified from this dross. Laying aside the suspicious forms of hallucination and of delirious vision, the Israelitish prophet became a convinced enthusiast, animated only by great ideas, just indignation and a sincere patriotism. In place of the semi-epileptics of primitive ages, appeared preachers, poets and divine singers, who were the censors and consolers of the people, a kind of tribuneship without official title, the whole power of which resided in the prestige of character and the support lent by conscience. It is there that the difference between prophetism and sacerdotalism shines forth. In contrast to sacerdotalism, the tendencies of which are always conservative, prophetism is essentially reformatory. Sacerdotalism is aristocratic, prophetism is democratic. It takes the part of the poor against the rich, of the weak against the strong, of the people against their kingly oppressors, of strict monotheism against the polytheistic and idolatrous corruptions of pure religion—finally, against sacerdotalism, which compromises and disgraces it by its rapacity or by its ambition. There are still here and there some features which recall its origin, something abrupt and sudden, in the appearances of the prophets. He who in the evening was only a herdsman or an ordinary citizen, begins the next day to preach, to discourse, to censure kings, judges, priests and nations. The prophet Elijah does nothing but appear, and disappear in order to appear again, and always in some unexpected way. When Amos of Tekoa was possessed by the spirit of Jahveh and began to prophesy, the priest Amaziah, whom his free speech offended, said to him, "O thou seer, go, flee thee away into the land of Judah, and there eat bread and prophesy there: but here is the king's chapel, and it is the king's court." Then Amos answered, "I was no prophet, neither was I a prophet's son;[1] but I was a herdsman and a gatherer of sycamore fruit: and the Lord took me and said unto me, Go, prophesy unto my people Israel."[2] We here find an echo of that rude accent which characterized primitive prophecy.

Nevertheless, it is much changed. The prophet is self-possessed; and if he always speaks by inspiration, in beautiful language poetic and imaginative, we can no longer reproach him with being only a visionary, a man of illusions. Far from furnishing arguments in favour of superstition, it is he who fights against it. We incontestably owe to the prophets the finest fragments of Hebraic literature, and they were the promoters of the religious progress by which we all benefit in the present day. Shall we quote the splendid vision of Elijah the Tishbite, when, flying from the persecution of king Ahab, he retired into a cave of Mount Horeb, hoping that there Jahveh would appear to him? We see in this vision, in symbolic form, an abridged development of the religious idea. A mysterious voice said to the prophet, "Go forth, and stand on the Mount before the Lord. And behold

---

[1] That is, disciple of a prophet.   [2] Amos vii. 12—16.

the Lord passed by, and a great and strong wind rent the mountains and brake in pieces the rocks before the Lord; but the Lord was not in the wind: and after the wind an earthquake; but the Lord was not in the earthquake: and after the earthquake a fire; but the Lord was not in the fire: and after the fire a still small voice. And when Elijah heard it, he wrapped his face in his mantle, and went out and stood at the entering in of the cave."[1]

This is very fine. The God of the prophet is not the visible phenomenon, magnificent or terrible, which ravages, which destroys, which devours; he is not the storm, nor the earthquake, nor the fire which consumes; he is the "still small voice," which the religious ear perceives and enjoys, which the eye cannot see, but to which the soul listens with delight as well as with reverence. Mysticism, however legitimate or wholesome, has never sounded sweeter chords.

It is the eminently religious principle of prophetism, its direct and immediate relation with the divine spirit, which renders it confident and powerful in its reformatory work. Another prophet, Isaiah, son of Amos, rose against the superstition of sacrifices. That which a priest would never have said, he taught—that the true service of Jahveh consisted in doing right, in succouring the unfortunate, in redressing injuries, and not in multiplying immolations. "To what purpose is the multitude of your sacrifices unto me?" says Jahveh himself through the medium of his prophet; "I am full of the burnt-offerings of rams and the fat of fed beasts..... Bring no more vain oblations; incense is an abomination to me, your new moons and your sabbaths..... Yea, when you make many prayers, I will not hear: your hands are full of blood..... Wash you; cease to do evil; learn to do well; seek judgment, relieve the oppressed, judge the fatherless, plead for the widow."[2] No religious teaching had ever uttered such exalted language. It was one of the first outbursts of the reforming spirit in religion.

[1] 1 Kings xix. 11—13.   [2] Isaiah i. 11—17.

Prophetism in Israel was very patriotic. It foresaw the misfortunes which were about to fall on its unfortunate country; but it rendered her the greatest service which can be rendered to a ruined country, that which consists in maintaining the sacred fire of patriotic faith, hope and confidence in the national destinies; and in the presence of a people ready to abandon themselves to despair, it struck the note of the *Sursum corda*. We know something of that. In the very midst even of the apparent annihilation of his nation, the prophet Ezekiel conceived his magnificent vision of the resurrection of dry bones, which were re-animated, joined together, clothed with flesh, and once more filled with the sounds of life the immense plain over which the silence of death had previously reigned.[1] Again, it was Isaiah, in the presence of Babylon the Great, so proud of her riches, her power and her impregnable walls, that Babylon who seemed to have for ever rivetted the chains of Israel's captivity, who described what will happen when she in her turn must submit to the yoke of the conqueror and descend to the pit, the subterranean vault in which the dead sleep. Then, in a magnificent prosopopœia, he paints the astonishment of the dead when they see the daughter of Babylon, the star of the morning fallen from heaven, arrive among them. "How! art thou also become one of us?"[2] It is in him also that we detect the hint of the first rationalism. How he satirizes the idolaters who make to themselves deaf and blind gods! "The carpenter stretcheth out his rule; he marketh it out with a line; he fitteth it with planes, and he marketh it out with the compass, and maketh it after the figure of a man, according to the beauty of man, that it may remain in the house. He heweth him down cedars, and taketh the cypress and the oak..... Then shall it be for a man to burn: for he will take thereof and warm himself; yea, he kindleth it and baketh bread; yea, he maketh a god and worshippeth it; he maketh it a graven image and falleth down thereto. He burneth part thereof in the fire; with part thereof he eateth flesh; he

---

[1] Ezekiel xxxvii.   [2] Isaiah xiv.

roasteth roast and is satisfied: yea, he warmeth himself and saith, Aha, I am warm; I have seen the fire: and the residue thereof he maketh a god, even his graven image: he falleth down unto it, and worshippeth it, and prayeth unto it, and saith, Deliver me, for thou art my God."[1] And again: "They lavish gold out of the bag, and weigh silver in the balance, and hire a goldsmith, and he maketh it a god..... They bear him upon the shoulder; they set him in his place and he standeth; from his place shall he not remove; yea, one shall cry unto him, yet can he not answer."[2]

No doubt, even in Israel, prophetism did not always maintain this high level of religious sentiment and sound reason. It had also its share of defects and of narrow-mindedness; it frequently made terms with the abuses which it ought to have opposed; its patriotism was often unjust or chimerical. Men who live only for their one idea are rarely clever politicians, and help to foster great illusions. We find also by the side of the sincere and disinterested prophet, the *nabi*, as he henceforward called himself—that is to say, inspired—the pretended "seer," who adapted his visions to his covetous desires or to his ambition. Every allowance being made for defects or infidelities, the prophetism of Israel none the less remains one of the most remarkable phenomena of religious history, and we owe too much to these inspired men not to be indulgent to their errors.

If it be characteristic of sacerdotalism to endure under forms always identical, it is even more the essence of free prophetism to be intermittent, to shine at one moment with the brightest lustre, then to be extinguished in order to appear again under other conditions. The Israelite prophetism gradually became extinct after the return from Babylon. The scribe, the man of law, of tradition and of the letter, succeeded it, and undertook to interpret the text in place of propounding it. But it had its revival. If we seek among the constituent elements of the people and of the history of Israel for that which engendered the move-

[1] Isaiah xliv. 13—17. [2] Isaiah xlvi. 6, 7.

ment whence the gospel arose, it is evidently prophetism which we must select. Jesus was a prophet in all the force of the term. It is this which best defines his person and the nature and the tendency of his teaching. It is always the same principle of internal individual persuasion, which respects sacred tradition, but which knows how to emancipate itself from it when it comes in the way of *fulfilment,* or of innovations suggested by a purer and more refined religious feeling. Traditionalists, formalists, the priests—that is to say, Scribes, Pharisees, and the sacerdotalism of Jerusalem—were all soon in opposition to Jesus.

Prophetism was not confined to the limits of the Israelitish nation. Analogous phenomena are frequent among other Semitic races. Islamism, the second of the great universalist religions which Semitism bequeathed to the world, springs from the same source. The Arab reformer Mahomet is also and especially a prophet.

In other regions and among other races religious progress is also brought about by the action of prophetism, although under different forms. There is, in spite of all differences, a close analogy between the Israelitish prophet and that Buddha who abandons his rank, his riches and his princely life, in order to go about preaching deliverance, the abolition of caste, the emancipation of nature, and a morality of sublime purity. When Greco-Roman paganism, on the point of dying, endeavoured to reform itself, it was a kind of prophet complete in all parts which it strove to create in order to regain its lost ascendancy. Apollonius of Tyana was a prophet, almost a pagan Christ.

Prophetism is, then, a reforming religious power more widely spread than is ordinarily believed. But all these characteristics are ancient; they belong to a bygone period, to a state of mind far removed from our own. Has it ceased to exist?

In our view, it has only changed its name, and has been divided into several distinct branches which were united in the beginning and formed only one common trunk.

The successors of the ancient prophets are those great religious individualities who have made their mark in history as liberators and reformers of oppressive traditions.

To prophetism also it belongs to carry out the great enterprizes of moral reform attempted in the name of a religious principle. When Theodore Parker, the illustrious American preacher, sacrificed his learning, his repose, his safety, even his life itself, in order to plant throughout the Union the banner of freedom for the slaves—when he raised his powerful voice against the evils and the infamies of slavery—when he repeated on each note of the gamut, to a nation which began to listen only when he was about to die exhausted, "You are on the brink of a red sea, of a sea of blood"—Theodore Parker was a prophet, and resembled the prophets of the old time in being misunderstood.

There was an element of the prophet also in St. Bernard when he sought to reform the Church both in its head and in its members. There is prophetism in all really eloquent religious preaching; for the prophet, from the simple ecstatic seer which he was in the beginning, became an impassioned preacher.

Finally, primitive divination itself is not without its counterpart in our times. If the ancient prayer which pointed out to the divine Power what he should do for our good, is summed up in the act of implicit faith which consists in saying, Thy will be done! the ancient claim to divine the future in its details and its possible accidents is enlarged and rationalized in the philosophy of history. This kind of study does not enable us to predict what will happen to-morrow or the next day, nor to satisfy puerile curiosity like an almanac or an ecstatic somnambulist, but to deduce from the confused course of events the permanent laws of history. It is by this method that we may foresee the consequences which the tendencies, the faults, or the good deeds of nations entail upon them. Political science will be originated when a sufficiently wide generalization from an adequate number of facts shall have shown the certain result of the guiding causes of national life. Already ancient prophetism, in its later period, inclined to that side. Its last echo was the Apocalypse, a strange and stormy composition of obscure design, which has, however, had much light thrown on it in the present day, showing it to be of very simple interpretation, and laying bare the illusions of its authors. It was none the less the first attempt at a systematization of history in accordance with a certain symmetry.

In one word, prophetism is not dead; it expands and is perpetuated under other names. Religious reform, religious spirituality, emancipation from oppressive authority, war against corrupt institutions, religious poetry, the philosophy of history, &c., are various titles of its representatives in the modern world. It is the old trunk which has spread out into branches.

VI.

RELIGIOUS AUTHORITY.

Whether religion be purely mythological, or legalistic, or dogmatic, it always engenders a certain number of common beliefs of which every one who lives under its influence ought to take cognizance.

In speaking of the first ages of religion among the human race, we stated that there had certainly been among primitive tribes individuals more highly endowed than the rest, possessing more intense religious feeling, a more lively imagination, who would determine the ideas of their kind by giving them a concrete, precise and figurative form, which they would not have found by themselves, but which they had adopted without reflecting about it. The reason of this easy acceptance is, that fundamentally the initiators shared the intuitions and notions which were common to them along with those around them. They gave a fixed form to that which existed already confusedly in the soul; and, in fact, religious progress was never effected otherwise. The first direction given to thought is always very powerful. Say to a young child when showing him the moon, "See this head, this mouth and these eyes which look at you!"—the child sees the head, the mouth and the eyes, and shows them to his little companions. At Geneva may be seen the emperor Napoleon I. buried up to his chin in the eternal snow of Mont Blanc. It is somewhat difficult to bring oneself to realize it, but when we are once at the right point, and have seized the resemblance, we see it always, and cannot understand why we did not see it at once. In like manner, with primitive humanity, the first mythological notions, uttered by poets unconscious of their poetry, became the property of those who heard them. Fathers and mothers transmitted them to their children. Succeeding imaginations found themselves urged in the same direction. These notions acquired the character of truths or of axioms which no one questioned, and thus a tradition arose.

This tradition, once formed, derived great force from the feeling which isolated man has of his weakness, especially in religious matters. It obtruded itself on succeeding generations with a prestige which time, as it went on, could only increase. It registered the narratives which the old never wearied of repeating, nor the young of hearing. It recommended rites, observances, sacrifices, the first signification of which had been long forgotten, but which were scrupulously performed, because this was the hereditary custom. The more destitute of critics was the age with which it had to do, so much the more authoritative was tradition. It is very rarely that a savage knows the meaning of his religious customs. Almost always, when he is asked for explanations, he contents himself with replying that his fathers taught him to act in this way, and he is surprised that such an answer does not satisfy the inquirer. When, in fact, the origin of a tradition is sought, the age of simple faith has already passed away. In such an age, tradition has authority in virtue of its antiquity, or, better, of its apparent eternity. For in minds little developed, antiquity and eternity are confused. The man who has never travelled and never read, imagines that people everywhere see and think as he does, and that they have always thus seen and thought. Our own age is certainly the one of all others in which an interest in history has been the most generally diffused. We carry this taste even into our furniture. Antiquity scarcely knew it. The greatest painters up to the last century had no idea of it. This explains the docility with which successive generations accept the tradition transmitted to them, and never even think of examining it in order to ascertain whether it is worthy of belief.

In religion, especially, the power of tradition is great; for it idealizes the most common things by giving them the stamp of antiquity. A brick of modern manufacture does not attract our notice; but if it comes from Babylon or Nineveh, we contemplate it with devotion. Religious creeds and religious symbols become more venerable when they are embalmed in antiquity. They seem thus to enter into the order of eternal things. As long as the spirit of criticism remains unaroused, innovation appears irreligious. It is this veneration for the ancient which explains more than one strange usage in religious rites and customs. Why, for instance, in many a religion, are iron instruments proscribed in all which concerns religious acts properly so called, and only stone ones admitted? This must date from the time in which metal instruments were introduced. They were easily adopted in ordinary use. But there seemed something audacious and sacrilegious in using them in religious ceremonies also. In our own day, we have seen pious persons shocked at the idea of lighting our old churches with gas, as if this worldly, commercial light, of recent invention, was less religious than the old smoky lamps flickering beneath the arches. There, again, the synthetic character of religion reveals itself, seeking to connect the individual with the Eternal Spirit. While all passes away, changes and disappears, it seems to man that in allying himself with something which persists, he unites himself to the immutable.

We must admit, on the other hand, that this docility in regard to tradition is associated with a very moderate regard for truth. We do not know whether the legitimate horror which intolerance inspires in those who are sufficiently instructed to know the lamentable pages which it has added to the book of history, has not often prevented historians and philosophers from perceiving a thing which is nevertheless very evident—that it is to the excess of religious fanaticism that we owe the importance ever since attached to the question of truth in all departments. The executioners have been not less instructive than the victims. That men, incapable of crime in all other respects, should allow themselves to be carried away to the extent of pitiless fury against those whom they accused of denying the truth, proves the value which they attached to it; and we may with good reason ask ourselves if the passionate love of truth in all things which has produced modern science would have been possible, or at least would have become very general, if Europe had not passed through centuries of intolerance. It is the fact that antiquity was acquainted with this noble passion in a much less degree than we are.

But before coming to that, in developed religions, man, without calling tradition in question, perceived that it ran the risk of being changed or lost if nothing was done to protect it against the causes of change or of oblivion. Naturally it was the priesthoods or the corporations of priests who furnished the usual conservators and continuers of ancient traditions. A class of men living apart, bound by their profession to know the theory and practice of religious things better than all others, would be held pre-eminently fitted to be the depository of tradition. The authority of this tradition thence became sacerdotal authority. The ordinary man, in his weakness and in his ignorance, must appeal to the priests in order to know exactly what he must believe and do. The priest was quite disposed to add this incalculable power to that which he already possessed as sacrificer and indispensable intermediary. It would have been conferred upon him even if he had refused it. The priesthood has often been accused of ambition and of love of rule; and the fact is that it has only too often laid itself open to such an accusation. But we cannot conceal that this has been much oftener an effect than a cause.

The authority of the priesthood was greater still where for a long time it retained the monopoly of that knowledge which was the most indispensable to social life, when it had to fix the calendar, to establish the laws, to digest the annals. If its power was less in Greece than everywhere else, that was not only because it failed in organization and centralization, but it was because it never had exclusive possession of enlightenment. The care of the religious traditions was confided at least as much to the poets as to the priests. This is why, throughout all antiquity, Greece was distinguished among all nations as the country of free thought.

In Rome, religious tradition was an affair of the state, like the priesthood itself. The senate was by right its guardian. That body legislated for religion as for everything else; and when the Greco-Roman paganism persecuted, it did so from essentially political motives.

The case was otherwise in India and in Persia, where the priesthood defended the truths of which it was the guardian for entirely religious reasons. In order to that, as in other regions where it assumed the same part and made the same claims, it raised the superiority which it claimed to the absolute; that is to say, it laid claim to infallibility, as though its doctrinal decisions had been dictated by the Divinity himself. Thus *orthodoxies* were formed; that is, systems of belief held to be right, pure from all alloy, and offered as indispensable of adoption by all who would live in communion with the divine Power. And such is the need of authority in matters of religion, that this claim was admitted not only in the bosom of Christianity, but in many other religions, and notably in Brahmanism and Buddhism. In the Christian Church, the episcopate once constituted, considered as the sole competent guardian of apostolic tradition, set up in œcumenical or general councils for the infallible organ of truth. The tendency to recognize authority, without having many other proofs of its legitimacy than the need man has of it, did not stop there. The time came when it was found that the councils met rarely, were difficult to assemble, that they were not always in accord, that their decisions allowed of differing interpretations, and that it would be much better to possess a permanent living organ of eternal truth, and it was sought to centralize in a single man, in a single bishop, the authority previously dispersed throughout the whole body of the Church. And in spite of obstacles, of resistance and of innumerable objections, the partizans of this personal infallibility carried it through, because their position, based on the need of authority, was logically sound. We have not yet done. The infallibility of the Pontiff to be complete and quite reassuring, supposes his impeccability. For, in fact, it is of little use to possess a personal infallible organ of eternal truth, unless it is certain that he *would* never from motives of personal interest withhold nor alter that truth. This is the final and the inevitable result of religious authority conferred upon the priesthood.

But this sacerdotal privilege is not the only form which the authority of tradition has assumed. There is an intermediate method, less rigorously logical, and thence leaving more scope for intellectual freedom and for varieties of thought, arising also out of the need of settling precious traditions, of preserving them from oblivion and change, and of transmitting them to posterity as the touchstone of faith. We allude to sacred books.

Not all religions have them, but many among the most important possess them. Brahmanism has its Vedas and its laws of Manou; Mazdeism has its Zend Avesta; Buddhism, its Tripitaka (the three baskets); China has its Kings; Islamism, its Koran; Judaism, its Bible, which is also that of Christianity, with the addition of the New Testament.

Sufficient information as to the way in which the greater part of these sacred books or holy scriptures was formed is wanting. But analogy allows us to suppose that one and the same law of formation directed their appearance. We know very well how the Holy Scriptures of the Jews and of the Christians were codified, and that is enough to enable us to give an account of the process followed in editing or in arranging the others.

Why, for instance, did the Jews, who in the time of ancient Israel dispensed with sacred books, proceed to form them in the period which elapsed between the return from captivity and the Christian era?

We have already seen, in speaking of the contemporaneous institution of synagogues, that with the Jews it became a question of not losing the memorials of the past, menaced as they were by revolutions, deportations, and all that had destroyed the national existence. Prior to the great catastrophe, several writings had already been composed. There were collections of laws—one especially, the sudden appearance of which in the reign of king Josiah made a great sensation. Other codes had been drawn up during or shortly after the captivity. A collection of these was made in combination with several historical narratives turning on the antiquities of Israel. From this work resulted the Pentateuch, or, as the Jews say, the Law. There were a certain number of prophets whose discourses had been committed to writing. These discourses were added to this first collection. Finally, there circulated a considerable number of hymns, of sayings, of annals and of chronicles. This made a third division, which was not hermetically closed like the first two, but which in the time of Jesus Christ already included the books which actually compose it in the Hebrew Bible. The mere fact of uniting all these books, differing in date and contents, was not enough to confer upon them the dignity of sacred books. They simply formed a library of great interest in regard to the political and religious history of the Israelitish nation. But they were very speedily used in the worship of the synagogues. Every day some fragment of these venerated books was read, commented on and explained. These books were then placed on a real pedestal and set apart from all others. They became pre-eminently the Scripture, the Bible, or the Book. They came to be considered as the source and the foundation of beliefs, and this conferred upon them a quite special and unique character. At length the people deified them as much as books can be deified—that is to say, they considered them as dictated by the mind of God himself. This was the point of departure of a number of rabbinical subtleties. They went so far, for instance, as religiously to reproduce the faults of copyists which had crept into the text, and to discover a world of mysteries in the number of letters which each of the writings in the sacred collection contained.

The origin of the New Testament does not differ essentially from that of the Old. It also is composed of different books, written by various authors at different dates, and certainly none of these authors foresaw that posterity would join his work with twenty-six others in order to form a new Holy Scripture. This work of union dates from the second century, when the Christian churches were invaded by Gnostic doctrines, a mixture of Oriental speculation, of polytheism and of Christianity, very much the fashion at that period—religion has its fashions and its temporary infatuations—which threatened to drown Christian tradition in a deluge of strange notions and bewildering dreams. A conservative instinct led to the desire of possessing written, incontestable monuments of the Christian teaching of early days, and a certain number of gospels, epistles, apostolic histories, &c., dating or supposed to date from the age of the apostles, was collected. This collection, which was not definitively settled until later, but which very early contained the principal books of which it is now composed, thence became the model, the official document, of true Christian tradition. These books, like those of the Old Testament, were read in the religious assemblies. There was no delay in conferring the same sacred character upon them.

In the beginning, there was no sort of conflict between the sacerdotal authority, complete in all parts, and this authority of the book which each one could read. On the contrary, the Christian priest was the principal collector of the new selection and gave his sanction to it. He made it the text of his teaching, and believed that he found in it confirmation of his authority, only he more and more reserved to himself the right of determining its interpretation. He founded Christian orthodoxy on those texts henceforth considered canonical, and he forgot absolutely that they presented several very different types of doctrine. But it is an illusion, common to those who read the sacred books without a spirit of independent criticism, not to see the doctrinal differences which distinguish some from the others.

See what now happened. The living and speaking authority of the priesthood gained the ascendant over the authority of the book, which was less and less read. Christian tradition, like all prolonged tradition, augmented and loaded with heterogeneous elements, deviated in many respects from its primitive lines; and the moment came in which the book, which had not changed, found itself in disagreement with the priesthood, which had greatly changed. Such was the antagonism which broke out in the Reformation. To sacerdotal tradition, Protestantism opposed the tradition deposited in the holy book.

An important step towards the emancipation of religious thought was certainly then taken. A book, serving as the basis of a religious society, ought to be read; and to read, is already to arouse reflection, examination and individual decision. Every Protestant, with a Bible in his hand, soon became a pope. Then, as this Bible was not always clear, not always in agreement with itself on all points, dogmatic differences were not slow to arise. We may remark here that, in its enthusiasm for its traditional written chart, Protestantism, like Judaism, fell into veritable bibliolatry. It made the Bible a miraculous writing, and, as its adversaries often reproached it with, a paper pope.

Nevertheless, it is to this ardent study of the Bible that we owe the scope of historical criticism. Nations who are educated in this reading acquire ideas concerning antiquity—concerning other races than their own—concerning the manners, customs, ideas of ages long gone by—of which nations submitted to sacerdotal authority remain destitute. It is not at all the result of chance that the great works of historical criticism and of comparative history have until now been carried on much more actively in Protestant countries than anywhere else. They find a public which interests itself in them, prepared beforehand to like and to understand them.

Finally, the ultimate result is evolved from these researches. There is no more of the supernatural in the authority of the sacred books than in that of the priesthood. According to periods, populations and states of mind, these two authorities have shown themselves in turn beneficent or oppressive. Religion itself is independent of both. Both have been specially constituted as protectors of tradition. The sacred books in each religion remain pre-eminently the documents which enable us to go back with certainty to their principle and to their original spirit. Whatever is the worth of a religion, that is the value of its sacred book. In virtue of this, the Bible remains always worthy of our respect and of our liveliest interest. Nothing can prevent it containing a great number of those words which humanity will never forget. But it has no right—we may add that it makes no claim—to enchain the liberty of the mind.

VII.

THEOLOGY.

The word theology has not a very good reputation in contemporary France. Many persons understand by it a science which they say is no science—in this sense, that it is governed by doctrines laid down *a priori* which do not leave it any real liberty of examination—a science consequently factitious, which is taught in the seminaries to young men destined to an ecclesiastical career, but which truly scientific men can never take seriously. This definition is much too limited; it confuses a particular form of its object with the object itself; and from our point of view we energetically challenge it.

It would not be very logical to strike out from the course of scientific studies those branches of knowledge which are not universally recognized as positive and susceptible of exact demonstration. There are people who believe neither in medicine nor in philosophy. We consider, however, that it would be very unwise to eliminate those studies from the programmes of instruction.

Everywhere, where observation establishes a group of facts, visible or invisible, linked together by an internal relationship, forming a class apart in the midst of all others, there is room for a special science.

Thus religion is the common cause of a mass of facts distinct from others—creeds, myths, symbols, rites, traditions, sacrifices, priesthoods, sacred books, &c.—and this mass constitutes the religious domain properly so called. Consequently, since the human mind has had capacity and leisure, it has looked at this with curiosity, it has sought to examine it, to understand it and to bring it into the forms and categories of reason; thence has arisen a special branch of human knowledge, to be called theology, or the science of God—more exactly, of all which concerns the divinity.

This science had not very brilliant beginnings, any more than its sisters. Much less ancient than its object, since it brings intelligence and reflection definitely into action, it bears, like all the sciences at their outset, that stamp of imagination, of poetry and of arbitrariness, which may charm æsthetically, but is anti-scientific in the highest degree. This is not a sufficient reason for disputing its existence. The true scientific spirit, for a moment caught sight of in ancient Greece, is in reality a very modern thing.

In the very fact of the elaboration of a myth, or of the organization of a rite, there is a work of arrangement and of systematization which proceeds from reflection. Where a religion turns in preference towards animism, and consequently towards sorcery, there are special theologians who claim to know the formulæ, the incantations, the mysterious signs, which compel the spirits entreated to intervene in a certain manner in human affairs. Where a religion gives rise to a complicated ritual, he who knows the rites well—the priest who knows the hymns which must be sung—how the victim is to be sacrificed and his entrails are to be interrogated—how he must be skinned and cut up on the altar—at what precise moment it is right to arrest the burning and to distribute to those present the portion which they share with the divinity—this priest, this great master of religious ceremonial, is learned in his part and has his theology at his fingers' end. Finally, when curiosity is aroused in the mind before it has lost its native credulity—when it seeks to know accurately all those beautiful histories which are related concerning gods and goddesses and their descent, and concerning the beginnings, those especially of the tribe or of the city—the theologian will be the priest or the poet who knows all that and who narrates it in order, in a language worthy of the subject, in fine flowing verses, harmonious or tragic.

For this reason, in Greek antiquity, the first theologian of renown is Hesiod, who described the beginnings of the world, of gods and of goddesses, their loves, their wars, how men lived at first, and how the great Olympian gods, gods in the regular order of things, ended by getting the better of monstrous disturbing powers, born of the first embraces of Heaven and Earth. Here we have a very primitive theology, which consists in a poetic account of old traditions and in their arrangement.

So long as we remain in the region of mythology, theology can scarcely be anything else. This arrangement has its special methods. For instance, it reconciles the different traditions revolving round the same natural fact, by establishing a relation of paternity between the different gods whom they concern. When Hesiod says that Kronos is the son of Uranus, and Zeus the son of Kronos, that is the same as saying that Uranus, Kronos and Zeus, are in fact the same being, Heaven. When it is related that the august Jupiter offered to others besides his rightful companion, Hera, the homage of his passion, translate: Hera, the goddess of the ethereal heights, was considered in most cities as the wife of Heaven; but in more than one place another companion was assigned to Heaven—the Earth, under the names of Demeter, Ceres, Leda, Danaë, Latona, &c., and that without thinking any evil. The poet of Ascra was not, however, an isolated phenomenon. Before his time, itinerant singers hawked about poems analogous to his, though probably less complete; and we find even in the Rig-Veda hymns which are nothing but attempts at systematization of the first Aryan mythology.

It was quite otherwise when philosophy had been born. In Greece, as in India, it formed a sort of philosophic theology, the characteristic of which was to introduce, under the forms, in the myths and the creeds, of the popular religion, ideas proceeding from philosophic speculation, but which, with some compromises, were amalgamated with the traditional forms, and appeared as making only one with them.

N

Among the philosopher-theologians of antiquity, we may name Pythagoras, who almost founded a religion, and in whom little was wanting to give to the West a sort of Buddha. Plato also contributes to theology, in the sense that he often interprets the popular traditions conformably to his own speculative ideas. Varro among the Romans, and Plutarch among the Greeks, come rather into the list of reciters and narrators. In India also schools flourish which are at once philosophic and religious, applying to the Vedic and Brahmanic traditions principles derived from sources external to them. We discern there the Vedantâ philosophy, implying a sufficiently decided monotheistic tendency; the Nyâya philosophy, occupying itself specially with logic and the sources of knowledge; the atomistic philosophy, called Vaiseshitra; and the system of pantheistic, even atheistic, tendency of Sânkhya. None of these philosophies appear separated from the Vedic religion; on the contrary, each claims to be its true interpretation.

Among the Jews, theology as a science was long unknown. The prophet, the psalmist, or the wise man of sententious speech, determined the direction of religious ideas among them. The Jewish theologian appeared with the lawyer, the scribe and the rabbi, chiefly in the character of interpreter of and commentator on the sacred books, particularly of the law. This primary Jewish theology, which produced the colossal work of the Talmud, is essentially a jurisprudence. But this book led to others. The Judaism which followed the captivity admitted doctrines which the old Mosaism did not know, or of which it possessed only the germs, such as the belief in good or bad angels, in Satan, in the Messiah, and in a future life under the form of corporeal resurrection. The rabbis for the most part adopted these innovations, arranged them in order and propagated them. Judaism, at the time when Jesus appeared, was thoroughly impregnated with them.

The same Judaism, but this time in Egypt, furnishes us with a new and very curious proof of the influence of philosophical ideas on the theological elaboration of religious ideas. We speak here of the school of Alexandrian Judaism so called, of which Philo the Jew is the most eminent representative. In him, the Old Testament and Plato meet and combine. The foundation is Platonic, the form is Biblical; but the foundation modifies the form, and reciprocally. What especially distinguishes the theology of Philo is that, without knowing anything of Christianity, by the simple application of his Platonic ideas to Hebraic tradition, he proclaims the theory of the Word, the Son of God, the intermediary between creation and the absolute Divinity, divine thought emitted before all time, and since then endowed with a personal existence, the revealer of truth, the redeemer of men. It is the Logos or the Word which, in the mind of the Alexandrian Jew, came forth from the absolute Being by an ineffable generation, just as, according to mythology, Pallas Athene sprang from the forehead of her father Jupiter. But what prodigious progress this speculative theory made! Hardly half a century had passed when an evangelist applied it to the person of Jesus. Two centuries later, the question which agitated the world was whether the Word or Son was, or was not, consubstantial with the Father; and the emperor Constantine, more disturbed by this difference than by the barbarians who thundered at the gates of civilization, assembled at his own cost the first great œcumenical council, and signed the famous formula of Nice, which proclaimed, in opposition to Arius, the consubstantiality of the Father and of the Son.

From this moment we enter fully on the theological period. For a long time theology will be the favourite intellectual occupation of both Pagans and Christians. Neo-platonism was especially a theology. The old paganism, on the eve of extinction, suffered its last spasm, its final resistance to the death-agony which had begun. The pagan reaction numbers very distinguished names—Libanius, Hierocles, Porphyrius, the emperor Julian, who also was a theologian. But this artificial theology had no chance against the Christian theology, which was however

not much more natural or scientific, but which had this enormous
advantage, that instead of being the theory of a dying religion,
it was that of a religion still young and possessing confidence and
hope. We must never confound the value of the great movements which carry away humanity with that of theories of
learned pretensions which may be based upon them. If our
French revolution had waited, before acting upon the world,
until one or more thinkers had given it a scientific formula, it
would have been waiting still.

There are two facts to be noticed at the point at which we
have arrived in this outline sketch of the history of theology.
The first is, that it is intimately connected with the history of
philosophy. In reality, theology ceases to be a simple arranged
statement of, or a mere commentary on, tradition, only when it
takes possession of that tradition in order to look at it in the
light of philosophic principles, and to submit it to forms corresponding to those principles. The second is, that the results of
this application of philosophical theories to the objects of religion become in their turn an integral part of the traditional faith,
and obtrude with the authority of immutable tradition on sub-
sequent theology. *Dogma* is born.

We have already remarked this very important element in the
history of religious ideas, that the establishment of the Christian
Church in the midst of populations fed on the old polytheistic
traditions had given an importance till then unknown to the
question of the true and the false in religion. We have shown
with what indulgence, which underwent only some momentary
interruptions, polytheism regarded this alternative. Prepossession
in favour of truth became so strong that, in Christianity especially,
we see a phenomenon also unknown to antiquity, the ardent
search after orthodoxy, that is correct belief. We have shown
how this ardent search invested the Christian priesthood with
the privilege of infallibility, and that orthodoxy consisted in
adhesion to the decrees issued by the councils or assemblies of
bishops. These decrees—those at least which aimed at deter-

mining the text of doctrines—became *dogmas*.[1] In theological language, a dogma is more than a doctrine, a disputable opinion to be modified in substance and in form. It is something absolute and invariable; and it is on the adhesion yielded to dogmas promulgated by the Church that orthodoxy depends. Consequently the explanation, the demonstration and the defence of dogma will be, until the moment when this authority shall be theologically disputed, the proper duty of theology.

We know how in the middle ages theology was the absorbing science, which comprehended all the others and was honoured by an undisputed pre-eminence. Then philosophy was declared its humble servant, *ancilla theologiæ*. It was not remarked that if the mistress had not first been in the school of her servant she would have had nothing to say, and would have continued to submit to her influence. The divinity of Jesus Christ and the divine Trinity imply a large element of Platonism; original sin, the redemption, the authority of the Church, the value of sacraments, the merits of the saints and their reversion to the faithful, &c., depend upon the principles of realism, which make out of the generality, out of the common element of collectivity, out of the *idea* of a whole, a concrete reality which is again Platonism. It is true that all these beliefs, in old times theological theses, had been raised to the dignity of definitive dogmas. But among chosen spirits, faith aspired after rational expression, *fides quærens intellectum*. Then arose scholasticism, the

---

[1] The word dogma, δόγμα, signifies primarily simply a plausible opinion, a thesis sure of approval. The Stoics gave it a stricter sense in applying it to decrees defining articles of the sovereign law or moral precepts. Cicero, *Acad. Quæst.* iv. 9, gives us this explanation of it: *Quæ (sapientia) neque de seipsa dubitare debet, neque de suis decretis quæ philosophi vocant δόγματα, quorum nullum sine scelere prodi potest. ... Non potest igitur dubitari, quia decretum nullum falsum possit esse, sapientique satis non sit non esse falsum, sed etiam stabile, fixum, ratum esse debeat, quod movere nulla ratio queat.* A little further on, *ibid.* 43 : *Ne incognito assentiar, quod mihi tecum est dogma commune.* It is in the same sense that we find the word used by Marcus Aurelius, Ἐις ἑαυτον, ii. 3 : ταῦτα σοι ἀρκείτω, ἀεὶ δόγματα ἔστω. This philosophical acceptation of the word *dogma* arose, according to all appearances, from the term, ἔδοξε, δέδοκται, *it seems*, or *it has seemed good, it is resolved*, which is put at the head of decrees emanating from public authorities.

daughter of Aristotle, but knowing very little of her father.
During several centuries there was a series of formidable doctors
who consecrated a phraseology of great subtlety and vigour to
definitions and demonstrations of the dogmas of the Church.
It was among them that the dawn of free thought threw its
first ray, thanks to Maître Abelard, much more celebrated in
the present day through his misfortunes than through his *Sic
et Non*. Nevertheless, the *Sic et Non*, the Yes and the No of
tradition—as if she could contradict herself!—was an event.
Bernard de Clairvaux, a mediocre theologian, but a great preacher
and a man of incomparable ardour, had as it were a vision of
the ravages which this rising criticism would one day make in
the edifice consecrated by ages. Twilight lasted long; and
while it still continued, the majestic *Somme* of Thomas Aquinas
appeared, an alarming work of credulous analysis and of scho-
lastic dulness. We might describe it as an immense Gothic
cathedral without taste or grace. It has never been surpassed
in its kind, and it is not without good reason that it is com-
mended as the last word of human wisdom for those who
believe that the safety of humanity is bound up in the religious idea as it was understood and developed by the angel of
the school. Thomas Aquinas had rivals and even adversaries, of
whom Duns Scotus was one. The quarrel of nominalism and
of realism, originally only philosophical, re-acted upon theology.
The nominalist doctors were usually of a much less assured
orthodoxy than the others. But Christian theology remained
without any notable change until the Reformation.

Then there was a bifurcation, a Catholic theology and a Protestant theology, guided by different principles and having different ends in view. About the same period, sciences of various
names detached themselves, like so many children emancipated
from the lap of their foster-mother, who, less alert and less shrewd,
had great difficulty in following them and often relinquished the
attempt. Theology was scarcely more than a science of application, studied by those who sought to enter the service of

one or other of the two Churches. Dogma was on both sides the principal study, to which all the others were subordinate. In the mean time, Protestant orthodoxy was establishing itself with a rigour almost as exclusive as that which distinguished its rival; and when we study its history, we perceive that it had, after its bold movement in the sixteenth century, its middle age and its scholasticism during the seventeenth and a great part of the eighteenth century. We see again that dreary, circumstantial and subtle method of discussing dogma, of which the doctors of the middle ages furnished the model. Let us add, that the controversy between the two hostile Churches absorbed the thoughts and labour of theologians almost entirely.

However, we already see two tendencies developing which are destined to be very powerful in the future. Protestant theologians, in their criticisms on the Catholic dogmas of transubstantiation, of sacraments in general, of the infallible authority of the Church, opened the way for a bold rationalism which could not fail to extend itself to their own orthodoxy. The Socinian school did not hesitate to shiver it into fragments. On the other hand, led away by controversy into making the Bible the religious authority sovereignly deciding all differences, they read and studied it much, without daring to apply to it the processes of independent criticism. The veneration of which the Bible was the object went even to superstition, even to the deification of the book.

This explains why independent biblical criticism arose outside Protestantism, through the labours of an excommunicated Jew, Spinoza, and an erudite priest, Richard Simon. To the timorous objections which were made to the latter from the midst of the Catholic Church, he replied that Protestant theologians, having no other basis than the Bible to support their doctrines, were compelled to put it outside discussion; but that Catholic theologians, founding their teaching on continuous tradition and the infallibility of the Church, were much freer to investigate the origin and method of composition of the books of the Bible without departing from orthodoxy. This specious reasoning did not prevent the usual defenders of Catholic orthodoxy, Bossuet among others, from shaking their heads in defiance, auguring nothing good from this "libertine criticism which threatens to invade everything." Richard Simon was censured, molested and somewhat persecuted; and his example was so little encouraging that he remained without successors. The valiant Benedictine school of the last century published some very remarkable works of erudition relating to the first centuries, and hunted out, as was then said, a certain number of male and female saints; but it exerted no influence on ecclesiastical theology properly so called. The inheritance of Richard Simon was acquired chiefly by Protestant theologians. It could not in the end escape them that the Bible itself, in its formation and in the way in which it has reached us, rests on the principle of tradition. Who gathered together the different books? Who decided that these books, and no others, ought to compose it? Who has guaranteed to us that in course of time no curtailments and no additions have been made? These questions were bound to obtrude themselves, and to compel Protestant theology to treat them scientifically.

In the mean time, philosophy had been enriched and transformed. Through Descartes, Spinoza and Leibnitz, it had put in circulation many new ideas and methods. Once more the law which ordains that theology shall always sooner or later yield to the ascendancy of philosophy, was about to be verified. Protestant theology had its Leibnitzian, or rather Wolfian, period,— Wolf, the disciple of Leibnitz, having chiefly contributed to propagate the ideas of his master in the Universities. The prestige of traditional dogma had much diminished, and we in France can scarcely form an idea of the incredible mass of learned works which German theology produced in the two neighbouring domains of biblical criticism and of ecclesiastical history. Later still, German theology had its Kantian period, then its Hegelian period; then it underwent a reaction in the sense of a return to old dogmas. But the ancient dogmatic theology, founded at first sight on the authority of a revealed dogma, no longer existed. Since then we have seen the profession of theology, such as we understand it in the present day—that is to say, a whole formed of critical, historical and philosophical knowledge—concerning itself with all religious matters, and specially, but no longer exclusively, with the origin and the history of Christianity. The course, the first lessons of which are to be found in a condensed form here, is in truth a course of theology, but of theology absolutely laic. We recognize, indeed, in truly scientific theology, that Christianity cannot be understood, that the Bible cannot be soundly appreciated, except on the condition of comparing the one and the other with the religions of the whole world, with their traditions and their sacred books. This point of view in no way invalidates the legitimacy of the theological studies pursued in view of the ministry in any church. All things being equal, it is infinitely better that the ministers of a religious society should be instructed and scientifically prepared for their functions, than that they should be left without defence against the illusions of ignorance. But we can claim for the position in which we have placed ourselves the advantage of entire disinterestedness, and we measure our sympathies for ecclesiastical or for applied theology by the degree of independence and of really scientific spirit of which they give proof.

To sum up: theology is to religion what all methodic knowledge is to a determinate group of facts. Sometimes in advance of progress in other directions of the human mind, sometimes in the rear, theology passes through three phases: in the first, it records and arranges traditions; in the second, it defines, demonstrates and develops the dogmas in force in a religious society; in the third, it gradually emancipates itself from the dictatorial authorities which limit the free scope of religious science, and, except in the case of its special application to religious societies at present constituted, it moves henceforth as boldly and freely in the field of inquiry as any other branch of knowledge. Finally, whether the philosophy by which it is inspired be ancient or recent matters little; it is the fact that theology is always determined or modified by the course of philosophical ideas. Dogma itself is never anything but philosophical interpretation embalmed in a sacred formula of traditional facts.

It is, then, above all necessary, in order to grasp the true relations between religion and theology, to take account also of the relations of the former to philosophy.

VIII.

PHILOSOPHY.

We should be greatly embarrassed if, among all the definitions which have been given of philosophy, we had to choose that which would be considered as the most exact. Most frequently the proposed definition has been true only from the point of view of the particular system of which it formed a part. On the historical ground on which we have the right, or rather the duty, of remaining, we take the whole of the works which, by common consent, are ranked under the category of philosophical works. We observe that they all have as a condition full liberty of thought; that they take their rise first of all from intellect, while religion takes its rise in the first instance from feeling; that they are ordinarily consecrated to the search after first principles, while establishing themselves, consciously or not, on the sum of the knowledge acquired at the moment at which these attempts are perfected; that, finally, that which concerns the soul, the thinking *ego*, human destiny, forms part of their field of inquiry to a quite special extent.

Thence, historically, we have the right of thus defining philosophy: it is the free search after higher truth in the world and in man on the basis of acquired knowledge in general and of observation of human nature.

The affinity between religion and philosophy arises from this—that both aspire after the highest or sovereign truth. Religion springs from the spontaneous sentiment of it which man possesses, and which he interprets first of all without reflection, as also without method, under the preponderating influence of the imagination. Philosophy springs from the need which man experiences of correcting by rational formulæ the inspirations of feeling. They are, however, two sisters, offspring of the human mind, and each of them in her own way renders homage to this impulse which urges the human mind to seek the supreme unity of things, to seize it when it believes it has found it, to set to work again when it perceives that it does not possess it. Of what importance from this point of view are the aberrations whether of philosophy or of religion? Each has a great charge; but it is not the result which we must weigh; it is the tendency and the effort; and the two efforts are parallel.

Nevertheless, their harmony is often disturbed by bitter and fierce disputes.

Religious tradition, always formed in a period of relative ignorance, proposes to the reason assertions which the latter after a certain time can no longer admit, which even offend it. Sometimes a religious genius, reforming and transforming religion, raising the religious level of the soul to a height previously unknown, removes the difficulty, and becomes the point of departure of a new tradition. But such an event is very rare. Long periods pass during which religious tradition remains unchanged. Each time, also, discontented reason seeks the satisfaction which tradition refuses her, and seeks it outside the latter.

Philosophy, consequently, from its first appearance, presents itself in a condition of detachment from religious tradition, and starts from a supposition more or less hostile to it. Our attention has been called to the fact that where, as in Greece, the authority of this tradition is ill-defined and hazy, theoretic antagonism is only feebly felt. Nevertheless, the example of Socrates and of some other thinkers of antiquity is there to prove to us that this antagonism might very easily pass into action and assume a tragic form.

It is always by a compromise that philosophy and religion can live on terms of peace for any length of time. Philosophy accepts the forms and symbols of tradition, and translates its speculations and its favourite ideas into traditional language.

We see remarkable examples of this in India, among the Pythagoreans and the Platonists, in Neo-platonism and in Alexandrian Judaism, which was persuaded that Plato and Moses were in complete accord, although it unfolded a system in which neither Plato nor Moses would have recognized themselves. Tradition then becomes philosophical, and philosophy becomes a theology.

But that cannot continue indefinitely. This agreement is more diplomatic than real. New evolutions of free thought may place it in an antagonism to tradition also penetrated by philosophical ideas. It may besides happen, and it does happen, that philosophy may be irreligious in its tendency.

It is so when it rests on chance as the last word of things. In truth, that synthesis which is the fundamental claim of religion, its *raison d'être* and its constant ambition, is no longer possible if, instead of a centralizing and co-ordinating principle of things, thought has nothing for its supreme standpoint but this irrational category, absolutely opposed to the most imperious postulate of the mind, which we call chance. This is why in pagan antiquity the philosophical school which was always the most suspected in the eyes of religious men was Epicurism. It mattered little that, more or less seriously, Epicurus admitted the existence of the gods. He recognized no real connection between them and the world; and as for the latter, its existence, its organization and its continuance, arose from a fortuitous concourse of infinitely numerous atoms involved by an undefinable force in an eternal fall. Such a system is irreligious, because it banishes mind from the universe. Religion knows not to whom or to what to cling. Since there is no more any thought in the world, human thought cannot attach itself to anything analogous to itself. Nothing any longer answers to the idea of permanence or of immutability. Man cannot logically find a standpoint even in the admission of eternal laws affecting the very essence of things. If the universe is in effect nothing but a fortuitous combination, who may assure us that this combination may not to-morrow, in an hour, or even in a moment, have exhausted its chances of duration, and that the kosmos, the organized world, may not be replaced by an indescribable chaos in *ictu oculi* ?

This will always be the weak side of a purely atomistic philosophy, even when it has more than once usefully re-acted against the hollow speculations of a metaphysical system too disdainful of experience. We may add that philosophy has very rarely made atheism a principle. It is an abuse of words to address this reproach to schools which, like the positivism of the present day, simply conclude our mental impotency in the search after the final cause. It is not detracting from this theory, supposing it admitted, to ask the question, *What next*, and *next ?*— and in default of a reply which shall in all points satisfy the requirements of strict logic, to collect and question the indications of human nature, with its needs, its spontaneous tendencies, and its aspirations towards the ideal.

As a rule, however, religion finds itself more in harmony with philosophies which possess a metaphysical system in itself religious, and which can give a reason to man when he desires to unite himself with the sovereign spirit, the supreme being, the constant thought and director of things, the real ideal, or any other name which it suits him to apply to the being whom ordinary language calls God. It is thus that Platonism and Stoicism in antiquity—the systems of Descartes, of Spinoza, of Leibnitz, of Kant and of Hegel—have given a great impulse to religious thought and have powerfully modified it. But we must not, therefore, say that it is philosophy which makes religion. That is not true in the beginning; it is only to a certain extent true in the sequel. Philosophy can influence only the doctrinal theory of religion or theology. Each system of philosophy has its day. It appears; it puts itself forward; then it falls to pieces and gives place to another. Only the really powerful systems of philosophy do not disappear without leaving in the general thought some elements which survive them, and which become henceforth a part of the general inheritance. Has not Plato bequeathed to us idealism ; Descartes, the autonomy of the mind; Spinoza, anti-dualism; Leibnitz, the idea of substantive force; Kant, that of the sovereignty of duty in life; Hegel, that of becoming or of developing by the opposition of contraries? So many indestructible furrows ploughed on the field of the mind, so many precious pearls with which the treasury of humanity is enriched, and which henceforth form part of its inalienable dowry.

But before these religious thinkers themselves, religious tradition often recoils in fear, and through the medium of its official theologians declares violent war against them.

This tradition, impregnated with philosophical ideas of the past, would intrude itself as a supernatural revelation, and does not intend that it shall be lawful to seek truth outside itself. The autonomy of the mind seems to it hostile to the rights which it arrogates; with still greater reason when this philosophy teaches doctrines in open opposition to its dogmas. Then it accuses it, not only of temerity, but even of impiety and of blasphemy. It assumes the offensive. It demands from the wisdom of this world an account of its errors and of its extravagances, and proclaims itself infinitely more rational than its rival.[1] Too often it

---

[1] We still remember very distinctly an address which we heard more than thirty years ago in Paris, in the Church of the Assumption. The preacher was that Father Ventura who had his season of celebrity, and whom a certain reputation for liberalism had preceded amongst us. An Italian, he spoke French with a marked accent, but with much facility and even with elegance. His subject was the demonstration of the superiority of Catholic theology over philosophy. With unpitying eloquence and real erudition he enumerated all the errors, all the nonsense, all the follies, of which philosophy had been guilty from ancient times down to our own day. It was an interminable string of blunders, of which several very comic ones almost provoked the laughter of the numerous audience assembled in the sacred place. At bottom the effect was saddening, inasmuch as one was present at the caricature of poor human reason. The audience, educated young men for the most part, seemed much struck with it. Could not the preacher have foreseen that among them he might probably find some who were also studying theology, and that, without any pretension to know all that it could teach them, they knew enough already to feel that his argument might be turned against him, and that if one was to set in a line all the errors committed by theologians—and among the number are some very lamentable ones—we should encounter a list at least as long as could be drawn from philosophy? We quote this example to show that it is not in small points, in detail, that it is desirable to treat these great questions. With such a method we can never escape recriminations.

does not hesitate to seek confirmation of the victory which it has adjudged to itself, in recourse to weapons which are anything but rational, which impose the silence of fear, not that of acquiescence.

We are happily delivered from any such apprehension. But the struggle in the domain of ideas is not finished and will probably never be finished. It recurs again in that of liberty and of authority. From our historical point of view, we cannot discuss the relative legitimacy of either the one or the other of these two claims. Relative or historical legitimacy supposes, not an absolute right, but a relative right depending on the wants which any institution or power is alone in a condition to satisfy. The fact is that, since the day in which reflection dominated individual and collective life, it has been no more possible to dispense with religious tradition than with philosophy. What would the ignorant multitude do without a certain authority, telling them at least which path to follow? And what stifling despotism, what mortal stagnation, when authority is not tempered and in the end rectified by liberty! We think we need not affirm that, wherever the battle is being fought, we are on the side of liberty. In the best regiment there are always some soldiers who do it little honour; and perhaps, taking them all in turn, we should find in each of them vices of constitution or of character. But in time of war we do not pause before such details. We look, before all, at the banner; and if this banner be that of national independence, of our country and of freedom, it is not the moment to talk about trifles; we rush on to fire with the rest, and we think only of the great ideas which its symbolical folds represent, and of all the brave men who are ready to die in its defence.

But it is not being unfaithful to the cause of liberty to try if we cannot find the terms, if not of an impossible agreement, at least of a *modus vivendi* which would allow of the maintenance of pacific relations. It is clear that there can be no question of a submission which would be equivalent to suicide. The first condition of the indefinitely prolonged truce which we should like to see accepted on both sides is the persuasion that we must resign ourselves to the co-existence of the two adversaries. Traditional theologians have often denied the right of independent thought, but can we say that philosophers and their partizans have always done justice to the opposite point of view?

We have said that dogmatic theology always arose from the fusion of philosophical doctrines with elements furnished by tradition. It has many times happened to philosophy not to recognize itself in dogma, and while believing that it was fighting against a foreign power, it was upon itself that it directed its blows. Then it was said, It is the fault of the theologians; why did they not present their philosophical doctrines under their authentic form? Why have they mixed up and disguised them? Simply because theologians did not deal with abstract theory, but with concrete, positive religion, having to do with real life.

Take, for instance, from the historical point of view, and without seeking either to confirm or to oppose it, the dogma of the divinity of Jesus Christ. This dogma is the result of two great movements of idea, one of purely philosophical origin, the other of religious origin. The latter has for its point of departure the sentiment of a divine ideal of moral beauty, of purity, of obedience and of heroism, such as is revealed in the person of Jesus. This sentiment is carried very far, becomes enthusiastic, and very soon finds its Jewish formula in this expression: Jesus is the Messiah. After his death he is the Risen One who now dwells in heaven. The apostle Paul arrives upon the scene. Already the historical features of the Son of Man begin to be effaced in the dazzling nimbus with which the veneration of his followers has surrounded his head; and although still forming part of humanity, the Christ of Paul is so heavenly, so sublime, that he begins to leave history in order to enter into metaphysical regions, and to become the centre, the means and the end of creation. Jesus, borne up by the enthusiasm which he has inspired in his disciples, then slowly rises towards God by a continuous ascent.

But in the midst of Hellenic Judaism, and without any relation of origin with the gospel, a metaphysical theory arose and was also propagated, that of the Word, this God of second rank, this organ of creation and of revelation, who concentrates in himself and displays to the world the divine idea as opposed to matter, to the flesh and to darkness. The religious movement which led to the exaltation of Jesus coincides with the philosophical movement of which the theory of the Word is the essential idea. Scarcely a century had rolled away and already the fusion took place. Jesus, ascending to God, meets the Word, which descends from him; soon they become only one; and evangelical history in its turn is transmuted into the same sense by the pen of the Philonian author of the fourth Gospel.

There is thus a confluence of philosophy and of religion, which—after interminable debates, after Sabellius, Paul of Samosatus, Arius, Macedonius and others, had been rejected by the episcopal majority; after Nice, after Constantinople, Ephesus and Chalcedony—ended at last in the orthodox dogma of the Trinity as it is unfolded in the creed attributed to Athanasius, the *Quicumque*.

As a result of this, if later philosophy feels bound to attack this dogma, it ought not to forget that after all it was philosophy which gave rise to it. If it had not produced the metaphysical theory of the Word, the first Christian generations would not have been led away by it, and would not have applied it to the person of Jesus. Such was the prestige exerted by this personage, that both sides, Jew and Greek, thought they could not too highly honour him. The Jew, who could conceive nothing superior to his Messiah, said, It is he! And when Christianity began to speak Greek, the Greek, who could conceive nothing higher, after God, than the divine Word, also said, It is he! But it must be admitted that, if there is a culprit, it is Platonism. It is because they desired to think philosophically, because they sought to arrange their creeds, their sentiments and their primitive traditions, in a rational form that Christian thinkers applied the notion of the Word to Jesus Christ.

But, then, whence comes it that dogma, born of the engrafting of philosophy on religion, extends and expands under conditions with which philosophy and reason have nothing to do?

The chief cause of that is, that dogma seeks to satisfy other needs than those of reason. If it is possessed by a notion or by a philosophical theory, it is not for the sake of the lovely eyes of philosophy, but for the exclusive satisfaction of the religious sentiment. That done, it marches onwards, bold, imperturbable, not stopping even before the contradictory or the absurd, often even enjoying it with transport, as if it saw there a mark of divine favour. That does not prevent it from employing in its course a number of notions and of definitions which it borrows from philosophy, but its logic is absolutely controlled by the end at which it aims. It has raised Jesus so high, that it has made of him a divine being. Let us admit that it is right. It will not henceforward be content until it has established at Nice that the Son is of the same substance with the Father. That again will not suffice. This eternal Son is incarnate, and it is because he is made man that he has worked out the salvation of men. It is thence necessary to maintain his true humanity not less carefully than his divinity. Ephesus and Chalcedony are the complement of Nice, and from them will go forth the doctrine of "the two natures," or of the God-man, possessing at once, distinctly and yet without separation, the divine nature and the human nature in the unity of his person. That is not yet all. The human nature is endowed with will, the divine nature also; and what would happen if the human will and the divine will contradicted each other in the person of the God-man? To escape this peril, the *monothelites* claim that in him the divine will exists alone. But to suppress the human will is to do violence to the integrity of human nature. Orthodoxy, fixed at this point at Constantinople in 680, thus consists in believing that there are in the God-man a divine will and a human will, but that the human will is always and necessarily in accord with the divine will. All that is excessively subtle, but inexorably logical in view of the end pursued. On the other hand, it cannot be denied that throughout this history philosophy plays a great part, although subordinated to the religious sentiment seeking its satisfaction; and while this sentiment retains its power and its prestige, the objections of reason will have little influence on dogma.

We might make the same remarks on other dogmas, such as that of the Fall, or of the Redemption, or of the authority of the Church. Historical science is still very recent, since it does not date beyond this century. It has, however, produced in Germany works of the highest order on the *History of Dogma*. These show clearly the persistent advance of the human mind on the domain of religious thought. They show also how dogmas are born, how they grow and spread, how at last they decline and end by dying. That last moment comes in which they have nothing more to say to the religious sentiment. Then reason resumes all its rights, and judges as a monarch. There are dogmas in Christianity which have become extinct, as, for example, the nearly approaching end of the world. There are others which tend to extinction, such as those which maintain the existence of demons and the reality of their relations with men. What educated and sensible man in the present day still believes in sorcerers?

To sum up: Religion, the daughter of spontaneous feeling, and Philosophy, the daughter of free reason, are two sisters of unequal age, who often quarrel, but can never dispense one with the other. According to our view, there is a common ground on which, the legitimacy of the principle of each of them being admitted, it would be possible to establish a continuity of pacific relations and of reciprocal services. There should be, on the religious side, gratitude for the part which philosophy has always taken in the development of religious thought and in the intellectual forms which give it its normal expression; on the philosophical side, a sympathetic rallying to the most liberal and the most scientific evolution of religious thought in a fixed period.

But even outside this solution, for which only a small number on each side are sufficiently prepared, the conviction that the co-existence and the mutual action of these two great powers form a part of the normal, natural and necessary development of the human mind, already suffices for mutual regard to replace former acrimony, and of this conviction religious history furnishes peremptory demonstration.

IX.

MORALITY.

RELIGION, which aspires to secure to man the harmonious synthesis of his personal life with the universe, of which he occupies one point, thence finds itself in close relation with those higher conditions of human life which lead to the triple category of the true, the good and the beautiful. When studying its historical relations with theology and philosophy, we looked at its relations with the true; we must now consider those which it sustains with the good—that is, with *morality*.

From the historical point of view, morality may be defined in two ways: either it is the realization in life of the ideal of good such as man conceives it, or it is the philosophical theory and the rule of this realization.

Clearly, we have to concern ourselves with the history of practical morality rather than with the systems of moralists. Morality is much older than moralists, just as religion by a long way preceded theologians. We must devote some moments to an inquiry into its origin or its principle. We here find ourselves in the presence of two theories. One supposes that morality springs from a natural disposition of the human mind to make the judgments which it applies to acts and intentions depend on a notion *sui generis*, that of duty, which must not be confounded with any other, not even with that of utility. The other will have it that it is only a transformation of this notion of the useful. The numerous variations, the very contradictions in the moral sense, the desire of explaining everything in human nature without having recourse to principles existing outside it and certain sensual and materialistic tendencies, have led some people to see in morality only a superior form of intelligent, experienced egotism, which discovers at last that it is more advantageous to resist blind allurements, and to submit to that which, in the sequel, takes the name of duty. For instance, every man has an innate tendency to appropriate everything within his reach which can procure him comfort. As far as that goes, every man is the plunderer of his neighbour. *Homo homini lupus.* He began in that way, it is said; but with growing reflection he perceives that such a system, very far from increasing his comfort, diminishes it, and that, in the name of his own interest well understood, it will answer far better to lay down a general rule that each one shall enjoy only the fruits of his own labour, or of that which he can peaceably obtain from others by way of voluntary exchange. Thence the social precept which forbids theft, and the constitution of a social force to prevent it or to punish the thief. Generations succeed and are brought up with the idea that theft is an evil thing; the evil thing becomes disgraceful; and by heredity the precept becomes axiomatic in the conscience. The same genesis is applicable to all other moral rules.

We must begin by admitting that historically this second point of view can be supported by many apparent confirmations. It is a fact that, wherever we can trace them, the beginnings of morality, like those of religion, are very humble. In the present day among populations who have remained very nearly in a primitive state, the elementary principles of that which constitutes morality for us seem for the most part wholly unknown. There are others among whom that which seems to us a frightful crime—infanticide, for instance, or parricide—is a usual and lawful thing. We cannot dispute either the influence of education or that of heredity. Finally, we know the celebrated utilitarian reasoning: there is only one impulse, one motive in man; each loves himself above all; if a man happens to act under the inspiration of love for his friend, it is because he would suffer if he acted otherwise, because he finds happiness in the sympathetic act; it is always his own satisfaction that he seeks; and the only difference between him and the vulgar egotist is reduced to a difference of taste.

All that is very true, but nothing in it all will account for the moral sentiment. Vauvenargues, in the last century, had already observed that the question was to distinguish those who love themselves well from those who love themselves ill. The unity of motive in no way explains the diversity of direction. Heredity, education and custom, are very powerful in determining the permanence of characteristics of race; but how will they explain the first appearance of these characteristics? Say that morality is formed by the action of moral educators—is not this to reason like those who maintain that religion was primarily the work of the priests? And if we cannot imagine the effect of any education on beings who are not capable of being educated—in other terms, if all education implies that the end which it proposes to itself already virtually exists potentially in the being who receives it—what could moral education do for man if he had not been endowed with the moral faculty? Let us take care that we are not led away by words. Utilitarian experience may very well teach us that a society in which theft is prevented and punished, finds itself in a much happier position than if it allowed it free scope unpunished. But it will never convince us that we ought to subordinate ourselves and to sacrifice ourselves to the general interest and abstain from theft, if we could commit it quite safely. If we deceive ourselves in our calculations of self-interest, we may experience vexation; but this sentiment has nothing in common with that of moral grief or of remorse. What do we say? When we hesitate as to the judgment to be pronounced on those of our actions the consequences of which are to be regretted, we are happy if we can say sincerely that we have been unskilful or improvident, but that we had no bad intention. The sentiment of moral innocence thus consoles us for defective utility. Utilitarians too often forget that there is no logical connection between the experience of the useful and the moral facts which they contend spring out of it. The greater part of us may certainly be more than once in a position to recall the old adage, "*Fais ce que dois, advienne qui pourra!*" Substitute for this noble motto, Do what is most useful to you, come what may—do you not see that you change it into a maxim by which the vilest rascals would profit?

We must, then, in morality, as in religion, recognize in the human mind a spontaneous disposition, *sui generis*, arising from its natural constitution, destined to expand in the school of experience, but which that school can never create.

This expansion, however, is not more primitive in humanity than in the case of a child newly born. It is not more astonishing to see primitive or undeveloped people commit without any remorse what we should call a great crime, than it is to learn that they can consider as personal and adorable beings so many inanimate things which are completely strange to the life of the mind. Mark always, that if a people absolutely destitute of any religious notion has never been discovered, we also know none whose moral life is absolutely *nil*. On this point also we must renounce the beautiful dream of the last century. There is no more a primitive morality lovely and pure, than there is a primitive religion simple and free from error. Morality, like religion, began very low to rise very high; and in the two spheres, the progress made by one part of the species, or by its chosen ones, does not prevent the rest from long remaining in the prejudices and the ignorance of a prior age. There are superstitions in morality as well as in religion.

This parallelism in moral development and in religious development does not prevent religion and morality being in principle, and during a great part of their history, independent. It in no way follows from the definition of them that they must necessarily coalesce. Religion desires to realize the synthesis of the human spirit and of the superior spirit whose existence and sovereignty man believes that he discerns in the world. There is nothing there which is beforehand and specifically moral. It may even happen that, with the idea of attaining to the union which he seeks with the divine spirit, man may have recourse to means which morality rejects. To that end he represents to himself the object of his adoration in such a way that, in order to please him, he believes himself obliged to perform acts which his conscience condemns in relation to his kind. Nations who have for ages renounced anthropophagy, have long persisted in offering human victims as food for their gods. In certain sanctuaries, thousands of women have made the grievous offering of their chastity to divinities of fierce sensuality; and if man imagines that his god demands before all things an undivided dominion for his orthodoxy, he devotedly abandons himself to the crimes of fanaticism, and inoffensive and gentle beings become like ferocious animals.

Morality, in its turn, forms and unfolds itself independently of religious tradition. The gods of paganism are dissolute, arbitrary, vindictive and pitiless. That does not prevent their worshippers from attaining notions of moral purity, of justice and of clemency, which definitively take their place in the general conscience. The Old Testament very often speaks of a terrible Jahveh, a destroyer, wreaking fearful vengeance on those who have offended him; nevertheless, on this very ground sprang up the morality pre-eminently of mercy and of pardon. In short we see every day that the real morality of men is by no means necessarily proportionate to the intensity of their religious feelings.

But let us guard against supposing this reciprocal independence as definitive and absolute. Religion in the end attracts morality into its sphere, and morality investigates and corrects religion. Everything, in fact, is interdependent in man and in history, as in the world. The first intervention of the moral order in the religious order, and reciprocally, took place when man rose to the notion that his gods are the founders and sustainers of the general order of the world. If the world is not chaos—if day, night, seasons, follow a regular course—it is because the gods watch over and maintain the order of things against the ill-omened powers who would disturb it. But it is not only in the physical world that order should be maintained by divine power—it is also in human society, in the family and in the city. There also the law of order is laid down. Who has ordained it? Who maintains and sanctions it? The gods. And, according to the polytheistic method of the division of divine labour, the developed mythologies attribute the care of certain moral laws to certain divinities. Vesta is the protectress of domestic happiness; Juno presides over conjugal fidelity; Jupiter chastises perjurers and the violators of hospitality; and the terrible Eumenides pursue to the ends of the earth the unpunished criminals who fly from the presence of their crime.

Elsewhere—in Persia, for instance—physical evil and moral evil form only one single whole; it is the same with physical and moral good; and religion consists in a continuous dramatization of the struggle between these two powers. This dualist notion is carried into Christianity, in which for so long the prince of darkness and of evil, Satan, was considered as an actual rival, a furious antagonist, of the Eternal Father. In China, the conservative laws of the empire are emanations from heaven. In India, Brahmanism envelopes the whole life in a network of precepts. Morality is nothing more than the systematic application of the religious idea to life. By a rebound, in the original Buddhism, morality supplants religion. At least Buddhism, which denies on principle all concrete religion, admits a sovereign moral order, and logically ought not to recognize any other sovereignty.

This entrance of moral prepossession into the sphere of religious beliefs will have the effect of determining in a very exact sense the direction of ideas relating to a future life. Life beyond the tomb, which also formed a part, though sometimes in a very vague way, of the universal beliefs, assumes another character when seen from the moral point of view; it becomes the place of divine rewards. This forms a new chapter of religious history.

The connection between religion and morality becomes still closer in monotheistic religions. There is there no longer any division of divine labour. Everything—the physical world, human society, human personality—has but one master, and that master all-powerful. Moral order is his work by the same right and as completely as the visible order. Obedience to the moral law is, then, essentially a religious duty. *Per contra*, the progress of moral ideas re-acts upon the notion which is formed of their supreme source. In monotheism, man does not admit that there can exist any moral perfection which would not coincide with the divine will. Consequently his religious ideal rises and becomes purified at the same time as his moral ideal. We may even say that in the gospel religion and morality are no longer easily to be distinguished. At least, when by the light of modern criticism we go back to the personal teaching of Jesus, we find this characteristic trait, that upon the basis of the monotheistic principle and of the affinity of nature between man and God (an affinity which is expressed by the *filial* relation of man with God), the religion of Jesus moves on independently of dogma and of rite, consisting essentially of strictly moral provisions and applications.

We ought to ask ourselves if morality has gained or lost by this close alliance with religion. The answer to this question, so much debated in the present day, cannot be very simple. In a general way, we may say that the characteristic of the religious sentiment, when it is associated with another element of human life, is to render this element much more intense and more powerful. Who does not know the exceptional vigour which patriotism, the spirit of sacrifice, sustained activity and devotion under all its forms, borrow from their alliance with the religious sentiment? Seeing that the moral weakness of man is as evident as the necessity for the moral life, we have the right to conclude from this simple observation that as a general rule morality gains in attractiveness, in power and in strength, by its alliance with religion.

But it cannot be denied either, that too often unenlightened religion has perverted the moral sense or weakened it.

Thus the external sanction promised to morality by so many religions often risks the debasement of human morality to the level of the most utilitarian calculation. Good, to be done, ought to be loved for its own sake ; evil, to be seriously avoided, ought to produce horror. Could we put much confidence in the probity of a man whom fear of the police and of the law alone prevented from stealing? So, paradise and hell correspond to really moral notions only when they are divested of their mythological garb, and we are convinced of the truth that the good man carries heaven in his heart—and that if the wicked man is not in hell, hell is in him. The only consideration in extenuation of this judgment is, that in the infancy of the mind, individual or collective, it is difficult to rise to this height of view. As an apostle has said, childhood is the age of law, which encourages and punishes ; in the age of reflection, it is the charm of goodness and its supreme beauty, which preaches morality.

In the second place, the junction of morality and of religion often leads to that exaggeration of morality called *asceticism*. This is the principle in virtue of which the natural appetites and desires should be not only controlled and governed, but fought against, weakened and as far as possible annihilated. Asceticism invents suffering where nature itself has not provided it. It condemns comfort as a thing in itself reprehensible. The reduction of the body to the condition of a corpse would be its ideal. Most of the religions which have assigned a large place to morality have foundered on this rock, especially Brahmanism, Buddhism, and the Christianity of the middle ages. Not only has true morality had nothing to gain from the extravagances of asceticism, not only does this religious error render man incapable of acquitting himself of his duties towards human society, but too many instances prove that, there as elsewhere, nature, which yields to rational order, revolts against violence. We recall the words of Pascal, so true in spite of their coarseness, concerning what happens to man, who is neither angel nor beast, when he conceives the unfortunate idea of wishing to become an angel.

A third kind of wrong which religion can do to morality occurs when it does not distinguish morality from ritualism. Religion, we have seen, always gives birth to a certain symbolism, and this symbolism to a ritual. Nothing can be more legitimate up to the moment in which confusion, ordinarily sufficiently self-interested, arises between moral duty and ritualistic observance, and this moment arrives when religion establishes equality between the two obligations. Often there results, from the extreme importance attached to the performance of the rite, this very demoralizing consequence, that the punctual observer of the rite is considered to be more nearly united to God or to the normal ideal of life, notwithstanding terrible violations of the moral law of which he may be guilty, than the good man who has neglected or refused to submit to ritual obligations. The rite may thus become an anæsthetic of conscience. Exactly the same remark applies to religions which make orthodoxy or the accuracy of belief a primary obligation imposed on man.

It is, then, by utilitarianism, asceticism, ritualism, and the absorbing prejudice in favour of orthodoxy, that the alliance of religion and of morality may be injurious to the latter. The evil effects of this alliance proceed from an evil direction given to religion itself. Religious history records, along with these deviations of the religious sentiment, the rectifications which the prophetic spiritualist and reformer suggests and ends by achieving.

Finally, let us notice the important part which the moral view, once developed, has taken in the modification and direction of religious thought.

Man, in possession of a moral sense of some delicacy, is not slow to perceive that he is always, do what he may, inferior to his moral ideal. In the religions which promise a reward founded on moral merit or demerit, the fear of divine chastisement adds a very considerable weight to all that which urges man to seek in religion the synthesis of the contradictions of destiny. It is that which gives rise to all the expiatory rites which occupy so large a place in the history of religions, and to the doctrine of an original fall, which we discover elsewhere than in Christian tradition. It is the same feeling also which has given so much power to religions offering a *redemption* to man—that is to say, a means or method of returning to peace with them. This is the domain in which mythology longest endured, as may be seen in the history of the dogma of redemption; it is also that in which religious philosophy can best succeed in disengaging the sublime truth which it expresses with more or less clearness throughout the definitions of traditional dogmatics.

We have not to take part in the debate going on in the present day between the adversaries and the partizans of what is called independent morality. We have shown that we have little taste for these radical divisions which are claimed to be established between neighbouring questions, which may be distinct, but which always end by joining together again when their lines are prolonged. It is clear that this question will be resolved differently according as it is looked at from the social or from the individual point of view. The want of evidence of religious truth, which arises from the very fact of the extreme diversity of creeds, makes us unable to seek in a religious doctrine the foundation or the principle of social life. On the other hand, no society could subsist if it did not start from certain principles determining the social relations of its members, and these principles come into the sphere of morality. It may be said perhaps that moral truths are not always more evident than religious truths. That is true; but there is here a *force majeure;* and society, which gets on very well with several religions, could not adapt itself to several public moralities. From the social point of view, morality is, then, independent of all the rest, and ought to be so considered.

But, from the individual point of view, the question which the spiritual tribunal of each one of us is alone qualified to decide is, whether we ought not to congratulate the man who derives from his religious convictions, freed from narrowness, from utilitarianism and from superstition, the source, the charm and the vigour of his moral life. Without condemning any one, but persuaded that for most men the alliance thus understood between religion and morality cannot but be salutary, we pronounce in the affirmative.

X.

ART.

Art is the domain of the beautiful, as morality is that of the good, and religious synthesis ought to include it also among its various tributaries. Numerous definitions of it have been given. The only one which can embrace all its forms—which applies to arts of sight, such as dancing, architecture, sculpture and painting, as well as to arts of hearing, like music, poetry and eloquence—is that which sums it up as the penetration of the ideal and of matter effected by the will and the labour of man.

It has been sometimes sought to reduce art to an imitation as exact as possible of nature, and this definition is found in Plato and in Aristotle, who in proposing it have not given proof of great perspicacity. *Still life deception* would then be the end of art. If architecture had done nothing but imitate nature, it would have produced only grottos, beavers' huts, bee-hives, ant-hills and birds'-nests. Music would have limited itself to offering us warblings, hummings and croakings. Even in arts such as painting and sculpture, where imitation is of unquestionable importance, it is necessary that it should derive its inspiration from art.

The wax figure, which resembles the living body to such an extent as to challenge the greatest masterpieces of statuary, can never be worth so much from an artistic point of view as the smallest terra-cotta in which the genius of a true artist is revealed.[1]

---

[1] This is why, even in portraits, photography, however highly perfect it may be, even if it should paint colours with as much accuracy as it draws lines, will never replace the pencil. The reason is, that the expression of the face constantly changes,

It results from the definition given, that religion and art are by nature independent of each other, but this independence does not exclude intimate and frequent relations.

Art, for instance, will penetrate into the religious domain much more easily than into the philosophical, because religion is a concrete and real thing, while philosophy is the reign of abstraction. How can any one clothe in artistic forms the moral theory of Kant or the dialectics of Hegel? Religion, the daughter of sentiment, which seeks its rational expression in theology, but which, always preserving its mystic nature, speaks to the heart and to the imagination not less than to the intellect, will lend itself infinitely more readily to the exigencies as well as to the efforts of art.

Art and religion met very early in symbolism. We may remember that the symbol rests on the sentiment of an analogy uniting together things of very different nature, and giving visible and tangible form to ideas which have, however, nothing really in common with the object which they profess to represent. Symbol is, then, like art, the combination of an idea and of a sensible object. Only this combination is merely external, a simple juxtaposition, while art is the penetration of one by the other. The symbol tends to become a work of art, and art furnishes the most beautiful symbols.

But a long time must elapse before religion and art coincide at the point of coalescing in finished works, and in some sort combining their two natures. Religion begins by demanding genuine service from art. The first symbols are ordinarily very rude. The *menhirs*, pious images made of clay to represent some divinity, the idols of savage nations, have nothing in com-

---

and that the art of the portrait-painter, whether he takes it into account or not, consists in seizing the central expression, that to which all the others relate, that which photography can never give. There are portraits which some find very like, others pronounce failures. Why? It is because the painter could reproduce only an accidental expression of the subject. This central expression, which the portrait-painter seizes when he has the genius of his art, does not exist in reality. It must be imagined, not copied. Art is, then, something quite different from simple imitation.

mon with art. This is so because the religious impression and the æsthetic impression fundamentally differ. In the churches which admit the worship of holy images, is the devotion of the crowd directed towards the masterpieces? Would it be the Madonna of Raphaël, or the Descent from the Cross of Rubens, or the Moses of Michael Angelo, which would attract the mass of worshippers? Not at all. The crowd neglects them, and greatly prefers to offer its adoration to vulgar images, which appeal much more forcibly to their dense sense and to their imagination, which delights in the mysterious rather than in the beautiful.

In the midst of relative civilization, and when the means of execution are well perfected, art is still the subordinate of symbol. We may apply this remark to the religious art of ancient Egypt, of India, of China and of Asia Minor, with their monstrous divinities, in which the animal type combines with the human type to result in hideous compositions—gods and goddesses with eight arms, to show that their action extends everywhere; human busts, surmounted by the head of a bull, or of a dog, or of a hawk; colossal sphynxes, with a human head coming out of a lion's neck; goddesses of enamelled clay, with bodies covered with breasts, as if they would thus indicate that the immovable earth is the universal mother, &c.

Architecture attained perfection much sooner than the other arts, entirely through subordinating itself to the exigencies of a religious idea. This arises from the forced simplicity of its means of expression. The Babylonian temple, with its superposed stories, directed towards heaven, as though it would reach thither—and when the Hebrews became acquainted with the great temple of Babel, they had no doubt that such had been the intention of its builders—has something very imposing in its effect. It expresses haughtiness, pride of sovereignty, and expresses it well. The Egyptian temple, with the avenues of towering sphynxes which led to it—its massive masonry—its dimly-lighted apartments—its sanctuary, inaccessible to ordinary mortals—is the eloquent symbol of a religion which makes special appeal to the sentiment of mystery, and which insists on the calm regularity of the divine life—the type of what human life should be. The immense temples of India—not built, but hollowed out of the interior of granite or porphyry mountains, subterranean cathedrals—well denote the colossal, paradoxical character of the Brahman religion, in which man seeks less to rise towards the divinity than to enter into it, in order to be swallowed up in it. It is in the Greek temple that pure art displays itself in intimate harmony with a religion of light and of serenity. It is in Greece also that mythological monsters are humanized and take the actual human form, which made Hegel say that the sphynx at Œdipus was nothing else than the religious enigma propounded by Egypt and solved by Greece.

But there, again, we see that religious development and that of art remain really distinct, even when they seem to blend together. If the Greek religion excels in beauty all others of antiquity, it is far from having attained the highest rank in other respects. It always remains very puerile in its principles, and its moral influence is very small. In return, other religions which are superior to it from the point of view of earnestness and of moral influence, show themselves rather antipathetic to the arts—at least to the arts of sight, such as sculpture and painting.

Art, precisely because it has a sensible or material aspect, may be a danger to religion quite as much as an auxiliary. Here we must always make a distinction. There are religions which reject works of art, somewhat as the fox in the fable disdained the grapes. When, for example, Tacitus tells us of the Germans that they refused to represent their gods under human forms, we may ask how they could have contrived to sculpture or to paint them. The same question may be put in reference to the nomad Semites of the patriarchal periods. But it was not the same with the Persians in the time in which Mazdeism so greatly flourished, nor with the Israelites after the Babylonish captivity, nor with the Mussulmans; and among Christian churches we may remark a salient and well-known difference on the subject of the intervention of certain arts in religious worship.

In antiquity, this rejection of the arts relating specially to sight is associated with the sentiment that any material form given to the divinity belittles him, and has in consequence the effect of profanation. And, from the religious point of view, the most artistic of profanations remains always a profanation. Among the polytheists of Greece and of Rome, there were not wanting reflecting minds who regretted that the vulgar piety was linked as it was with material representations, and who recalled with satisfaction that in the early times religion dispensed with idols. It is, in fact, the consecration of divine images in places of worship which almost inevitably instigates in the mind of the ignorant crowd what is called *idolatry*—that is, adoration, no longer of the divine Being represented by the image, but of the image itself elevated to the rank of a conscious person. Thence also they adore as many distinct divinities as there are renowned images of the same divinity. This explains the implacable war which the prophets and the partizans of strict monotheism, in Arabia as well as in Israel, declared against "graven images." This repugnance did not extend to other arts which did not suffer from the same objection, such as architecture, music or poetry. There are on this point very subtle gradations in the religious sentiment. Thus the Greek Church, faithful to Byzantine tradition, willingly admits pictures painted without perspective, while it rejects statues—that is, it tolerates colour and proscribes relief.

It is remarkable that in the history properly so called of Christianity, we see the reproduction of various phases which run through the religious sentiment in relation to art in religious history in general. Primitive Christianity, in reaction against polytheism, repudiates images and removes them from its sanctuaries. Still, art very early made its way into the Church by the door of symbolism. We see this especially on the tombs in the catacombs. Little by little, this symbolism ascends to the light of day and penetrates into the places of worship, not without provoking some opposition,[1] and at the end of a certain time it becomes confused with art. From that time the veneration of images has a large place in Christian worship. This custom is of great help in the work of converting barbarian masses. There was, however, a very energetic reaction in the East in the time of the iconoclastic emperors, and in the West under Charlemagne, when the Council of Frankfort sought to interdict the worship of images. But it was not of long duration, and the Catholic of the middle ages could appeal to all the arts to display the magnificence of the city of God descended upon earth. Abuse, it is true, showed itself closely allied to use, and the schism of the sixteenth century widely divided Christianity on this point.

It will, then, be interesting to examine a little more thoroughly the question of the relation of art and of religion, not, of course, to discuss theologically the question in debate between the two principal forms of Christianity, but to understand how the religious sentiment has been able in the domain of art to adopt two such opposite courses.[2]

While art, defective, it is true, and without elevation, lent itself in India to materialize the poetic religion of the Vedas, so superior in its purity to the extravagances and quaintnesses of

---

[1] One of those incidents which denote how orthodoxy may vary with epochs is that which St. Epiphanus, the great destroyer of the heretics of his time, relates of himself. He indignantly tore down a velum hung at the entrance of a sanctuary in Palestine, on which was painted a picture of Christ or of some saint. (*Epiph. ad Johann. Hierosol.* Opp. II. 317.)

[2] In considering the above, we may thus distinguish between Catholicism and Protestantism: Catholicism is the expansion of the Christian idea; Protestantism, its concentration. In the first, the Christian idea spreads itself as far as possible over everything at the risk of volatilization, even of loss by spreading itself over that which it ought to repress. In the second, the Christian idea comes back, as it were, upon itself, seeks to seize anew its primary energy at its source, at the risk of ending in a narrow Puritanism, excluding all which is not itself. If we will take account of this distinction, which does homage to the relative greatness and legitimacy of these two large branches of Christianity, at the same time that it indicates beforehand their dangers and their defects, we shall be able to explain most of the differences which separate them, and understand also how the most sincere piety on the one side is scandalized by that which supports and strengthens the other.

Brahmanism, it raised the religion of the Greeks to the highest degree of perfection of which it was capable. The nature and the forms of a religion may, then, undergo grave modifications in consequence of the application of art to its visible manifestations. But so much the more may we ask whether, in proportion as the religious sentiment ascends, it does not detach itself from certain arts which had long afforded it real satisfaction, or rather—and that really comes to the same thing—if all the arts lend themselves in the same degree to serve as the expression or symbol of a religious sentiment become more delicate and purer.

We have mentioned dancing among the arts. It is so in fact. It is the penetration of the common walk and gesture by a certain ideal of measure, of rhythm, of harmony, with a view to expressing a thought. Dancing has been among all nations a religious art. Even at the present day populations called savage know scarcely any other. With us, dancing is an art only at the opera, in the kingdom of the fairies; elsewhere it is simply an amusement enjoyed by the young. Nothing would be more contrary to our ideas of everything than to endeavour to make it once more a part of religious ceremonies. Why?

Because, of all the arts, dancing is the least independent of its material form, which is the human body itself and its locomotion. Instead of elevating its subject and transfiguring it, it tends on one side to lower it. It is difficult to take in earnest the man who dances; he is so like a jumping Jack. He seems to resign all liberty in order to submit himself servilely to a measure and a cadence which are imposed upon him.[1] Louis XIV., who was a great master in all that concerned personal dignity, discountenanced the custom which required the king of France to figure in the ballets. In a word, the material in this art too much conceals the ideal for the purified religious sentiment to be able to find expression in it.

[1] It is on this account that at the present day, even at the opera, the *male* dancer is infinitely less appreciated than the *female* dancer, woman not losing grace of motion so much as man when subjected to a slavish rule.

Dancing is not the only art which has suffered from the same incoherence between it and the religious sentiment revealing itself after a certain time. Another art, much more noble, the appanage of all civilization, and more than ever appreciated among ourselves—the dramatic art—gives rise to a like observation. It is of religious origin, in Greece as in modern Europe. Among us, at the beginning, it was approved and encouraged by the Church. Then it detached itself from the latter, separated itself, in proportion as it attained excellence, and the Church ended by condemning it. If even this severity were relaxed, it is no less true that no one now would dream of restoring to this art the part in Christian worship which in former times was assigned to it. Without doubt, the infinitely greater liberty which the dramatic actor displays as compared with the dancer—the effort of intelligence and of observation which he must make to identify himself with his part—the infinite resources of which he must avail himself in order to awaken the whole gamut of human sentiment—all this raises the dramatic art incomparably higher than that of dancing. Nevertheless, if it is a question of representing beings who are the objects of religious veneration, a certain uneasiness takes possession at once of the author and of the spectator. We endure the devil on the scene, because we scarcely believe in him; but we could not bear to see Christ there, because, even in the absence of faith, we venerate him; and if any one sought to edify us, as in the middle ages, by setting a beautiful girl to ride upon an ass, or by dressing her in such a way as that she may represent the Virgin Mary, we should all, believers and unbelievers alike, see in it only a profanation. There, again, the ideal and the artistic material can no longer penetrate each other;[1] there is jarring—that is, there is a disproportion between the person who is to be represented, the sentiments which his thoughts arouse, the ideas of which he

---

[1] The animated representation of the Passion, periodically performed in the village of Oberammergau, in Bavaria, which is said to be very successful, proves by its exceptionality how much this kind of drama has become foreign to our actual ideas.

forms the centre, and his visible representation. The part is always too high, the actor too low.

This must be one cause of a quite similar, though less generally admitted feeling, through which the religious sentiment turns aside from seeking in pictures and statues the kind of satisfaction which it demands in worship. We do not mean by this to say that the same man who objects to worship images (pictures or statues) does not taste enjoyment of the highest order in contemplating them from an artistic point of view. But then it is the ideal of the painter or of the sculptor which he admires; his own individuality is not concerned in it. If there seems to him disproportion between the work and his idea, his religious feeling is not wounded by it. On the other hand, it must be understood that all do not share this repugnance; and, especially if the worshipper is accustomed to accept passively the religious ideal which is imposed upon him, he will be much less sensible of this disproportion than the man who has laboured to form this ideal for himself.

On the other hand, arts such as architecture, because of the simplicity of the idea which it expresses—music, the most immaterial of all the arts—poetry and eloquence—this last peculiarly appreciated in monotheistic teaching and propagandist religions—are of undisputed religious application. They have also the advantage, as M. de Remusat has very judiciously observed, of producing a *collective* effect—that is, influencing the great mass; and religious sentiment finds quite special pleasure in large gatherings.

To sum up: religion and art are two independent spheres, the constant and reciprocal penetration of which history shows us; and the more an art causes its ideal side to predominate over the material which it employs for its manifestations and the more it aims at collective effect, the more also its alliance with religion is admitted and enjoyed by the religious sentiment.

XI.

CIVILIZATION.

CIVILIZATION is the resultant of all the efforts which man makes to live the true human life, superior to the instinctive and animal life—in one word, the life of the spirit.

Here, again, we find ourselves in the presence of a difficulty of definition. Civilization is not one of those well-marked categories which are clearly distinguished from all which is not them. There is nothing very evident except the two ends of the chain. When we hear of peoples who ignore clothing, the cultivation of the soil, even elementary industry—who live solely on the fruits of the forest, roots, the chances of the chase and of fishing—among whom the law of the strongest alone rules—we say without hesitation that they are savages. If, on the contrary, we see a settled industrious people, organized in such a way that the weak are protected against the violent, that they construct edifices and cultivate the arts and sciences, we should with the same certainty acknowledge that this is a civilized people.

In fact, civilization thus understood is as yet the portion of a minority only of the human race, and races absolutely savage are very rare. But shall we call the Negro tribes civilized, because they are ordinarily sedentary and agricultural; Kaffirs and Hottentots, because they possess numerous herds; the Esquimaux, because they are clothed, and because they take care to lay in a store of dried fish and train oil?

This would be absurd; nevertheless, they are above absolute savagery.

We should be tempted to say rather that civilization begins from the moment when a people possesses a history. Savage peoples have in fact no history. Years and centuries pass with them in the monotony of an existence always the same, giving rise at most only to vague mythical recollections. Civilized peoples have a history, because their life, incomparably richer and more full of incident, passes through crises and revolutions which are prominent points in their development. But this would be to take one of the signs of civilization for civilization itself.

Let us add that, even where it displays itself most powerfully and strikingly, civilization is never finished. It marches onwards towards an ideal always very remote. This ideal is composed of knowledge, of morality or of justice, and of beauty. And in proportion as this is approached, the principle of justice joined to that of humanity requires that participation in civilized life should become more and more general. If anything militates in favour of our modern civilization as compared with the ancient, it is this universalist characteristic—equality in the best sense of the word—which distinguishes it. It is not enough for us, as it was for the ancients, that the higher life of the spirit should be the lot of a few privileged ones; we mean that all shall more and more participate in it. We desire that the sun of the spirit, like that of nature, shall shine on the whole world.

As a consequence of this view, we recognize the beginnings of civilization wherever we find institutions having the culture of the spirit as their end. Thenceforth the wild stock may be considered as having been grafted. It will now depend on many circumstances whether it will bear fruit quickly, good fruit, and abundantly. But from this moment we may say that civilization has entered upon its *being*. The culture of the spirit is, then, the index of an actual and advancing civilization.

But this culture in its turn supposes conditions which are not yet civilization, but which are indispensable to its growth; and these conditions resolve themselves into two fundamental ones, personal security and the division of labour.

If we transport ourselves into the mode of existence of tribes entirely destitute of civilization, we see that both these conditions are reduced to zero. The savage lives in perpetual apprehension of the causes of destruction which menace him, and he must himself make his own weapons, his hut, his canoe, his tools. Association does not make individual efforts converge towards an end of collective interest. It is only in view of some fighting or hunting expeditions that the savage elects a chief. Primordial progress is thus that of a military and judicial organization which shall protect the individuals associated in the primitive clan or horde, and which shall deliver them from this permanent state of defiance and of fear. Then they will be able to labour in some security. Labour, in its turn, will bring about its appropriate division; for diversity of skill and of power will not be long in revealing the superiority of the products of the most practised hands in any kind of definite work. Divided labour induces exchange, consequently commerce; this leads to the adoption of a representative sign of value. Finally, individual security increases with the sense of resources in excess of needs which accumulated labour procures. Man no longer fears dying of hunger, or being devoured by wild beasts, or being brutally destroyed by one stronger than himself.

It is then that new and higher wants, of which no one had previously dreamed, arise. Man has henceforth security, leisure and taste, to exercise his intellect and to relish enjoyments which he never knew before. Useful arts, those which augment his power, his gains, his safety—reading, writing, and calculation—lend a charm to his existence, and urge him in the direction in which, having become in their turn the simple means of progress, they render science, politics and art possible. In that way the conditions of primary security go on improving. He sets himself to make roads, to cross the sea, to transport to distant regions the products of the soil, in order to bring back those which the soil does not produce. Intercourse is established between all the branches of the human family. The relations of nation to nation become marvellous agents of progress. The edifice of civilization is raised. Let us note these two essential points—the solidarity established first between the members of the same human group and then between the different groups; secondly, the incessant, productive labour, indefinitely multiplying its results—which form the necessary, permanent base of this edifice. But it has for its highest crown the triumph of justice, of truth and of beauty, on the earth. Simply material civilization does not rise above the category of mere means.

From these very general considerations—which, however, in our opinion, recommend themselves by their accuracy—result the notions which we must maintain concerning the relations of religion and civilization. This is a subject in regard to which there is in the present day no lack of exaggeration on both sides, one side considering civilization the fruit exclusively of religion, the other looking upon the latter as almost its worst enemy.

History confirms neither of these absolute pretensions.

We had reason to see in one of the early parts of our course, that the only thing which explains the strange separation of the populations of the globe into civilized nations, or those qualified to become civilized, and into nations incapable by themselves or through contact with others of attaining to civilization, is a primordial difference in the religious intuition of the world. It is certain that there is no civilization the cradle of which was not religious. Even in the present day we cannot define the civilization to which we ourselves belong except by the name of Christian civilization. There is a community of moral atmosphere which we all breathe, whatever may be our individual views, which surrounds unbelievers as well as believers, and the reality of which we never recognize more fully than when we are transported into regions holding another tradition. This atmosphere, whatever one may say, is of Christian origin.

Further, if it is true that civilization proceeds from the solidarity which is established among men, and which succeeds the unsocial isolation of savage life, it ought also to be true that all which tends to take them out of this isolation, to bring them together, to lead them to live a life in common, ought also to be favourable to the civilizing movement. On this account, religion, as a powerful means of bringing together and of uniting men, entreating them on that behalf even in virtue of this tendency to inquire into the sympathetic echoes and the concordant emotions which we have observed in the religious sentiment, ought to have been, and in fact has been, a great agent of civilization.

If, further, civilization aims at an end superior to that which would consist solely in developing material well-being—if it aspires after realizing the full life of the spirit—religion has been and always is the vehicle which carries man far from the commonplace of simply animal life, and enables him to discover horizons of supreme beauty, of which he brings back a deep impression, elevating his thoughts, purifying his tastes, preparing him for that life of the spirit of which religion itself forms a part, and which is the real end of civilization.

Finally, labour, which is properly speaking the generator of civilization, is a moral fact, since it supposes effort, foresight and self-control. The savage is always extremely idle. Religion, which concerns itself with the moral province, acts thus also in this way as a civilizing element.

The special history of each religion will show how it has been able to widen or to contract the scope of civilization by the principles which it has propagated, and by the applications of them which it has made to social life.

We say widen or contract, because in fact religious influence has not always borne happy fruit. For example, instead of bringing men together, of uniting them in the sentiment of their solidarity, it has many times succeeded in separating them into bitterly hostile camps and in sowing fanatical hatreds. Religious persecutions, religious wars, religious punishments—those horrible things which would make one believe in Satan if it were possible to believe in him—are in all our memories, and it is unnecessary to dwell upon them.

Religion has always been prejudicial to civilization when it has cherished a spirit of superstitious routine, which places itself obstinately in the way of all scientific progress, of all social reforms, of all the freedom claimed by the human spirit.

It has been its enemy, whether, as in antiquity, it has sanctioned the letting loose of the most shameless passions, or whether, inspired by an absurd asceticism, it has turned man aside from marriage, from the family and from labour.

In other words, religion is civilizing only if it is in harmony with the conditions of civilization. That is, if it can so adapt itself as not to be in conflict with the necessities and the ideas which each new period of human history sees disclosed. An institution, a religious form, which at its first appearing may have been eminently civilizing, may later be like the leading-strings which helped us to take our first steps, but which would singularly hinder us now if we had still to wear them. The investigation of the social effects which each religion has produced will be an interesting chapter in the studies which we devote to the history of religions, and we see in accordance with what principles we may be able to form a sound judgment.

XII.
SCIENCE.

ALL that has gone before justifies us in abridging what we have to say in the name of history concerning the relations of religion with that other queen of the human mind, *science*—that is, the methodical, experimental and constantly verified knowledge of facts of all kinds that the world offers to our observation.

Religion, under all its forms, proposes to man a synthesis between him and the *non-ego*, by uniting him to the spirits, or to a sovereign spirit, which governs all beings. Man delights in the consciousness of this union, and consequently it pleases him to cherish it and to keep it alive by all the means at his disposal.

But the form under which he represents it to himself, the conditions which he believes necessary to its reality, depend upon the notions which he has formed of this world, in which he has felt the active presence of the divinity. Hence, in the beginning, religion is clothed in forms suggested by a very imperfect knowledge of things. For a long time these forms, become traditional, are identified with religion, and it is not difficult to suppose that the latter is indissolubly bound up with the childish ideas in the midst of which it has had its birth.

Science, then, even in virtue of its progress, cannot at the end of a given time do otherwise than unsettle religious traditions, in so far as they imply false ideas which had been previously formed concerning the world and the mode in which it is constituted. The alterations which have thus to be made in the frame necessarily change the picture considerably. Then arises another illusion, which consists in believing that religion itself perishes with its traditional form. History shows that in such a case it never fails to be transformed, and that it does not die.

It would, nevertheless, be an error to think that there is always and necessarily a conflict between religion and science. On the contrary, they can count up periods of union and of reciprocal support. It was most frequently among the primitive priesthoods that the first lines were drawn of what we call science. It was very confused and very elementary; but this embryo science was all the more precious inasmuch as there was no other. It must be said also that the scientific spirit, with the ardour and the complete independence which we recognize in it, is in truth quite a modern thing. Even during all that great period of civilization commencing with Pericles and ending with the Roman empire, in spite of the labours of such men as Aristotle, Archimedes, Hippocrates, Galen, Pliny and certain astronomers and geographers, science continued very timid, and did not succeed in changing to any marked extent the ideas which had been formed of the world. Even among those who were detached from the vulgar polytheism, the pagan principle, the tendency to personify the inanimate, still exercised a great influence, and nothing could be more opposed to scientific progress. For example, even learned men would explain the phenomena of tides as the respiration of the sea, which alternately raised and lowered its vast bosom. The best taught of the ancients looked upon the stars as animated and conscious beings. The bent of the mythological spirit still remained among those who had repudiated mythology itself.

Jewish monotheism, which freed the mind from this kind of polytheistic prejudice—which summed up all divine existence and divine power in the only God, supreme over all the world—ought, it would seem, to have given greater encouragement to the awakening of the scientific spirit. But it also had its drawbacks. Itself quite strange to experimental and methodic science, it sought in divine power the immediate cause of all phenomena. If the thunder rolled, if the sun followed his course, if the seasons succeeded each other, it was because God thus willed it, and that took the place of any other explanation.

The idea has been suggested that it was Christianity which, by absorbing the mind and occupying it in the exclusive domain of religious discussion, had distinctly arrested the sciences which were about to take their upward flight. This is not true. Christianity became absorbing only at the end of the third century. It was not till then that it touched the higher social classes, the only ones in regard to which there could be any question of scientific development. During all the previous period, if the ancient world had been really capable of it, this development would have come into action; but it found no place. After that time, indeed, theological controversies occupied all minds; then the barbarians arrived, and the night was long and dark.

We have said and we repeat, in spite of the paradoxical appearance of the assertion, that it was the orthodox intolerance of the Church in the middle ages which impressed on Christian society this disposition to seek truth at any price, of which the modern scientific spirit is only the application. The more importance the Church attached to the profession of the truth—to the extent even of considering involuntary error as in the highest degree a damnable crime—so much the more the sentiment of the immense value of this truth arose in the general persuasion, along with a resolve to conquer it wherever it was felt not to be possessed. How otherwise can we explain that science was not developed and has not been pursued with constancy, except in the midst of Christian societies? Does not this remarkable phenomenon denote the indirect influence at any rate of previous education? The fact is, that it is only in virtue of this ruling passion that very religious men, such as Bacon, Copernicus, Galileo, Kepler, Pascal, Newton and Linnæus, were able to lay the foundations of the edifice which we admire in the present day.

We need not enlarge on the lamentable history of the conflict which every one knows. The Church, which had at first smiled at the early efforts of modern science, became alarmed for its tradition, founded on a notion of the world which this science modified from day to day. Like the Wagner of the German poet, it was terrified because it could not send back to its prison the genius which it had unchained. Rather it claimed to direct it itself, to dictate to it what it should say, to impose silence on it. Vain efforts! Science has been victorious over tradition. God did not create the world in six days; Joshua did not make the sun stand still; the latter, any more than the moon and the stars, was not fixed in the firmament by the Creator's hand in order to give light to the earth; Jonah was not able to live in his great fish; and the clever and contemptible Pope Alexander VI. would have done better not to have divided the world between the Spaniards and the Portuguese, giving the latter all the East and the former all the West. But to what good end do we multiply all these examples? We are still engaged in this conflict of science and of religious tradition. And what it is important to say is, that neither religion nor science will die of it, and that, as neither can dispense with the other, the philosophic mind ought to consider the means of compassing and of favouring their co-existence.

Science has certainly a right to the most complete autonomy. Her admirable conquests justify all her claims in this respect, and we may look upon the cause of her full and entire liberty as gained.

On the other hand, a certain modesty becomes her. Her progress, however considerable it may be, does not prevent her from coming in contact on all sides with the unknown. Further, she ought to guard against decreeing for herself an apotheosis which more than once already the course of time has invalidated. What will our contemporary sciences be in the eyes of our successors in the year 2000? If the scientific movement goes on as we hope it will, they will be for them what the science of the seventeenth century is for us, as yet little developed in spite of real and important progress. The results of science, moreover, have been very far from negative for the religious soul. Our heaven, in which numberless worlds gravitate like dust—the incalculable periods during which all that now exists was preparing—all these imposing grandeurs of time and space which science has revealed to us—have they not furnished food for the religious sentiment which it never tasted before? He who never ceases to feel the breath of God throughout the immensity of the universe, has the right to re-assure himself in view of all the discoveries yet to be made; and fortified by the experience of ages, he may console himself by the fact that whenever man has succeeded in seizing truth in the world, he has uniformly found it a hundred times more beautiful than anything that he had dreamed.

But, above all, it is well to recognize that definitively, and when thoroughly understood, religion in itself and independent science never ought to be hostile, because in fact they do not respond to the same needs and cannot be substituted the one for the other. If science springs out of the intellectual need of knowing the real and the true in everything, religion meets aspirations of another kind which are not less natural, less inherent in the human spirit. Science proceeds methodically, using hypothesis provisionally only, always subject to experience. It is essentially analytic; and it is on that account that it cannot end in the universal synthesis which the spirit nevertheless also demands. No; even were there nothing hidden in the facts with which it occupied itself—if it could pass without a moment of uncertainty from the formation of nebulæ to that of the latest infusoria, it would have attained only to a certain part; and the universe is more than a part, it is infinite. How, then, will science experimentally disengage the unity binding together the totality of beings? How will it determine the whole course of a river, the source and the mouth of which equally escape it? Science, sovereign mistress in the domain of the finite, cannot go beyond it without contradicting itself. It sometimes happens to some of its least qualified representatives, influenced as they are by their exclusively analytic habits of thought, to imagine that they alone have made the synthesis, because they have carefully enumerated the facts, little and great, the series of which constitutes the object of study. You have, let us suppose, demonstrated that there are only mechanical, physical and chemical laws in action in the human body, and that formerly men were dreaming when they spoke of vital force or of animal spirits; you have labelled all the parts and all the convolutions of the human brain, and have determined with precision the function of each of them in mental operations. It is wonderful; but do you think that you have by that means given the shadow of an explanation of life and thought? And the convergence and the guiding cause, and the source of harmony and of permanent co-ordination, where is it? It is there, however, and it escapes you. Much more would it be the case if it were a question of the synthesis of the universe!

It is then that Religion, not merely in one only of its traditional forms, but in its fundamental and persistent claim, speaks in its turn. "That which you cannot do," it says, "I do; that which you dare not utter, I proclaim; the immense void which your greatest researches always leave, I fill. I am the indestructible aspiration of the human heart. I am the voice of the depths of the soul. I am the bond which unites human dust to absolute thought; and in this bottomless abyss, on the edge of which, in virtue of your very processes, you inevitably arrive, I perceive the supreme reality, that which truly is; I hear from the unfathomable gulf a voice which calls me; I see a light which attracts me. Ah! I may be deceived in the ideas I form. It may be that I possess very little—only symbols, only reflections. What matter? Are you very sure, men of science, that you know exactly the nature of the sun, and does that prevent you from lighting yourselves by his light, from warming yourselves by his heat? In like manner, I venture to affirm the reality of my object, independently of the ideas which I try to form of it, and that satisfies me. Continue your useful, your admirable labours. You worship the Eternal in seeking your aspect of truth; leave me to seek in Him the complete ideal, the presentiment of which raises me from earth, the prevision of which procures me ineffable delights, and let us live in peace."

It is the ardent effort of humanity to respond to this mysterious appeal that we shall endeavour to narrate.

Prospectus of the
THEOLOGICAL TRANSLATION FUND.

As it is important that the best results of recent theological investigations on the Continent, conducted without reference to doctrinal considerations, and with the sole purpose of arriving at truth, should be placed within the reach of English readers, it is proposed to collect, by Subscriptions and Donations, a Fund which shall be employed for the promotion of this object. A good deal has been already effected in the way of translating foreign theological literature, a series of works from the pens of Hengstenberg, Haevernick, Delitzsch, Keil, and others of the same school, having of late years been published in English; but—as the names of the authors just mentioned will at once suggest to those who are conversant with the subject—the tendency of these works is for the most part conservative. It is a theological literature of a more independent character, less biassed by dogmatical prepossessions, a literature which is represented by such works as those of Ewald, Hupfeld, F. C. Baur, Zeller, Rothe, Keim, Schrader, Hausrath, Nöldeke, Pfleiderer, &c., in Germany, and by those of Kuenen, Scholten, and others, in Holland, that it is desirable to render accessible to English readers who are not familiar with the languages of the Continent. The demand for works of this description is not as yet so widely extended among either the clergy or the laity of Great Britain as to render it practicable for publishers to bring them out in any considerable numbers at their own risk. And for this reason the publication of treatises of this description can only be secured by obtaining the co-operation of the friends of free and unbiassed theological inquiry.

It is hoped that at least such a number of Subscribers of *One Guinea Annually* may be obtained as may render it practicable for the Publishers, as soon as the scheme is fairly set on foot, to bring out every year *three 8vo volumes*, which each Subscriber of the above amount would be entitled to receive gratis. But as it will be necessary to obtain, and to remunerate, the services of a responsible Editor, and in general, if not invariably, to pay the translators, it would conduce materially to the speedy success of the design, if free donations were also made to the Fund; or if contributors were to subscribe for more than one copy of the works to be published.

If you approve of this scheme, you are requested to communicate with Messrs. Williams and Norgate, 14, Henrietta Street, Covent Garden, London, and to state whether you are willing to subscribe; and if you are disposed to assist further, what would be the amount of your donation, or the number of additional copies of the publications which you would take.

We are, your obedient servants,

JOHN TULLOCH,	H. J. S. SMITH,
H. B. WILSON,	H. SIDGWICK,
B. JOWETT,	JAMES HEYWOOD,
A. P. STANLEY,	C. KEGAN PAUL,
W. G. CLARK,	J. ALLANSON PICTON,
S. DAVIDSON,	ROBT. WALLACE,
JAMES MARTINEAU,	LEWIS CAMPBELL,
JOHN CAIRD,	RUSSELL MARTINEAU,
EDWARD CAIRD,	T. K. CHEYNE,
JAMES DONALDSON,	J. MUIR.

A Committee selected from the signataries of the original Prospectus agreed upon the works to commence the series. Of these, the following were published in

The *First* Year (1873): 3 vols., 21*s.*

1. KEIM (TH.), HISTORY OF JESUS OF NAZARA. Considered in its connection with the National Life of Israel, and related in detail. Second Edition, re-translated by Arthur Ransom. Vol. I. Introduction; Survey of Sources; Sacred and Political Groundwork; Religious Groundwork.

2. BAUR (F. C.), PAUL, THE APOSTLE OF JESUS CHRIST, his Life and Work, his Epistles and Doctrine. A Contribution to a Critical History of Primitive Christianity. Second Edition, by Rev. Allan Menzies. Vol. I.

3. KUENEN (A.), THE RELIGION OF ISRAEL TO THE FALL OF THE JEWISH STATE. Translated by A. H. May. Vol. I.

The *Second* Year (1874): 3 vols., 21s.

4. KUENEN'S RELIGION OF ISRAEL. Vol. II. Translated by A. H. May.
5. BLEEK'S LECTURES ON THE APOCALYPSE. Edited by the Rev. Dr. S. Davidson.
6. BAUR'S PAUL; the second and concluding volume. Translated by the Rev. Allan Menzies.

The *Third* Year (1875): 3 vols., 21s.

7. KUENEN'S RELIGION OF ISRAEL; the third and concluding volume.
8. ZELLER, THE ACTS OF THE APOSTLES CRITICALLY EXAMINED. To which is prefixed, Overbeck's Introduction from De Wette's Handbook, translated by Joseph Dare, B.A. Vol. I.
9. EWALD'S COMMENTARY ON THE PROPHETS OF THE OLD TESTAMENT. Translated by the Rev. J. Frederick Smith. Vol. I. General Introduction; Yoel, Amos, Hosea, and Zakharya 9—11.

The *Fourth* Year (1876): 3 vols., 21s.

10. ZELLER'S ACTS OF THE APOSTLES. Vol. II. and last.
11. KEIM'S HISTORY OF JESUS OF NAZARA. Vol. II. Translated by the Rev. E. M. Geldart. The Sacred Youth; Self-recognition; Decision.
12. EWALD'S PROPHETS OF THE OLD TESTAMENT. Vol. II. Yesaya, Obadya, Mikha.

The *Fifth* Year (1877): 3 vols., 21s.

13. PAULINISM: a Contribution to the History of Primitive Christian
15. Theology. By Professor O. Pfleiderer, of Jena. Translated by E. Peters. 2 vols.
14. KEIM'S HISTORY OF JESUS OF NAZARA. Translated by A. Ransom. Vol. III. The First Preaching; the Works of Jesus; the Disciples; and the Apostolic Mission.

The *Sixth* Year (1878): 3 vols., 21s.

16. BAUR'S (F. C.), CHURCH HISTORY OF THE FIRST THREE CENTURIES. Translated from the third German Edition. Edited by the Rev. Allan Menzies (in 2 vols.). Vol. I.
17. HAUSRATH'S HISTORY OF THE NEW TESTAMENT TIMES. The Time of Jesus. Translated by the Revds. C. T. Poynting and P. Quenzer (in 2 vols.). Vol. I.
18. EWALD'S COMMENTARY ON THE PROPHETS OF THE OLD TESTAMENT. Translated by the Rev. J. Frederick Smith. Vol. III. Nahum, Ssephanya, Habaqquq, Zakharya 12—14, Yeremya.

The *Seventh* Year (1879): 3 vols., 21s.
19. KEIM'S HISTORY OF JESUS OF NAZARA. Vol. IV. The Galilean Storms; Signs of the approaching Fall; Recognition of the Messiah.
20. BAUR'S CHURCH HISTORY. Vol. II. and last.
21. EWALD'S COMMENTARY ON THE PROPHETS. Vol. IV. Hezeqiel, Yesaya xl.—lxvi.

The *Eighth* Year (1880): 3 vols., 21s.
22. HAUSRATH'S NEW TESTAMENT TIMES. The Time of Jesus. Vol. II. and last.
23. EWALD'S COMMENTARY ON THE PSALMS. Translated by the Rev.
24. E. Johnson, M.A. 2 vols.

The *Ninth* Year (1881): 3 vols., 21s.
25. KEIM'S HISTORY OF JESUS OF NAZARA. Vol. V. The Messianic Progress to Jerusalem.
26. EWALD'S COMMENTARY ON THE PROPHETS. Vol. V. and last. Haggai, Zakharya, Malaki, Yona, Barukh, Daniel.
27. A PROTESTANT COMMENTARY ON THE BOOKS OF THE NEW TESTAMENT: with General and Special Introductions. Edited by Professors P. W. Schmidt and F. von Holzendorff. Translated from the Third German Edition by the Rev. F. H. Jones, B.A. (in 3 vols.). Vol. I. Matthew to Acts.

The *Tenth* Year (1882): 3 vols., 21s.
28. EWALD'S COMMENTARY ON THE BOOK OF JOB. Translated by the Rev. J. Frederick Smith (in 1 vol.).
29. PROTESTANT COMMENTARY. Vol. II. The Pauline Epistles to Galatians.
30. KEIM'S HISTORY OF JESUS OF NAZARA. Vol. VI. and last.

The *Eleventh* Year (1883-84): 3 vols., 21s.
31. PROTESTANT COMMENTARY. Vol. III. and last.
32. REVILLE (Professor ALB., D.D.) PROLEGOMENA OF THE HISTORY OF RELIGIONS. Translated by A. S. Squire. With an Introduction by Professor Max Müller.
33. SCHRADER (Professor E., D.D.) THE CUNEIFORM INSCRIPTIONS AND THE OLD TESTAMENT. Translated by Professor Owen C. Whitehouse. Vol. I. Map.

The *Twelfth* Year (1885-86):
34. PFLEIDERER (Professor O.) THE PHILOSOPHY OF RELIGION ON THE BASIS OF ITS HISTORY. Translated by the Rev. Alex. Stewart and the Rev. Allan Menzies. Vol. I. Spinoza to Schleiermacher.

Beyond these, the following Works are in the hands of Translators, and will be included in the next years' Subscriptions:

SCHRADER (Professor E.) THE OLD TESTAMENT AND CUNEIFORM INSCRIPTIONS. Vol. II.

PFLEIDERER'S PHILOSOPHY OF RELIGION. Translated by the Rev. Alexander Stewart, of Dundee, and the Rev. Allan Menzies Vols. II.—IV.

CONTENTS OF THE
THEOLOGICAL TRANSLATION FUND LIBRARY.

A Selection of Six or more volumes may be had on direct application to the Publishers, at 7s. per volume.

1. **Baur (F. C.) Church History of the First Three** Centuries. Translated from the Third German Edition. Edited by the Rev. Allan Menzies. 2 vols. 8vo. 21s.
2. **Baur (F. C.) Paul, the Apostle of Jesus Christ, his** Life and Work, his Epistles and Doctrine. A Contribution to a Critical History of Primitive Christianity. Second Edition. By the Rev. Allan Menzies. 2 vols. 21s.
3. **Bleek's Lectures on the Apocalypse.** Edited by the Rev. Dr. S. Davidson. 10s. 6d.
4. **Ewald (H.) Commentary on the Prophets of the** Old Testament. Vol. I. Yoel, Amos, Hosea, Zakharya, c. 9—12. Vol. II. Yesaya, Obadya, Mikha. Vol. III. Nahum, Ssephanya, Habaqquq, Zakharya, c. 12—14, Yeremya. Vol. IV. Hezeqiel, Yesaya, c. 40—66. Vol. V. Anonymous Pieces, Haggai, Zakharya, Malaki, Yona, Barukh, Daniel, Index. Translated by the Rev. J. Frederick Smith. 5 vols. 8vo. Each 10s. 6d.
5. **Ewald (H.) Commentary on the Psalms.** Translated by the Rev. E. Johnson, M.A. 2 vols. 8vo. Each 10s. 6d.
6. **Ewald (H.) Commentary on the Book of Job,** with Translation by Professor H. Ewald. Translated from the German by the Rev. J. Frederick Smith. 1 vol. 8vo. 10s. 6d.
7. **Hausrath (Professor A.) History of the New Tes**tament Times. The Time of Jesus. By Dr. A. Hausrath, Professor of Theology, Heidelberg. Translated, with the Author's sanction, from the Second German Edition, by the Revs. C. T. Poynting and P. Quenzer. 2 vols. 8vo. 21s.
8. **Keim (Th.) History of Jesus of Nazara.** Considered in its connection with the National Life of Israel, and related in detail. Vol. I. Survey of Sources, Paul, Gospels, the Sacred Groundwork. Vol. II. The Sacred Youth, Self-recognition, and Decision. Vol. III. The Galilean Springtime. Vol. IV. The Galilean Storms, Recognition of the Messiah. Vol. V. The Messianic Progress to Jerusalem, the Decisive Struggle, the Farewell, the Last Supper. Vol. VI. The Messianic Death, Burial and Resurrection, the Messianic Place in History. Translated by Arthur Ransom and the Rev. E. M. Geldart. 6 vols. 8vo. Each 10s. 6d.

9. **Kuenen (A.) The Religion of Israel to the Fall of** the Jewish State. Translated by A. H. May. 3 vols. 8vo. 31s. 6d.

10. **Pfleiderer (Professor O.) Paulinism**: a Contribution to the History of Primitive Christian Theology. Translated by E. Peters. 2 vols. 21s.

11. **Pfleiderer (Professor O.) The Philosophy of Religion** on the Basis of its History. I. History of the Philosophy of Religion from Spinoza to the present Day. Vol. I. Spinoza to Schleiermacher. Translated by the Rev. Allan Menzies and the Rev. Alex. Stewart, of Dundee. 10s. 6d. (Vol. II. in the Press.)

12. **Protestant Commentary on the New Testament;** with General and Special Introductions to the Books, by Lipsius, Holsten, Lang, Pfleiderer, Holtzmann, Hilgenfeld, and others. Vol. I. Introduction, the Gospels, the Acts. Vol. II. Epistles to the Romans, Corinthians, Galatians. Vol. III. Ephesians, Philippians, Colossians, Thessalonians, Pastoral Epistles, Revelations. Translated by the Rev. F. H. Jones. 3 vols. 8vo. 31s. 6d.

13. **Reville (Rev. Dr.) Prolegomena of the History of** Religion, with Introduction by Professor Max Müller. 10s. 6d.

14. **Schrader (Professor E.) The Old Testament and** the Cuneiform Inscriptions. Translated by the Rev. Owen C. Whitehouse. (In 2 vols.) Vol. I. Map. 10s. 6d. (Vol. II. in the Press.)

15. **Zeller (E.) The Acts of the Apostles Critically** Examined. To which is prefixed Overbeck's Introduction from De Wette's Handbook. Translated by Joseph Dare. 2 vols. 8vo. 21s.

The price of the Works to Subscribers, 7s. per vol.

Works in the Press:

Pfleiderer (Professor O.) The Philosophy of Religion. Translated by the Rev. Alexander Stewart, of Dundee, and the Rev. Allan Menzies. Vols. II.—IV.

Schrader's Old Testament and Cuneiform Inscriptions, Vol. II.

All new Subscribers may purchase any of the previous volumes at 7s. instead of 10s. 6d. per volume. A selection of six or more volumes may also be had at the Subscriber's price, or 7s. per volume, upon direct application to the Publishers.

THE HIBBERT LECTURES.

1886.—**Professor J. Rhys. Lectures on the Origin and** Growth of Religion as illustrated in Celtic Heathendom. 8vo, cloth. 10s. 6d.

1885.—**Professor O. Pfleiderer. Lectures on the Influence** of the Apostle Paul on the Development of Christianity. Translated by the Rev. J. F. Smith. 8vo, cloth. 10s. 6d.

1884.—**Professor Albert Reville. Lectures on the Ancient** Religions of Mexico and Peru. 8vo, cloth. 10s. 6d.

1883.—**The Rev. Charles Beard. Lectures on the Reformation** of the Sixteenth Century in its Relation to Modern Thought and Knowledge. 8vo, cloth. 10s. 6d. (Cheap Edition, 4s. 6d.)

1882.—**Professor Kuenen. Lectures on National Religions** and Universal Religions. 8vo, cloth. 10s. 6d.

1881.—**T. W. Rhys Davids. Lectures on the Origin and** Growth of Religion as illustrated by some Points in the History of Indian Buddhism. 8vo, cloth. 10s. 6d.

1880.—**M. Ernest Renan. On the Influence of the Institutions,** Thought and Culture of Rome on Christianity, and the Development of the Catholic Church. Translated by the Rev. Charles Beard. 8vo, cloth. 10s. 6d. (Cheap Edition, 2s. 6d.)

1879.—**P. Le Page Renouf. Lectures on the Origin and** Growth of Religion as illustrated by the Religion of Ancient Egypt. Second Edition. 8vo, cloth. 10s. 6d.

1878.—**Professor Max Müller. Lectures on the Origin** and Growth of Religion as illustrated by the Religions of India. 8vo, cloth. 10s. 6d.

Works published by the Hibbert Trustees.

Illustrations of the History of Medieval Thought in the Departments of Theology and Ecclesiastical Politics. By REGINALD LANE POOLE, M.A., Balliol College, Oxford, Ph.D. Leipzig. 8vo, cloth. 10s. 6d.

The Objectivity of Truth. By GEORGE J. STOKES, B.A., Senior Moderator and Gold Medallist, Trinity College, Dublin; late Hibbert Travelling Scholar. 8vo, cloth. 5s.

An Essay on Assyriology. By GEORGE EVANS, M.A., Hibbert Fellow. With an Assyrian Tablet in Cuneiform Type. 8vo, cloth. 5s.

The Development from Kant to Hegel, with Chapters on the Philosophy of Religion. By ANDREW SETH, Assistant to the Professor of Logic and Metaphysics, Edinburgh University. 8vo, cloth. 5s.

Kantian Ethics and the Ethics of Evolution. A Critical Study by J. GOULD SCHURMAN, M.A., D.Sc., Professor of Logic and Metaphysics in Acadia College, Nova Scotia. 8vo, cloth. 5s.

The Resurrection of Jesus Christ. An Essay, in Three Chapters. By REGINALD W. MACAN, Christ Church, Oxford. 8vo, cloth. 5s.

The Ecclesiastical Institutions of Holland, treated with Special Reference to the Position and Prospects of the Modern School of Theology. By the Rev. P. H. WICKSTEED, M.A. 8vo. 1s.

WILLIAMS AND NORGATE,

14, HENRIETTA STREET, COVENT GARDEN, LONDON;
AND 20, SOUTH FREDERICK STREET, EDINBURGH.

14, Henrietta Street, Covent Garden, London;
20, South Frederick Street, Edinburgh.

CATALOGUE OF SOME WORKS

PUBLISHED BY

WILLIAMS & NORGATE.

Agnostic's Progress, An, from the Known to the Unknown. 268 pp. Crown 8vo, cloth. 5s.

Alviella (Count Goblet d') The Contemporary Evolution of Religious Thought in England, America and India. Translated by J. MODEN. 8vo, cloth. 10s. 6d.

Baur (F. C.) Church History of the First Three Centuries. Translated from the Third German Edition. Edited by the Rev. ALLAN MENZIES. 2 vols. 8vo. 21s.
—— Vide Theological Translation Fund Library.

Baur (F. C.) Paul, the Apostle of Jesus Christ, his Life and Work, his Epistles and his Doctrine. A Contribution to the Critical History of Primitive Christianity. Edited by E. ZELLER. Translated by Rev. ALLAN MENZIES. 2 vols. 8vo, cloth. 21s.
—— Vide Theological Translation Fund Library.

Beard (Rev. Chas.) Lectures on the Reformation of the Sixteenth Century in its Relation to Modern Thought and Knowledge. Hibbert Lectures, 1883. 8vo, cloth. [Cheap Edition, 4s. 6d.] 10s. 6d.

Beard (Rev. Chas.) Port Royal, a Contribution to the History of Religion and Literature in France. Cheaper Edition. 2 vols. Crown 8vo. 12s.

Beard (Rev. Dr. J. R.) The Autobiography of Satan. Crown 8vo, cloth. 7s. 6d.

Bible for Young People. A Critical, Historical, and Moral Handbook to the Old and New Testaments. By Dr. H. OORT and Dr. J. HOOYKAAS, with the assistance of Dr. KUENEN. Translated from the Dutch by the Rev. P. H. WICKSTEED. Vols. I. to IV., Old Testament, 12s.; V. VI., New Testament, 8s. Maps. 6 vols. Crown 8vo, cloth. 20s.

Bleek (F.) Lectures on the Apocalypse. Edited by T. HOSSBACH. Edited by the Rev. Dr. S. DAVIDSON. 8vo, cloth. 10s. 6d.
—— Vide Theological Translation Fund Library.

Channing's Complete Works, including the "Perfect Life," with
a brief Memoir. Centenary Edition. 868 pp. Crown 8vo, 1s.; cloth, 2s.
—— The same, large type, 4to, cloth. 7s. 6d.

Cobbe (Miss F. P.) The Hopes of the Human Race, Hereafter and
Here. Essays on the Life after Death. With a Preface having special
reference to Mr. Mill's Essay on Religion. Second Edition. Crown 8vo,
cloth. 5s.

Cobbe (Miss F. P.) Darwinism in Morals, and (13) other Essays
(Religion in Childhood, Unconscious Cerebration, Dreams, the Devil, Auricular
Confession, &c. &c.). 400 pp. 8vo, cloth. (pub. at 10s.) 5s.

Cobbe (Miss F. P.) The Duties of Women. A Course of Lectures
delivered in London and Clifton. Second Edition. Crown 8vo, cloth. 5s.

Cobbe (Miss F. P.) The Peak in Darien, and other Riddles of Life
and Death. Crown 8vo, cloth. 7s. 6d.

Cobbe (Miss F. P.) A Faithless World. With Additions and a
Preface. 8vo, cloth. 2s. 6d.

Cobbe (Miss F. P.) Broken Lights. An Inquiry into the Present
Condition and Future Prospects of Religious Faith. Third Edition. Crown
8vo, cloth. 5s.

Cobbe (Miss F. P.) Dawning Lights. An Inquiry concerning the
Secular Results of the New Reformation. 8vo, cloth. 5s.

Cobbe (Miss F. P.) Alone to the Alone. Prayers for Theists, by
several Contributors. Third Edition. Crown 8vo, cloth, gilt edges. 5s.

Davids (T. W. Rhys) Lectures on the Origin and Growth of Religion, as illustrated by some Points in the History of Indian Buddhism.
Hibbert Lectures, 1881. 8vo, cloth. 10s. 6d.

Echoes of Holy Thoughts: arranged as Private Meditations before
a First Communion. Second Edition, with a Preface by the Rev. J. HAMILTON THOM, of Liverpool. Printed with red lines. Crown 8vo, cloth. 2s. 6d.

Evolution of Christianity, The. By CHARLES GILL. Second Edition,
with Dissertations in answer to Criticism. 8vo, cloth. 12s.

Ewald (Professor H.) Commentary on the Prophets of the Old Testament. Translated by the Rev. J. FRED. SMITH. Vol. I. Yoel, Amos,
Hozea, and Zakharya ix.—xi. Vol. II. Yesayah, Obadya, Micah. Vol. III.
Nahum, Sephanya, Habaqquq, Zakharya xii.—xiv., Yeremiah. Vol. IV.
Hezekiel, Yesaya xl.—lxvi., with Translation. Vol. V. Haggai, Zakharya,
Malaki, Jona, Baruch, Appendix and Index. Complete in 5 vols. 8vo,
cloth. each 10s. 6d.
—— Vide Theological Translation Fund Library.

Ewald (Professor H.) Commentary on the Psalms. (Poetical Books of the Old Testament. Part I.) Translated by the Rev. E. JOHNSON, M.A. 2 vols. 8vo, cloth. each 10s. 6d.
—— Vide Theological Translation Fund Library.

Ewald (Professor H.) Commentary on the Book of Job. (Poetical Books, Part II.) Translated by the Rev. J. FREDERICK SMITH. 8vo, cloth. 10s. 6d.
—— Vide Theological Translation Fund Library.

Gould (S. Baring) Lost and Hostile Gospels. An Account of the Toledoth Jesher, two Hebrew Gospels circulating in the Middle Ages, and extant Fragments of the Gospels of the First Three Centuries of Petrine and Pauline Origin. By the Rev. S. BARING GOULD. Crown 8vo, cloth. 7s. 6d.

Hanson (Sir Richard) The Apostle Paul and the Preaching of Christianity in the Primitive Church. By Sir RICHARD DAVIS HANSON, Chief Justice of South Australia, Author of "The Jesus of History," "Letters to and from Rome," &c. 8vo, cloth. (pub. at 12s.) 7s. 6d.

Hausrath. History of the New Testament Times. The Time of Jesus. By Dr. A. HAUSRATH, Professor of Theology, Heidelberg. Translated, with the Author's sanction, from the Second German Edition, by the Revds. C. T. POYNTING and P. QUENZER. 2 vols. 8vo, cloth. 21s.
—— Vide Theological Translation Fund Library.

Hibbert Lectures, vide Beard, Davids, Kuenen, Müller, Pfleiderer, Renan, Renouf, Reville, Rhys.

Horne (Rev. W.) Religious Life and Thought. By WILLIAM HORNE, M.A., Dundee, Examiner in Philosophy in the University of St. Andrews; Author of "Reason and Revelation." Crown 8vo, cloth. 3s. 6d.

Jones (Rev. R. Crompton) Hymns of Duty and Faith, selected and arranged. Second Edition. 247 pp. Foolscap 8vo, cloth. 3s. 6d.

Jones (Rev. R. Crompton) Psalms and Canticles, selected and pointed for Chanting. 18mo, cloth. 1s. 6d.
—— Anthems, with Indexes and References to the Music. 18mo, cloth. 1s. 3d.
—— The Chants and Anthems, together in 1 vol. 2s. 6d.
—— A Book of Prayer in 30 Orders of Worship, for Public or Private Devotions. 12mo, cloth, 2s. 6d.
—— The same with the Chants. 18mo, cloth. 3s.

Keim's History of Jesus of Nazara, considered in its connection with the National Life of Israel, and related in detail. Translated from the German by A. RANSOM and the Rev. E. M. GELDART, in 6 vols. 8vo, cloth. each 10s. 6d.
—— Vide Theological Translation Fund Library.

Knighton (W.) Struggles for Life. By WILLIAM KNIGHTON, LL.D.,
Vice-President of the Royal Society of Literature; Author of "The History
of Ceylon," "Forest Life in Ceylon," &c. &c. 8vo, cloth. 10s. 6d.

Kuenen (Dr. A.) The Religion of Israel to the Fall of the Jewish
State. By Dr. A. KUENEN, Professor of Theology at the University, Leyden.
Translated from the Dutch by A. H. MAY. 3 vols. 8vo, cloth. 31s. 6d.
—— Vide Theological Translation Fund Library.

Kuenen (Professor A.) Lectures on National Religions and Universal Religions. Delivered in Oxford and London. By A. KUENEN, LL.D., D.D.,
Professor of Theology at Leyden. Hibbert Lectures, 1882. 10s. 6d.

Macan (Reg. W.) The Resurrection of Jesus Christ. An Essay
in Three Chapters. Published for the Hibbert Trustees. 8vo, cloth. 5s.

Mackay (R. W.) Sketch of the Rise and Progress of Christianity.
8vo, cloth. (pub. at 10s. 6d.) 6s.

Martineau (Rev. Dr. James) Religion as affected by Modern Materialism; and, Modern Materialism: its Attitude towards Theology. A Critique
and Defence. 8vo. 2s. 6d.
—— The Relation between Ethics and Religion. 8vo. 1s.
—— Ideal Substitutes for God considered. 8vo. 1s.

Mind: a Quarterly Review of Psychology and Philosophy. Contributions by Mr. Herbert Spencer, Professor Bain, Mr. Henry Sidgwick,
Mr. Shadworth H. Hodgson, Professor Flint, Mr. James Sully, the Rev. John
Venn, the Editor (Professor Croom Robertson), and others. Vols. I. to XI.,
1876 to 1886, each 12s.; cloth, 13s. 6d. 12s. per annum, post free.

Müller (Professor Max) Lectures on the Origin and Growth of
Religion, as illustrated by the Religions of India. Hibbert Lectures, 1878.
8vo, cloth. 10s. 6d.

Oldenberg (Prof. H.) Buddha: his Life, his Doctrine, his Order.
Translated by WILLIAM HOEY, M.A., D.Lit., Member of the Royal Asiatic
Society, Asiatic Society of Bengal, &c., of her Majesty's Bengal Civil Service.
Cloth, gilt. 18s.

Peill (Rev. G.) The Three-fold Basis of Universal Restitution.
Crown 8vo, cloth. 3s.

Pfleiderer (O.) Paulinism. An Essay towards the History of the
Theology of Primitive Christianity. Translated by E. PETERS, Esq. 2 vols.
8vo, cloth. 21s.
—— Vide Theological Translation Fund Library.

Pfleiderer (Professor O.) The Philosophy of Religion on the Basis
of its History. I. History of the Philosophy of Religion from Spinoza to
the present Day. Vol. I. Spinoza to Schleiermacher. By Professor OTTO
PFLEIDERER. Translated by the Rev. ALLAN MENZIES and the Rev. ALEX.
STEWART, of Dundee. 8vo, cloth. 10s. 6d.
—— Vide Theological Translation Fund Library.

Pfleiderer (Professor O.) Lectures on the Influence of the Apostle Paul on the Development of Christianity. Translated by the Rev. J. FREDERICK SMITH. Hibbert Lectures, 1885. 8vo, cloth. 10s. 6d.

Poole (Reg. Lane) Illustrations of the History of Medieval Thought, in the Departments of Theology and Ecclesiastical Politics. 8vo, cloth. 10s. 6d.

Pratt (Dr. H.) New Aspects of Life and Religion. 440 pp. Crown 8vo, cloth. 7s. 6d.

Protestant Commentary, A Short, on the New Testament, with General and Special Introductions. From the German of Hilgenfeld, Holtzmann, Lang, Pfleiderer, Lipsius, and others. Translated by the Rev. F. H. JONES, of Oldham. 3 vols. 8vo, cloth. each 10s. 6d.
—— Vide Theological Translation Fund Library.

Renan (E.) On the Influence of the Institutions, Thought and Culture of Rome on Christianity, and the Development of the Catholic Church. By ERNEST RENAN, Membre de l'Institute. Translated by the Rev. CHARLES BEARD, of Liverpool. Hibbert Lectures, 1880. 8vo, cloth. [Cheap Edition, 2s. 6d.] 10s. 6d.

Renouf (P. Le Page) Lectures on the Origin and Growth of Religion, as illustrated by the Religion of Ancient Egypt. Hibbert Lectures, 1879. 8vo, cloth. 10s. 6d.

Reville (Prof. Albert) Prolegomena of the History of Religions. By ALBERT REVILLE, D.D., Professor in the Collége de France, and Hibbert Lecturer, 1884. Translated from the French. With an Introduction by Professor F. MAX MÜLLER. 8vo, cloth. 10s. 6d.
—— Vide Theological Translation Fund Library.

Reville (Prof. Albert) Lectures on the Origin and Growth of Religion, as illustrated by the Native Religions of Mexico and Peru. Translated by the Rev. P. H. WICKSTEED, M.A. Hibbert Lectures, 1884. 8vo, cl. 10s. 6d.

Reville (Rev. Dr. A.) The Song of Songs, commonly called the Song of Solomon, or the Canticle. Crown 8vo, cloth. 1s. 6d.

Reville (Rev. Dr. A.) The Devil: his Origin, Greatness, and Decadence. Translated from the French. Second Edition. 12mo, cloth. 2s.

Rhys (Professor J.) Lectures on the Origin and Growth of Religion as illustrated by Celtic Heathendom. Hibbert Lectures, 1886. 8vo, cl. 10s. 6d.

Samuelson (Jas.) Views of the Deity, Traditional and Scientific; a Contribution to the Study of Theological Science. By JAMES SAMUELSON, Esq., of the Middle Temple, Barrister-at-law, Founder and former Editor of the Quarterly Journal of Science. Crown 8vo, cloth. 4s. 6d.

Savage (Rev. M. J.) Beliefs about the Bible. By the Rev. M. J. SAVAGE, of the Unity Church, Boston, Mass., Author of "Belief in God," "Beliefs about Man," &c. &c. 8vo, cloth. 7s. 6d.

Schurman (J. G.) Kantian Ethics and the Ethics of Evolution. A Critical Study, by J. GOULD SCHURMAN, M.A. D.Sc., Professor of Logic and Metaphysics in Acadia College, Nova Scotia. Published by the Hibbert Trustees. 8vo, cloth. 5s.

Seth (A.) The Development from Kant to Hegel, with Chapters on the Philosophy of Religion. By ANDREW SETH, Assistant to the Professor of Logic and Metaphysics, Edinburgh University. Published by the Hibbert Trustees. 8vo, cloth. 5s.

Sharpe (S.) History of the Hebrew Nation and its Literature, with an Appendix on the Hebrew Chronology. Fourth Edition. 487 pp. 8vo, cloth. 7s. 6d.

Sharpe (S.) Bible. The Holy Bible, translated by SAMUEL SHARPE, being a Revision of the Authorized English Version. Fourth Edition of the Old Testament; Eighth Edition of the New Testament. 8vo, roan. 4s. 6d.

Sharpe (S.) The New Testament. Translated from Griesbach's Text. 14th Thousand, fcap. 8vo, cloth. 1s. 6d.

Smith (Rev. J. Fred.) Studies in Religion under German Masters. Essays on Herder, Goethe, Lessing, Franck, and Lang. By the Rev. J. FREDERICK SMITH, of Mansfield. Crown 8vo, cloth. 5s.

Spencer (Herbert) Works. The Doctrine of Evolution. 8vo, cloth.
First Principles. Sixth Thousand. 16s.
Principles of Biology. 2 vols. 34s.
Principles of Psychology. Fourth Thousand. 2 vols. 36s.
Principles of Sociology. Vol. I. 21s.
Ceremonial Institutions. Principles of Sociology. Vol. II. Part I. 7s.
Political Institutions. Principles of Sociology. Vol. II. Part II. 12s.
The Data of Ethics. Principles of Morality. Fourth Thousand. Part I. 8s.

Spencer (Herbert) The Study of Sociology. Library Edition (being the Ninth), with a Postscript. 8vo, cloth. 10s. 6d.
—— Education (Cheap Edition, Seventh Thousand, 2s. 6d.). 6s.
—— Essays. 2 vols. Third Edition. 16s.
—— Essays (Third Series). Third Edition. 8s.

Spencer (Herbert) The Man *versus* the State. 1s.; or on better paper, in cloth, 2s. 6d.

Spencer (Herbert) The Philosophy of M. Comte—Reasons for Dissenting from it. (Republished from "The Classification of the Sciences," &c., 1864.) 6d.

Spinoza. Four Essays, by Professors J. LAND, KUNO FISCHER, and VAN VLOTEN, and ERNEST RENAN. Edited, with an Introduction, by Professor W. KNIGHT, of St. Andrews. 8vo, cloth. 5s.

Stokes (G. J.) The Objectivity of Truth. By GEORGE J. STOKES, B.A., Senior Moderator and Gold Medallist, Trinity College, Dublin; late Hibbert Travelling Scholar. Published by the Hibbert Trustees. 8vo, cloth. 5s.

Strauss (Dr. D. F.) New Life of Jesus, for the People. The Authorized English Edition. 2 vols. 8vo, cloth. 24s.

Taylor (Rev. J. J.) An Attempt to ascertain the Character of the Fourth Gospel, especially in its Relation to the First Three. New Edition, 8vo, cloth. 5s.

Ten Services of Public Prayer, taken in Substance from the "Common Prayer for Christian Worship," with a few additional Prayers for particular Days.

    Ten Services alone, crown 8vo, cloth, 2s. 6d.; with Special Collects. 3s.
    Ten Services alone, 32mo, 1s.; with Special Collects. 1s. 6d.
    Psalms and Canticles. (To accompany the same.) Crown 8vo, 1s. 6d.
    With Anthems. 2s.

Thoughts for Every Day in the Year. Selected from the Writings of Spiritually-minded Persons. By the Author of "Visiting my Relations." Printed within red lines. Crown 8vo, cloth. 2s. 6d.

Theological Translation Fund. A Series of Translations, by which the best results of recent Theological investigations on the Continent, conducted without reference to doctrinal considerations, and with the sole purpose of arriving at truth, will be placed within reach of English readers. A literature which is represented by such works as those of Ewald, F. C. Baur, Zeller, Roth, Keim, Nöldeke, &c., in Germany, and by those of Kuenen, Scholten and others in Holland.

    Three Volumes annually for *a Guinea* Subscription. The Prospectus, bearing the signatures of Principal Tulloch, Dean Stanley, Professors Jowett, H. J. Smith, Henry Sidgwick, the Rev. Dr. Martineau, Mr. W. G. Clark, the Rev. T. K. Cheyne, Principal Caird and others, may be had.

36 *Volumes published* (1873 to 1886) *for* £12. 12s.

    Protestant Commentary, a Short, on the New Testament. 3 vols.
    Keim's History of Jesus of Nazara. 6 vols.
    Baur's Paul, his Life and Work. 2 vols.
    Baur's Church History of the First Three Centuries. 2 vols.
    Kuenen. The Religion of Israel. 3 vols.
    Ewald. Prophets of the Old Testament. 5 vols.
    Ewald's Commentary on the Psalms. 2 vols.
    Ewald. Book of Job.
    Bleek, on the Apocalypse.
    Zeller, on the Acts of the Apostles. 2 vols.
    Hausrath's History of the New Testament Times. 2 vols.
    Pfleiderer's Paulinism. 2 vols.
    Reville's Prolegomena of the History of Religions.
    Schrader's The Cuneiform Inscriptions and the Old Testament. 2 vols.
    Pfleiderer's Philosophy of Religion. 4 vols.

Theological Translation Fund—*(continued)*.

All new Subscribers may purchase any of the previous volumes at 7s. instead of 10s. 6d. per volume.

A selection of six or more volumes from the list may also be had at the Subscribers price, or 7s. per volume.

In the Press.
Schrader's Cuneiform Inscriptions, Vol. II.
Pfleiderer's Philosophy of Religion, Vol. II.

Vickers (J.) The History of Herod; or, Another Look at a Man emerging from Twenty Centuries of Calumny. 388 pp. Crown 8vo, cloth. 6s.

What I have taught my Children. By a Member of the Theistic Church. 12mo, cloth. 2s. 6d.

Williams (Dr. Rowland) The Hebrew Prophets. Translated afresh and illustrated for English Readers. 2 vols. 8vo, cloth. 22s. 6d.

Zeller (Dr. E.) The Contents and Origin of the Acts of the Apostles, critically investigated. Preceded by Dr. Fr. Overbeck's Introduction to the Acts of the Apostles from De Wette's Handbook. Translated by Joseph Dare. 2 vols. 8vo, cloth. 21s.
—— Vide Theological Translation Fund Library.

PAMPHLETS.

Athanasian Creed. Two Prize Essays. By C. Peabody and C. S. Kenny. 1s.
Beard (C.) William Ellery Channing. In Memoriam. A Sermon. 12mo. 6d.
Beard (C.) The Kingdom of God. A Sermon. 6d.
Beard (C.) The House of God, and two Sermons by Rev. R. A. Armstrong. 1s.
Butler's Analogy: A Lay Argument. By a Lancashire Manufacturer. 1s.
Hopgood (Jas.) Disestablishment and Disendowment of the Church of England. 6d.
Hopgood (Jas.) An Attempt to Define Unitarian Christianity. 6d.
Howe (Rev. C.) The Athanasian Creed. Two Discourses. 1s.
Jesus of Nazareth and his Contemporaries. 1s.
Journey to Emmaus. By a Modern Traveller. 2s.
Lisle (L.) The Two Tests: the Supernatural Claims of Christianity tried by two of its own Rules. Cloth. 1s. 6d.
Marriage of Cana, as read by a Layman. 6d.
Martineau (Rev. Dr. James) New Affinities of Faith; a Plea for free Christian Union. 12mo. 1s.
Must God Annihilate the Wicked? A Reply to Dr. Jos. Parker. 1s.
Reasonable Faith, A, the Want of our Age. 1s.
Savage (Rev. M. J.) Herbert Spencer: his Influence on Religion and Morality. 6d.
Sharpe (S.) Journeys and Epistles of the Apostle Paul. 1s. 6d.
Sidgwick (H.) The Ethics of Conformity and Subscription. 1s.
Tayler (Rev. J. J.) Christianity: What is it? and What has it done? 1s.

WILLIAMS AND NORGATE,
14, Henrietta Street, Covent Garden, London;
And 20, South Frederick Street, Edinburgh.